# Brazil's
# Second Chance

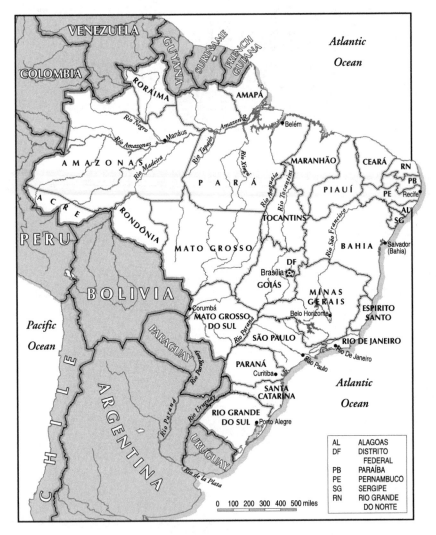

*Brazil and Its Neighbors*

A Century Foundation Book

# Brazil's Second Chance

## En Route toward the First World

LINCOLN GORDON

BROOKINGS INSTITUTION PRESS
*Washington, D.C.*

*Library of Congress Cataloging-in-Publication data*

Gordon, Lincoln.
  Brazil's second chance : en route toward the first world /
Lincoln Gordon.
    p.    cm.
  Includes bibliographical references and index.
  "A Century Foundation book."
  ISBN 0-8157-0032-6 (alk. paper)
  1. Brazil—History—1954–1964. 2. Brazil—History—1964–1985.
3. Brazil—History—1985–   . I. Title.
  F2538.2.G76 2001                    2001000442
  981.06—dc21                         CIP


9 8 7 6 5 4 3 2 1


The paper used in this publication meets minimum requirements of the American National Standard for Information Sciences—Permanence of Paper for Printed Library Materials: ANSI Z39.48-1992.

Typeset in Minion

Composition by Circle Graphics
Columbia, Maryland

Printed by R. R. Donnelley and Sons
Harrisonburg, Virginia

# Foreword

In modern economies, every downturn provokes a new round of explanations, usually emphasizing specific conditions that made a particular setback
inevitable. All booms, on the other hand, are likely to produce quite uniform
explanations for the good times. In fact, sustained periods of prosperity tend
to stimulate an astonishing amount of optimism about our ability to predict
and control our economic destiny. When subject to review, however, the
accuracy of such analyses of the recent past and forecasts of the near-term
future are far from perfect—even in advanced nations, where the economists and business observers who do this sort of explaining and predicting
are not only well trained, but also have access to good statistical data.

We should not be surprised, then, if the record is even more mixed for
those who study the economies of and offer prognostications for the less
developed world. After all, these efforts often depend on unreliable and less
than comprehensive information. Still, with so much at stake for the large
share of the globe's people who suffer from continuing widespread deprivation and poverty, the attempt to understand what actually makes break-
throughs in modernization possible remains compelling. Moreover, the
meteoric rise of some economies during the past two decades provides fresh
evidence that real progress is not only possible but often can exceed our
highest expectations.

It is cause for rejoicing when just about any third world nation finally
turns the corner toward sustained and significant economic growth. And,

when such a nation is one of the handful of large countries that seem destined for global significance, the consequences of success are likely to be of
great political and even historical importance. In South America, the nation
that has perennially attracted this sort of intense attention and high expectations is Brazil. Its history is, in a sense, a tale of a long struggle to modernize—
to fulfill the enormous potential suggested by its large territory and
population (it ranks fifth globally in both categories). In the pages that follow, Lincoln Gordon traces that fascinating story through the end of the
twentieth century, with a particular focus on the last few decades of that century when Brazilian leaders almost routinely had to struggle with the desta-
bilizing consequences of frequent economic turmoil, often including
near-runaway inflation.

Gordon, a guest scholar at the Brookings Institution, former assistant secretary of state for inter-American affairs, and former U.S. ambassador to
Brazil (1961–66), brings exceptional credentials to this task. In addition to
his deep experience with Brazil, he is an accomplished scholar and author.
His previous books include *Eroding Empire: Western Relations with Eastern
Europe* (coauthor, 1987), *Energy Strategies for Developing Nations* (coauthor,
1981), and *A New Deal for Latin America* (1963).

Gordon explains the gyrations of Brazil's stormy politics in the years since
the overthrow of the monarchy late in the nineteenth century. For Americans, his candid, often firsthand account of U.S.-Brazilian relations during
the cold war, when Brazil was a key prize in the decades-long competition
with global communism, is of particular interest. Gordon informs us in sat-
isfying detail about the crises in domestic politics that, from time to time,
seemed to overwhelm all other influences shaping Brazilian development.
With broad coverage of the topic, including social and political as well as
economic factors, he provides the reader with a solid basis for assessing the
current state of this South American colossus.

Today, Gordon notes, Brazil seems to have broken out of the past pattern
of two steps forward, one step back and is realizing significant gains both
economically and politically, although it still has far to go (its per capita
income is somewhat lower than Mexico's). It also must overcome the dead-
weight of a legacy of severe economic inequality.

This book is one in a long series of analyses of the nations to our south
that the Century Foundation has supported. A little more than fifty years
ago, we published George Wythe, Royce A. Wight, and Harold H. Midkiff's

*Brazil: An Expanding Economy.* Over the decades that followed, we published studies of individual nations in the region as well as broader works,
most notably in the 1960s a volume edited by Albert O. Hirschman, *Latin
American Issues,* and Hirschman's *Journeys toward Progress.* Then, in the
1980s, we supported a series of reports looking at the debt crisis in Latin
America, including *Latin American Debt* by Pedro-Pablo Kucynski and *The
Brazilian Quandary* by Marcilio Marques Moreira. We also supported a volume of essays in the early 1990s that reviewed the impact of that crisis and
looked ahead, *In the Shadow of the Debt: Emerging Issues in Latin America.*

Lest anyone become too sanguine, or too grim, about prospects for Brazil
or indeed of any developing country, it may be helpful to consider how
much we do not understand about economic and political development.
The history of the twentieth century is littered with embarrassing forecasts:
This will be the war to end all wars. No advanced country will revert to bar-
barism. Argentina is secure among the rich countries of the world. Africa is
already on the road to prosperity. South Asia is a basket case. In fact, while
there is little mystery about what produces economic development—steady
investment in people and physical capital in an environment that encour-
ages socially productive use of resources—there is every reason to doubt that
we know how to initiate and sustain such development. Political institutions, social classes, and vested interests have complex national and local histories that all but determine the future. Lincoln Gordon may well be right
in arguing that Brazil is breaking away from the limits to development that
its deep divisions by class and race have imposed in the past. His optimism
is based on his extensive knowledge of the subject and his experience, and
his case is strong. On behalf of the Century Foundation, I extend our appreciation for this timely work.

RICHARD C. LEONE
President
The Century Foundation
February 2001

# Preface

B razil and its people have attracted the interest of European and North American scholars and policymakers since independence from Portugal in 1822. The country's vast dimensions, natural beauty, variety of climate and resources, cultural achievements, engrossing political history, and friendly responsiveness to strangers all distinguish it from most of the third world. In the decades since World War II, Brazil has undergone basic transformations in demography, economics, politics, and social relations and has sought a position of increasing prominence on the world stage. Yet these advances have been punctuated periodically by setbacks, usually political in character, seemingly giving substance to the old and tired cliché, "Brazil is the land of the future, and always will be."

These features, both positive and negative, led me in the late 1950s to undertake a study of the respective roles and relationships of government and the private sector in Brazil's economic and social development, under the auspices of Harvard's then new Center for International Affairs. That work was put aside after the election of President John F. Kennedy in 1960, when I was asked to help in the development of the Alliance for Progress and then to go to Brazil as U.S. ambassador.

The origins of the present book date back to 1987. As a guest scholar at the Brookings Institution in Washington, I had just completed a study on Western policies toward Eastern Europe. The Brookings authorities kindly invited me to stay on and give thought to a new project. Brazil had only recently emerged from twenty-one years of military rule and was preparing a new democratic constitution. It seemed timely to take up again the central questions of the earlier research project, in a framework now enriched by thirty years of active international interest in economic and social development in the third world.

From the project's inception, the Twentieth Century Fund (now the Century Foundation) encouraged its development and offered financial support. I traveled to Brazil in 1988 and 1990, renewing former acquaintanceships and forming new ones in academic, governmental, political, business, labor union, and NGO (nongovernmental organization) circles. By 1992 several chapters were in draft. Then the work was interrupted on two accounts. On the Brazilian side, ten years of failed macroeconomic policies were undermining the hopes for sustained development. On my side, most working time was being preempted by service as an expert witness for the Department of Justice in lawsuits arising from industrial and mining pollution during World War II; the expertise was based on my wartime service as a high-ranking official of the War Production Board. I kept abreast of developments in Brazil, but faced with the "lost decade" traced here in chapter 7, I wondered from time to time whether this project should be abandoned.

Those doubts were dispelled by Brazil's fundamental policy changes of 1994, centered on the introduction of the *real*. At long last, the "second chance" of my title seemed to be taking on concrete form. The meaning of that title is fully explained in chapter 1. I then inquired of Richard Leone, the new president of the Century Foundation, whether the foundation was still interested in the project. The response was immediate, cordial, and positive.

My appreciation goes first to the Century Foundation, Richard Leone, and Marcia Bystryn for their continuing encouragement in the face of repeated missed deadlines. It goes in heartfelt measure to the Brookings Institution, which has been my office host for the last fifteen years. Presidents Bruce MacLaury and Michael Armacost and Foreign Policy Studies directors John Steinbruner and Richard Haass have provided steady encouragement from the top, while the staffs of the library and computation center have been unstinting in their assistance. I am also grateful for the stimulating companionship of fellow scholars in all of Brookings's research and teaching divisions. In the early phase of the project, I had the benefit of high-quality research assistance from Alison Sondhaus Carroll and Katherine Sieh, and more recently from Tatiana Martins. At the Brookings Institution Press, my thanks to Vicky Macintyre for her thoughtful editing, to Tanjam Jacobson and Janet Walker for seeing the book through production, and to Carlotta Ribar and Nedalina Dineva, who provided proofreading and indexing assistance.

Over these forty-five years, I have formed many friendships among Brazilians, American and European "Brazilianists," and others interested in Brazil, all of whom have had some influence on my attitudes and judgments. The acknowledgments here are necessarily limited to those providing assistance to the text as it stands, sometimes through critical review of early chapter drafts and often through insights based on much deeper experience than my own. I ask their forgiveness for omitting the courtesy titles normally attached to their names.

The roster includes Paulo Roberto de Almeida, Paulo Ayres Filho, Edmar Bacha, Werner Baer, Rubens Barbosa, Edmundo Barbosa da Silva, Luis Carlos Bresser Pereira, Roberto Campos, Eliana Cardoso, Claúdio de Moura Castro, Julian Chacel, Donald Coes, John Crimmins, Joan Dassin, Carol Evans, James Ferrer, Albert Fishlow, Paulo Tarso Flecha de Lima, David Fleischer, Norman Gall, Élio Gaspari, Carol Graham, José Augusto Guilhon Albuquerque, Peter Hakim, Margaret Daly Hayes, Hélio Jaguaribe, Alexandre Kafka, Jacob Kaplan, Peter Knight, Bolivar Lamounier, Carlos Geraldo Langoni, Melvin Levitzky, Pedro Malan, André Cezar Médici, Cândido Mendes de Almeida, Marcílio Marques Moreira, Samuel Morley, João Baptista Pinheiro, Murilo Portugal, Carlos Primo Braga, Trajano Pupo Neto, Raimar Richers, Rubens Ricúpero, Riordan Roett, Keith Rosenn, Margaret Sarles, Harry Schlaudeman, Mário Henrique Simonsen, Thomas Skidmore, Robert Solomon, Paulo Sotero, Amaury de Souza, Alfred Stepan, João Paulo dos Reis Velloso, Luis Viana Filho, Francisco Weffort, Howard Wiarda, and Jack E. Wyant.

LINCOLN GORDON

# Contents

# Brazil's Second Chance

# 1

## The Goal: Genuine First World Status

Brazil is the world's fifth largest nation-state in both area and population and ninth in total economic output. It accounts for more than
one-third of Latin America's total population and production. Its economy
in 1998 outranked that of all but the United States, Japan, China, and the
four leading countries of Europe. Among America's export destinations in
the Western Hemisphere, it is surpassed only by Canada and Mexico. It has
the world's eighth largest share of American direct foreign investments, far
exceeding those in any other Latin American country. In recent years, it has
also been a major destination for portfolio investment.

In the entire half century since World War II, Brazil has been a leader in
international trade governance and negotiation, playing an important part
in the development of the General Agreement on Tariffs and Trade (GATT)
and the World Trade Organization (WTO). At a regional level, it is the
major partner in Mercosur, which includes Argentina, Uruguay, and
Paraguay, and has negotiated special trading arrangements with Chile and
the Andean group. Mercosur has had unexpected success in expanding
trade, investment, and infrastructure cooperation between former political
rivals Brazil and Argentina and has given Brazil additional weight in negotiations toward a hemisphere-wide Free Trade Area of the Americas
(FTAA). It has also opened discussions with the European Union on the
possibility of region-to-region trade preferences.

In addition to economic issues, Brazil has taken an active part in regional
and global international affairs, following a tradition begun under its con-

stitutional monarchy (1822–89). Alone in Latin America, it has a well-educated and highly professional diplomatic corps, fluent in English, French, and Spanish and well versed in international politics and economics. It was the only Latin American country to participate actively in World War II, providing air bases on the northeastern hump and a full army division (under American command) in the difficult Italian campaign of 1944–45. For a brief period in the early 1960s, and again in the late 1970s, there were experiments in "independent" foreign policy and third world leadership, with a strongly anti-American flavor, but since the collapse of the Soviet Union, Brazil has returned to its older tradition, seeking collaboration with the United States while avoiding automatic concurrence or subservience. Brazil took the lead in 1998 in resolving a long-standing border conflict between Peru and Ecuador and has been an active and constructive participant in United Nations activities in peacekeeping, arms control (including nonproliferation of weapons of mass destruction), and environmental and human rights protection. It is unlikely, however, that Brazil will fulfill its ambition for a permanent place on the UN Security Council.

Brazil is currently in a critical phase of a decades-long transformation from a patrimonial society based mainly on the cultivation and export of sugar and coffee to a modernized industrial and service economy with effective democratic governance. Its political record since World War II has been erratic. That record includes one presidential suicide (Vargas, 1954); one unexpected resignation (Quadros, 1961); one removal by coup d'état (Goulart, 1964); twenty-one years of authoritarian military government (1964–85) under five army generals, one of whom became disabled by a stroke (Costa e Silva, 1969); one president-elect stricken by fatal illness on the eve of his inauguration (Tancredo Neves, 1985); and one elected president constitutionally impeached for corruption (Fernando Collor, 1992). Since 1950, only two civilian presidents have completed full terms: Juscelino Kubitschek (1956–61) and Fernando Henrique Cardoso (1995–98), who was reelected in 1998 to a second four-year term (1999–2002). The transition from military back to civilian governance was gradual, spread over a decade (1975–85), but relatively peaceful and consensual, with an amnesty law avoiding the recriminations commonly experienced in more abrupt political transitions.

The Constitution of 1988, drafted by an assembly composed of elected members of Congress (deputies and senators) and containing 245 articles and 70 "transitional provisions," reflected a populist reaction against the military regime. It gave constitutional protection not only for vital civil rights and liberties but also for social and economic privileges for a large array of special interest groups. Together with political party and electoral mechanics, which greatly overweight parochial interests and give undue strength to states and municipalities at the expense of the central government, it created high hurdles for economic and social reforms essential to full modernization.

Notwithstanding these gyrations, Brazil has made great strides toward first world status since the 1950s. Income per capita is about on a par with Central Europe's and roughly 30 percent of Western Europe's. Urbanization, industrialization, and modern services have displaced traditional agriculture as the dominant modes of life. Adult literacy has risen from 49 percent in 1950 to 84 percent in 1997, and average life expectancy from fifty to sixty-seven years. The most striking shortfall in the modernization process is the continuing gross inequality in income distribution, a pattern that contrasts sharply with the modernizing economies of East Asia. The remedies lie mainly in an overdue but ongoing reform of the educational structure and in a resumption of sustained economic growth.

In macroeconomic terms, Brazil's hallmark over the decades has been high inflation. The inflation rate per year averaged 34 percent in the 1970s, 428 percent in the 1980s, and almost 1,400 percent in the five years 1990–94, before being tamed by the ingenious Real Plan, which elevated Fernando Henrique Cardoso to the presidency in the 1994 election. In the following five years, the average inflation rate came down to 8.4 percent, but at the cost of a somewhat overvalued real. Growing deficits in the current balance of payments, together with financial crises in Asia and Russia, led to a run on international reserves and a substantial devaluation of the real in early 1999. A US$41.5 billion international aid package, backed by the International Monetary Fund (IMF), the U.S. Treasury, and other first world governments, warded off the threat of default on foreign obligations and a major economic setback. The new millennium opened in more promising macroeconomic conditions, but the government still faced difficult legislative battles for advancing badly needed economic and political reforms. The political climate was becoming more tense in preparation for mayoral elections in October 2000 and national and state elections in 2002 for president and vice president, deputies and senators, governors and members of state legislatures. The outcome may determine for many years whether Brazil can achieve full first world status and realize its potential for constructive worldwide influence or will relapse back into another "lost decade" like the 1980s and early 1990s.

## Brazilian Aspirations

In Brazil's nearly two centuries of independent statehood, elite opinion has always envisaged a future of *grandeza* (greatness) on the world stage. The national anthem somewhat naively foresees greatness as a necessary consequence of the country's huge size. This mind-set was fostered by the decades of political stability under the monarchies of Pedro I (1822–31) and Pedro II (1831–89), with their titled aristocracy, European-style royal institutions, and simulacrum of parliamentary government, albeit with a very limited franchise. Alongside the dominant patrimonial owners of sugar and coffee estates, based until 1888 on slave labor, there developed urban professional elites, often European-educated, who pressed for modernization on European or North American lines. Younger military officers became prominent in these groups, which played major roles in the antislavery movement, the overthrow of the imperial regime in 1889, and the drafting of a republican constitution in 1891. Although that constitution was patterned in form on the American model, in practice it weakened central government power and gave effective control to the coffee and cattle landowners of the two leading states, São Paulo and Minas Gerais. The stage was set for increasing tensions between a backward-looking oligarchical system and the modernizing professionals, both civilian and military. In the 1920s armed violence broke out in several states, often involving the state militia. In 1930 the modernizing forces joined in a Liberal Alliance to overthrow the Old Republic by coup d'état and install in the presidency Getúlio Vargas, the governor of Rio Grande do Sul. Vargas was to dominate Brazilian politics for the next twenty-four years.

In this turbulent era, significant changes took place in economic and social structures, gradually expanding manufacturing industry in textiles, shoes, and processed foodstuffs, especially in the growing metropolitan region of São Paulo. World War I had intensified these trends by cutting off traditional European sources of supply. In the depression years, manufacturing investment was also promoted by the government's policy of price support for coffee through purchases of huge quantities to keep the surpluses off the world market and enable the coffee barons to invest in industry. This anticipatory Keynesianism helped Brazil weather the depression better than many more advanced countries and fueled the Vargas administration's ambitions for economic expansion.

On the political side, fascist and communist movements became significant actors in Brazil, but Vargas warded off clumsy efforts at coups d'état from both left and right and centralized political power in his own hands.

He appointed mayors in the bigger cities and "interventors" in place of elected governors. In 1937 he assumed dictatorial power, promulgating by decree an authoritarian constitution for the so-called New State (Estado Novo), which included Italian fascist-style organization of labor unions and business associations on corporative lines.

Structural change, including urbanization and the expansion of manufacturing, was given further impetus by World War II, which also generated large export surpluses. National ambition was focused on the installation of heavy industry, starting with the government-owned National Steel Company (Companhia Siderúrgica Nacional) at Volta Redonda. Vargas hoped that active military collaboration with the United States might be rewarded by a political-economic "special relationship" after the war, with assistance for forced-pace industrialization. The seeds were thus planted for Brazil's postwar development policies, including substantial reliance on government ownership and a large component of economic nationalism. With the allied victory against fascist dictatorships, Vargas was forced out of office in 1945, but he secured a later political revival by creating two new parties in anticipation of renewed constitutional democracy. With their support, he won a three-man contest for the presidency overwhelmingly in 1950. In a wave of fervent nationalism, under the slogan "The Oil Is Ours," Congress created Petrobrás as a government-owned oil monopoly. The president elected in 1955, Juscelino Kubitschek, made "developmentalism" (*desenvolvimentismo*) the keynote of his campaign and his term in office. In one form or another, it has been a central theme of Brazilian national aspirations ever since.

## Genuine First World Status

On the broader global stage in the 1950s, international politics were increasingly dominated by the cold war. The world's nations came to be classified in three categories, separated by degrees and types of political-economic development. The first world comprised the "industrial democracies" of Western Europe, North America, Australia, New Zealand, and Japan—in effect the core membership of the Paris-based Organization for Economic Cooperation and Development (OECD).[1] The second world consisted of

1. The OECD was instituted in 1961 by the twenty nations involved in the Marshall Plan, eighteen from Western Europe plus the United States and Canada. Japan was added in 1964, soon followed by Finland, Australia, and New Zealand. Under political pressure from the United States, Mexico was admitted in 1994, but its financial crisis that year, subsequent macroeconomic instability, and single-

countries with centrally planned economies governed by Communist Party regimes. The collapse of the Soviet bloc in 1989, the end of the Communist Party's monopoly of power in Russia and Eastern Europe, and the weakening of central planning in China have reduced this category to North Korea and Cuba, so the term "second world" has gone out of use. In its place, the term "transitional economies" is now applied to Eastern Europe and the former Soviet republics, implying that they are all headed toward market-based economic systems and democratic polities, even though evidently not all at the same pace.

The original meaning of "third world" was political rather than economic, signifying nonalignment with either of the cold war blocs. By a gradual transformation in the 1950s and 1960s, however, it became equivalent to "underdeveloped" or "developing" countries, with relatively low degrees of industrialization and low incomes per capita. The third world thus defined included all of Africa, Latin America, and Asia except for Japan and China.[2] It was a huge and diverse category of about 130 units, with an enormous range of size and wealth. In United Nations debates on international economic policies, their representatives caucused together and often voted together as the "G-77."[3]

In the 1980s, the most advanced members of this group, marked by relatively high income levels and industrial sophistication, came to be called newly industrializing countries, or NICs. They included the four Asian "tigers" (South Korea, Taiwan, Singapore, and Hong Kong), possibly also Indonesia and Malaysia, together with Brazil, Mexico, and possibly Argentina, Chile, and Venezuela. By most measures, these NICs were much closer to the first world than to the average of their third world associates. While only Korea as yet regards itself—or is regarded by the rest of the world—as having fully completed the transition into the first world, it seems absurd to put in a single "third world" category countries as diverse as

---

party political tradition prevent its clear designation in the first world. Similar reservations do not apply to South Korea, which became a full OECD member in 1996, along with three former second world countries (Poland, the Czech Republic, and Hungary).

2. In Latin America, the first and third worlds are often referred to as "center" and "periphery," terms popularized in the 1950s and 1960s by Raúl Prebisch during his long tenure as secretary-general of the UN Economic Commission for Latin America (ECLA or CEPAL in Spanish, now ECLAC, the UN Economic and Social Commission for Latin America and the Caribbean).

3. There were seventy-seven members when the United Nations Conference on Trade and Development (UNCTAD) was launched in 1964. Since then about fifty-five more countries have been added as additional former colonial territories have achieved formal sovereignty and separate membership in the United Nations.

Argentina, Chile, Mexico, Malaysia, and Brazil at one end and Ethiopia, Mozambique, and Uganda at the other. The United Nations sometimes uses the terms "developed" and "developing," really meaning "rich" and "poor," but the World Bank has abandoned qualitative adjectives in favor of four categories based on per capita income levels: high income, upper middle income (which includes Brazil), lower middle income, and low income.[4] Yet the term "third world" (or "third world conditions") persists in common usage, without any generally accepted and clear-cut definition.

Apart from formal OECD membership, the first world is identified by three kinds of criteria: political, domestic economic, and external economic. The political criterion is easy to define, although not always easy to secure or maintain. It is a condition of stable pluralist democracy, with representative government based on free elections, competition among political parties, constitutional protection of individual and minority rights, and unconditional acceptance of electoral results.

The domestic economic criterion is harder to describe in a single sentence. It is not a mere matter of per capita incomes, although all present members enjoy levels above $15,000 per year (at 1997 prices, using "purchasing power parity" exchange rates) and the richest approach $30,000.[5] It includes a broad array of modern industrial and service activities, a high degree of urbanization, integration of agriculture into the money economy, access to advanced technologies, universal education for literacy and numeracy, some form of social "safety net" to prevent extreme destitution and provide access to health care, and general participation of the populations in modern institutions of trade and exchange.[6] On the external economic side, first world members are all actively involved in the late-twentieth-century international systems of trade, finance, and investment, institutionalized in the WTO, the IMF, the World Bank, and the network of private commercial and investment banks. During the 1990s, their openness to foreign trade and investment has come to be called globalization.

In the 1950s, the early period of active U.S. (and other first world) interest in overseas development, it was widely believed that all third world

---

4. See World Bank, *World Development Indicators, 1999* (Washington, 1999), p. xxiv. Largely overlapping the low-income group is a newly named category of highly indebted poor countries, for whom substantial debt forgiveness is planned early in the new millennium.

5. The data for all countries are readily available in World Bank, *World Development Indicators, 1999,* tables 1.1 and 1.6; and in United Nations Development Program (UNDP), *Human Development Report, 1999* (Oxford University Press, 1999), table 1, pp. 134–37.

6. I say "general" rather than "total" participation because several first world countries retain enclaves of preindustrial populations or regions, such as the Italian *mezzogiorno*.

countries would in due course undergo some form of transition to modernization, either into the first world or into the second. A major component of the American political interest in assisting development, although by no means its entire raison d'être, was the very issue of choice between "free" and "communist" worlds. Walt W. Rostow's widely read and influential book, *The Stages of Economic Growth* (1960), was subtitled *A Non-Communist Manifesto*. It predicted worldwide developmental patterns essentially similar to the nineteenth- and early twentieth-century experiences of Europe, North America, and Japan. In Rostow's view, the "take-off into sustained growth" had already taken place in Mexico and Argentina and was under way in Brazil and Venezuela as well as in China and India.[7]

For Simon Kuznets, on the other hand, the leading economic growth historian of that period, modernization could not be analyzed in such discrete stages and could be hampered by all kinds of political, social, and cultural constraints. The slowness of its spread was consequently not so surprising. In Latin America, Kuznets noted the delays occasioned "by a political and institutional framework that, at least until recent decades, permitted the small elites to profit from the economic advantages of their position, without embodying strong incentives and pressures for change that would spread the benefits and lay the foundation for greater modernization of the economic and social structure."[8] Yet he had little doubt that modernization would prevail in time. American policymakers under Dwight Eisenhower, John Kennedy, and Lyndon Johnson were confident that, with appropriate international assistance, the process could not only be accelerated but also steered toward assimilation into the first world rather than the second.

## The Brazilian Potential

That most Brazilians aspire to first world status, as thus defined, is scarcely in doubt. Advanced living standards for their children if not themselves, much less poverty and misery, a stable political structure providing democratic accountability and secure human rights—these are all widely shared

---

7. Walt W. Rostow, *The Stages of Economic Growth: A Non-Communist Manifesto* (Cambridge University Press, 1960), pp. 126–27. On the similarities and differences, see pp. 139–42, where Rostow takes explicit note of conflicts between "traditionalists" and "modernizers" and of institutional obstacles to modernization, but he concludes "with reasonable confidence" that in some sixty years "the world will contain many new nations which have achieved maturity." Forty years later, the pace appears to have been much slower.

8. Simon Kuznets, *Modern Economic Growth: Rate, Structure, and Spread* (Yale University Press, 1966), p. 475 and chap. 9 *passim*.

goals, even though many Brazilians would not state them in terms of first world versus third. These goals also have an intimate and long-standing connection with Brazilian nationalism.

In the early postwar decades, many Brazilian intellectuals would have defined greatness in socialist terms, but neither the Soviet Union nor China had much standing as models even then, and their glamour as ideals has now totally disappeared. More recently, Japan has received some attention as a country with "many qualities which other countries should imitate," but its appeal has declined with the long stagnation since 1990.[9] For a time in the 1970s, when the oil shocks had seemed to empower third world countries in a global struggle against the first world, a group of intellectuals on the left, including some professional diplomats, argued for Brazil to assume third world leadership. After years of sterile debates in UN bodies, and especially after the collapse of the Soviet Union, this line of thought dwindled to insignificance, again leaving Europe and North America as the dominant models. When pressed to identify specific countries, however, Brazilians I have consulted generally say that first world contents should be poured into a specifically Brazilian mold.[10]

On the political side, the basic commitment to democratic institutions and human rights was amply demonstrated during the recent period of military rule. Popular opinion had widely welcomed the ouster of President João Goulart in 1964 as an escape from the twin dangers of social chaos or populist dictatorship but by the early 1970s had already shifted to favor a democratic restoration. Even in the most repressive years, the dominant military faction rejected the idea of permanent authoritarian rule or single-party monopoly of power. From 1975 on, as the step-by-step processes of "relaxation" (*distensão*), "opening" (*abertura*), and redemocratization proceeded, the regime was kept under constant public pressure, culminating in the mass mobilization of 1984 favoring immediate direct elections to the presidency (*diretas já*). The restoration of civilian control in 1985 was immensely popular in all sectors of Brazilian society. In the same vein, spokesmen for all sectors, while acknowledging that the results were far from ideal, took pride in the intensely democratic procedures through which the Constitution of 1988 was prepared. Its human rights provisions are universally praised, in contrast to the controversial economic clauses. Notwithstanding the disappointments of economic and social performance in the

9. Instituto Gallup de Opinião Pública, *Research on International Problems,* November 1985, Question 23.

10. The notion of a fully modernized society with exceptional Brazilian traits was the central theme of Gilberto Freyre, *New World in the Tropics: The Culture of Modern Brazil* (Knopf, 1959).

first decade of the "New Republic," elections with freedom to form political parties and mass voting participation helped to distract attention from immediate woes and offered a hope for better times to come.

On the economic side, there is less consensus. Although first world levels of prosperity are widely desired, and only very small minorities believe that such levels could be achieved by Brazil in isolation from the world economy, there are deep differences on intermediate ends and on basic lines of policy. The economic record over the years has been disfigured by two great failures that are almost Brazilian hallmarks: (1) chronic inflation, verging on hyperinflation, and (2) extreme inequality in the distribution of incomes and wealth. But there is no general consensus on the remedies. These failures have been major obstacles to the achievement of genuine first world status. The efforts to overcome them, notably the Real Plan for financial stabilization introduced in 1994, are treated in later chapters.

Suffice it here to identify some of the major lines of cleavage in attitudes toward economic policies:

1. Regional tension between the Northeast and the more advanced Center-South goes back for generations. With its poles at Recife and São Paulo, the conflict pits the economic interests of a poor, relatively overpopulated, predominantly rural, and frequently drought-stricken group of northeastern states against the interests of the south-central region, whose dynamic growth in both industry and modern agriculture now extends from southern Bahia and Minas Gerais down to the Argentine and Uruguayan frontiers.

2. Conventional left-right political tension has developed in the wake of twentieth-century urbanization and industrialization. On the extreme left are former communists and socialists still devoted to direct state management of much of the economy and far-reaching intervention in the remainder; on the far right, there are intransigent free-enterprise liberals (defining "liberal" in the European manner, sometimes called "libertarian" in the United States), opposed to all forms of governmental intervention in the economy. Short of the extremes, the center-left protects the privileges of organized labor, especially in government service marked by redundant employment, early retirement, and extravagant pensions; it opposes privatization on principle. The center-right tends to resist agrarian reform and to move slowly on educational modernization. There is a substantial array of centrist groupings in between, but this tension is a central feature of both labor relations and party politics.

3. Until recently, there was also a sharp division on the proper role of foreign private investment and multinational corporations, arraying all-out opponents against all-out supporters. Today, while there are many more advocates of centrist positions on these issues, there remains a strong residue of nationalist antiforeign sentiment.

4. Overlapping all of the above, there is a cleavage between traditionalists and modernizing reformers. In the Brazilian context, this cleavage is as fundamental as Russia's classic division into Slavophiles and Westernizers. The traditionalists are the beneficiaries of the "three C's" of Brazil's socioeconomic history: clientelism, corporativism, and the cartorial (that is, overbureaucratized) state. In the countryside, especially in the Northeast, the traditionalist attitudes go straight back to colonial Brazil's patrimonial and slavery-based society. In commerce and industry, they seek to preserve the governmental subsidies and protection from competition developed in earlier stages of twentieth-century development. The modernizers want to break those molds, encouraging domestic competition and opening the economy to foreign competition. Exemplars of each side can be found in every walk of life: agricultural landowners, industrial owners and managers, bankers and businessmen in the newer service sectors, labor unions, the Church, universities, the liberal professions, the civil service, the military officer corps, and politics.[11]

These multiple cleavages might seem a prescription for paralysis, giving credence to the old saw that "Brazil is the land of the future and will always be so." Against that kind of pessimism, however, must be set the record of development in the twentieth century, especially in the postwar decades. In gross magnitudes, total economic output was multiplied elevenfold between 1947 and 1980, and per capita real output by four and a half times, while the structure of the economy was radically transformed.[12] That record gives assurance of Brazil's potential for complete transformation to first world status, whether or not the potential comes to be realized in the visible future.

---

11. As one acute Brazilian analyst put it to me in 1988, apropos of various provisions of the new constitution: "The real struggle in Brazil is between the Past and the Future; for the time being, I fear that the Past is prevailing."

12. Data calculated from national accounts summarized in Instituto Brasileiro de Geografia e Estatística (IBGE), *Estatísticas Históricas do Brasil, Séries Estatísticas Retrospectivas*, vol. 3, *Séries Econômicas, Demográficas e Sociais, 1550 a 1985* (Rio de Janeiro, 1987), pp. 111–12. A somewhat more conservative estimate gives a ratio of three and one-half times for per capita income; see Angus Maddison, *Monitoring the World Economy 1820–1992* (Paris: OECD, 1995), table D-1d, p. 203.

The first component in that potential is sheer size of territory and population. Size in itself is no guarantee of economic success, but it does provide real advantages: a wide array of natural resources within the national borders and a sufficient domestic market to promote industrial diversification. In the late 1990s Brazil was fifth in area, fifth in population, and ninth in economic output (table 1-1).

In per capita incomes, Brazil ranks somewhat below Mexico and Argentina and stands at about two-fifths of Spain's level and one-third of Western Europe's. It is far above the huge countries of India, China, and Indonesia. Brazil's middling per capita levels resemble southern Europe's in the 1950s. Combined with the population of over 150 million, they constitute a substantial domestic market. In broad terms, that market scale permits efficient production of the kinds of goods typical of the world's first and second industrial revolutions, including intermediate metal products, low-cost textiles and shoes, motor vehicles, electrical and chemical products, machine tools, and most consumer durables. For today's ongoing third industrial revolution of electronics and information, however, nothing short of a global market appears able to maintain the pace of technological advance.[13]

A rapid rate of population growth in a large and relatively poor country can be a drag on developmental potential, absorbing much of the available capital to provide basic goods and services at a subsistence level instead of raising per capita output and income. Brazil's census counts since 1872 are shown in figure 1-1, along with the intercensus rates of annual increase. The high growth in the early twentieth century mainly reflects heavy immigration, but the peak of 3.1 percent in midcentury is typical of the demographic transition, in which public health measures reduce mortality (especially infant mortality) while high birth rates continue. Notwithstanding the achievement of quite high levels of economic growth, the population surge sets limits to improvements in health and education and aggravates the inequalities in income distribution between geographical regions and social classes.[14] Since the mid-1960s, however, urbanization, extended education, and the spread of contraceptive practices have gradually brought the rate down to a level of

13. For smaller economies, such as Taiwan, Singapore, and Hong Kong, the limited scale of domestic markets has been compensated by aggressive export-oriented development policies, successful as long as the more industrialized first world remains receptive to their exports. Brazil's failure to exploit export market possibilities in the 1950s and 1960s certainly had some negative effect on its rates of economic growth, but that effect was greatly tempered by the availability of the large home market, much as in the United States and Germany in the late nineteenth and early twentieth centuries.

14. See Thomas W. Merrick and Douglas H. Graham, *Population and Economic Development in Brazil: 1800 to the Present* (Johns Hopkins University Press, 1979), pp. 294–96. For more recent

Table 1-1. *The World's Large Economic Units, 1997*

| Country | Area (thousands of km²) | Population (millions) | GNP (PPP) (billions of U.S. dollars) | GNP per capita (U.S. dollars) PPP | GNP per capita (U.S. dollars) World Bank Atlas |
|---|---|---|---|---|---|
| United States | 9,364 | 268 | 7,783 | 29,080 | 29,080 |
| China | 9,597 | 1,234 | 3,770 | 3,070 | 860 |
| Japan | 378 | 126 | 3,076 | 24,400 | 38,160 |
| Germany | 357 | 82 | 1,737 | 21,170 | 28,280 |
| India | 3,288 | 962 | 1,599 | 1,599 | 370 |
| France | 552 | 59 | 1,301 | 22,210 | 26,300 |
| United Kingdom | 245 | 59 | 1,222 | 20,710 | 20,870 |
| Italy | 301 | 58 | 1,156 | 20,100 | 20,170 |
| BRAZIL | 8,547 | 164 | 1,039 | 6,350 | 4,790 |
| Mexico | 1,958 | 94 | 765 | 8,110 | 3,700 |
| Indonesia | 1,905 | 200 | 679 | 3,390 | 1,110 |
| Canada | 9,971 | 30 | 659 | 21,750 | 19,640 |
| Russia | 17,075 | 147 | 631 | 4,280 | 2,680 |
| South Korea | 99 | 46 | 618 | 13,430 | 10,550 |
| Spain | 506 | 39 | 617 | 15,690 | 14,490 |
| Australia | 7,741 | 19 | 362 | 19,510 | 20,650 |
| Argentina | 2,780 | 36 | 360 | 10,100 | 8,950 |
| Netherlands | 41 | 16 | 332 | 21,300 | 25,830 |
| Europe (EMU) | 2,374 | 291 | 5,878 | 20,230 | 23,450 |

Source: World Bank, *World Development Indicators, 1999* (Washington, 1999), table 1.1, pp. 12–14.

1.4 percent in the late 1990s. Birthrates remain higher in the poor Northeast than elsewhere, but those regional disparities are also beginning to close.

Population stability, perhaps in the 250 million to 300 million range or even higher, cannot be expected until the mid-twenty-first century. New entries into the labor force are now at their peak, with a corresponding demand for investment and job creation. Regional migration, especially into the southern cities, places enormous demands on urban services. Neverthe-

---

surveys of research raising doubts about simplistic causal connections between economic stagnation and high rates of population growth, see National Research Council, *Population Growth and Economic Development: Policy Questions* (Washington: National Academy Press, 1984); and Allen C. Kelley, "Economic Consequences of Population Change in the Third World," *Journal of Economic Literature*, vol. 26 (December 1988), pp. 1685–1728.

Figure 1-1. *Population Growth, 1872–1996*

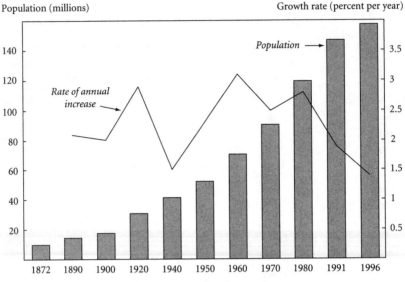

Population (millions)                                    Growth rate (percent per year)

Source: Instituto Brasileiro de Geografia e Estatística, periodic national censuses.

less, Brazil is now well advanced in the demographic transition inherent in modernization.

## Patterns of Development

The Brazilian economy in the decades since World War II appears as a belated but classic case of incomplete transformation from traditional stasis to modern economic growth. The old Brazil was mainly agrarian. Its commercial agriculture was concentrated in coffee and the lesser export crops of sugar, cotton, and cacao, and there was a large segment of subsistence agriculture. The economy had not been entirely stagnant in the prewar decades, as table 1-2 makes clear. Even before 1900, as already noted, a modest foundation for industry had been laid in São Paulo, mainly in textiles and food processing. Industrialization was given further impetus by World War I and the Great Depression. As a result, Brazil maintained a respectable annual growth rate of over 4 percent throughout the 1930s, when much of the richer world was in sharp decline. Nevertheless, almost 70 percent of the population still lived in rural areas in 1940, two-thirds of the adults were illiterate, and the rudimentary condition of communications and transport left large regions in isolation.

Table 1-2. *Five-Year Growth Rates, 1900–99*
Percent per year

| Period | Economic growth | Population growth | Per capita economic growth |
|---|---|---|---|
| 1900–05 | 4.0 | 2.1 | 1.9 |
| 1905–10 | 4.5 | 2.1 | 2.4 |
| 1910–15 | 2.9 | 2.1 | 0.8 |
| 1915–20 | 5.6 | 2.1 | 3.4 |
| 1920–25 | 3.9 | 2.1 | 1.8 |
| 1925–30 | 5.1 | 2.1 | 2.9 |
| 1930–35 | 4.3 | 2.1 | 2.2 |
| 1935–40 | 4.4 | 2.1 | 2.3 |
| 1940–45 | 4.2 | 2.4 | 1.8 |
| 1945–50 | 7.6 | 2.4 | 5.1 |
| 1950–55 | 6.7 | 3.1 | 3.5 |
| 1955–60 | 8.1 | 3.1 | 4.8 |
| 1960–65 | 4.3 | 2.5 | 1.8 |
| 1965–70 | 8.1 | 2.5 | 5.5 |
| 1970–75 | 10.3 | 2.8 | 7.3 |
| 1975–80 | 7.1 | 2.8 | 4.2 |
| 1980–85 | 1.4 | 1.9 | −0.5 |
| 1985–90 | 2.0 | 1.9 | 0.1 |
| 1990–95 | 3.1 | 1.4 | 1.7 |
| 1995–99 | 1.8 | 1.3 | 0.5 |

Sources: Economic growth rates between 1900 and 1947 are calculated from estimates of C. L. S. Haddad, *O Crescimento do Produto Real do Brasil* (Rio de Janeiro: Fundação Getúlio Vargas, 1978), as reported in Instituto Brasileiro de Geografia e Estatística (IBGE), *Estatísticas Históricas do Brasil, Séries Estatísticas Retrospectivas*, vol. 3, *Séries Econômicas, Demográficas e Sociais, 1550 a 1985* (Rio de Janeiro, 1987) (hereafter *Estatísticas Históricas*), p. 94; from 1947 to 1955, calculated from consolidated national accounts prepared by IBGE, as reported in *Estatísticas Históricas*, pp. 111–12; from 1955 to 1999, calculated from national accounts data prepared by IBGE, reported in "Conjuntura Estatística," *Conjuntura Econômica* (March 2000), p. vi.

Population growth rates between 1900 and 1920 and between 1920 and 1940 are the annual rates between the national censuses of those three years, as revised by Giorgio Mortara and reported in Merrick and Graham, *Population and Economic Development in Brazil*, p. 25. From 1940 to 1999, the growth rates are the annual rates between each pair of censuses, as reported by IBGE on the Internet.

Historical studies of today's first world countries identify four common patterns in the transformation to modern economic growth:[15] (1) acceleration in rates of overall and per capita output, involving radical changes in technology; (2) major shifts in the sectoral structure of income and employ-

15. The most comprehensive assembly of quantitative data on this transformation was the life work of the late Simon Kuznets, for which he received the 1971 Nobel Prize in economic science.

ment, away from agriculture and toward industry and services; (3) urbanization of the populations accompanied by the demographic transition from high to low death- and birthrates; and (4) changes in the composition and orientation of foreign trade related to the shifts in economic structure. Indispensable elements in this transformation are higher agricultural productivity and the accumulation of capital through private or public domestic saving, usually supplemented by foreign investment. The Brazilian experience, especially since 1945, fits very well with these patterns, as shown in tables 1-2 to 1-9 and figures 1-2 to 1-4. Each of those tables warrants a brief comment.

In every quinquennium since World War II, economic growth rates (table 1-2) were higher than at any earlier period, with two exceptions: the Goulart era of the early 1960s and the debt crisis era after 1981. Tables 1-3 and 1-4, together with figure 1-2, show the basic changes in economic structure, focused on the growth of industry and modern services. The sectoral shift in the work force became dramatic after 1950, cutting the share of the food and feed sectors by more than half from the 1950 level of 60 percent. The 1996 figure of 24½ percent, however, was still more than twice the first world average. The relatively low productivity in agriculture is demonstrated by the two tables taken together: 24½ percent of the work force produced only 8 percent of the gross domestic product (GDP).

Table 1-4 also points to the burgeoning of industrial output after 1955. That expansion was not merely quantitative; it moved from light industry into increasingly sophisticated consumer durable goods, intermediate goods, and a wide range of capital goods. With industrialization came more than a doubling of urbanization, as shown in table 1-5. The Brazilian definition of "urban" is more inclusive than for most countries, so the overall figure may be overstated, but it is significant that by 1993 the population in cities of over 1 million persons came to 32 percent for Brazil, close to the first world average of 36 percent.[16]

The other sections of table 1-5, together with table 1-6 and figure 1-3, show some of the fruits of economic development in terms of social welfare. From the 1940s to the 1970s, life expectancy was extended by twenty-two years, with the more advanced Southeast only eight years short of first world levels. A major reason for the remaining discrepancy is infant mortality;

---

See his *Modern Economic Growth* and the extensive collection of earlier articles and books cited therein. A much more recent review of available quantitative information is presented in Maddison, *Monitoring the World Economy 1820–1992*.

16. See World Bank, *World Development Report 1995* (Oxford University Press, 1995), p. 223.

Table 1-3. *Sectoral Distribution of the Work Force, 1920–96*[a]
Percent of total work force

| Sector | 1920 | 1940 | 1950 | 1960 | 1970 | 1980 | 1990 | 1996 |
|---|---|---|---|---|---|---|---|---|
| Total work force (in thousands) | 9,567 | 14,758 | 17,117 | 22,750 | 29,338 | 42,272 | 64,468 | 73,120 |
| Men (percent) | 84.7 | 81.0 | 85.4 | 82.1 | 79.1 | 72.8 | 64.5 | 59.9 |
| Women (percent) | 15.3 | 19.0 | 14.6 | 17.9 | 20.9 | 27.2 | 35.5 | 40.1 |
| Agriculture, livestock, hunting, and fishing | 66.7 | 65.9 | 59.9 | 54.0 | 44.8 | 30.2 | 22.8 | 24.5 |
| Industry, mining, construction, public utilities, transport, and communications | 13.2 | 17.3 | 21.6 | 22.2 | 26.2 | 33.6 | 26.6 | 23.6 |
| Services, all types | 15.8 | 16.1 | 18.2 | 22.1 | 27.5 | 35.5 | 50.6 | 51.9 |
| Commerce (except banking) | n.a. | 5.0 | 5.6 | 6.6 | 7.8 | 9.8 | 12.8 | 13.3 |
| Banking and finance | n.a. | 0.4 | 0.7 | 0.9 | 1.5 | 2.4 | 3.3 | 3.5 |
| Public administration | n.a. | 2.8 | 3.0 | 3.1 | 3.9 | 4.4 | 5.0 | 4.7 |
| (Armed forces) | n.a. | (0.7) | (1.0) | (1.0) | (0.9) | (0.6) | (0.5) | (0.5) |
| (Other) | n.a. | (2.1) | (2.0) | (2.2) | (3.1) | (3.8) | (4.5) | (4.2) |
| Education, health, recreation, and other liberal professions | n.a. | 2.0 | 3.0 | 4.3 | 6.3 | 9.8 | 29.5[b] | 30.4[b] |
| Personal services | n.a. | 5.9 | 5.9 | 7.3 | 8.1 | 9.1 |  |  |
| Unclassified | 4.3 | 0.7 | 0.3 | 1.7 | 1.5 | 0.7 | 2.8 | 1.9 |

Sources: For 1920 through 1980, calculated from data in the decennial censuses reported in *Estatísticas Históricas*, pp. 72–73. For 1990 and 1996, calculated from Household Sample Survey data, as reported in *Anuário Estatístico* (1993), pp. 2–51 and 2–73, and (1997), pp. 2–72 and 2–81, respectively.

n.a. Not available.

a. The categories used in 1920 and 1990 and 1996 are not strictly comparable with those in 1940 through 1980, but should be regarded as rough approximations.

b. Figure combines previous categories of "education, health, recreation, and other liberal professions" and "personal services."

Table 1-4. *Sectoral Distribution of Gross Domestic Product, 1947–96*
Percent of GDP

| Sector | 1947 | 1950 | 1955 | 1960 | 1965 | 1970 | 1975 | 1980 | 1985 | 1990 | 1996 |
|---|---|---|---|---|---|---|---|---|---|---|---|
| Agriculture, livestock, hunting, fishing | 20.7 | 24.3 | 23.5 | 17.8 | 15.9 | 20.2 | 11.2 | 10.0 | 9.8 | 8.1 | 8.0 |
| Industry, mining, construction, public utilities, transport, communications | 28.5 | 27.5 | 29.3 | 36.2 | 36.0 | 40.2 | 41.5 | 42.5 | 38.9 | 38.7 | 35.5 |
| Services | 50.8 | 48.2 | 47.2 | 46.0 | 48.2 | 48.3 | 47.2 | 47.5 | 51.3 | 53.2 | 56.5 |
| Commerce (except banking) | 15.8 | 15.6 | 16.2 | 16.9 | 16.6 | 16.4 | 16.5 | 14.5 | 12.9 | 8.3 | 7.3 |
| Banking and finance | 3.2 | 3.6 | 3.4 | 2.7 | 3.4 | 6.0 | 6.9 | 7.9 | 11.4 | 13.4 | 5.8 |
| Rents | 14.3 | 11.5 | 11.1 | 10.3 | 10.4 | 9.3 | 7.0 | 6.7 | 8.3 | 4.8 | 12.8 |
| Public administration | 6.1 | 6.6 | 6.1 | 6.3 | 8.0 | 9.2 | 7.8 | 6.3 | 6.6 | 14.1 | 14.8 |
| Other | 11.4 | 10.8 | 10.4 | 9.8 | 9.7 | 7.3 | 8.9 | 12.0 | 12.0 | 15.9 | 15.8 |

Sources: For 1947–85, calculated from data in the consolidated national accounts, as reported in *Estatísticas Históricas*, sec. 4.10, table 7, pp. 117–20; for 1990 and 1996, from data in *Anuário Estatístico* (1997), pp. 7–111.

Figure 1-2. *Sectoral Distribution of the Work Force, 1950–96*

Percent of total work force

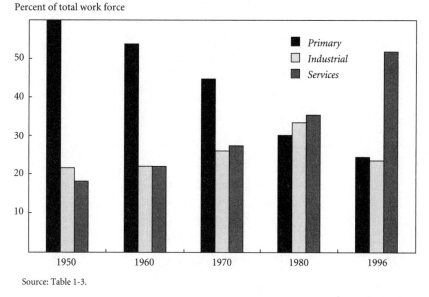

Source: Table 1-3.

although reduced by 75 percent since 1950, the overall rate is still several times the first world standard. Adult literacy (table 1-5) has been vastly improved but still has far to go, especially in the rural areas.

There have also been notable shifts in the volume, composition, and destinations of foreign trade. The first salient feature is a large overall increase in the volume of trade, although less than proportional to total output (table 1-7). The continuing low trade-dependency ratio results partly from Brazil's size but also reflects the inward-focused development strategy, which would have been a major constraint on overall growth rates in a smaller country. Notwithstanding that strategy, there was a striking change in the composition of exports from traditional tropical products to industrial goods and more variegated raw materials (table 1-8). Trading partners have also become more diversified, with Mercosur and other Latin American countries gaining a significant share (table 1-9 and figure 1-4).

At each stage in these transformations, there was strenuous controversy, both political and intellectual, concerning the strategies employed and the by-products in social terms. Looking back on the late 1950s, most analysts now believe that the Kubitschek government relied too heavily on industrialization through import substitution for consumer durable goods, to the

Table 1-5. *Urbanization and Adult Literacy, 1900–98*[a]

Percent

| Indicator | 1900 | 1920 | 1940 | 1950 | 1960 | 1970 | 1980 | 1991 | 1996 | 1998 |
|---|---|---|---|---|---|---|---|---|---|---|
| Urban population | n.a. | n.a. | 31.2 | 36.2 | 44.7 | 55.9 | 67.6 | 75.6 | 78.4 | n.a. |
| Literacy in adult population | 34.7 | 35.1 | 43.8 | 49.3 | 60.2 | 65.9 | 74.5 | 79.9 | n.a. | 86.2 |
| Urban | n.a. | n.a. | n.a. | n.a. | n.a. | n.a. | 83.2 | 85.8 | n.a. | n.a. |
| Rural | n.a. | n.a. | n.a. | n.a. | n.a. | n.a. | 53.7 | 59.5 | n.a. | n.a. |

Sources: Urbanization is calculated from census data as reported in *Anuário Estatístico* (1994), pp. 2–7, and (1997), pp. 2–36. Literacy is from census data as reported in *Anuário Estatístico* (1997), pp. 2–40; and for 1998, from the Ministry of Finance's Institute of Applied Economic Research (IPEA), based on the PNAD.

n.a. Not available.

a. In Brazil, the "urban" population is defined as those living in all urban and suburban zones of the administrative centers of *municípios* (counties) and districts, rather than according to the population level of a town or city. Compared with the population level of 20,000 or more standard in many other countries, this definition somewhat overstates the extent of urbanization in Brazil. Adult literacy is defined as persons aged fifteen or older who can read and write.

Table 1-6. *Life Expectancy and Infant Mortality, 1930–96*

| Indicator | 1930–40 | 1940–50 | 1950–60 | 1960–70 | 1980 | 1990 | 1996 |
|---|---|---|---|---|---|---|---|
| Life expectancy | | | | | | | |
| at birth (years) | 42.7 | 45.9 | 52.4 | 52.7 | 61.7 | 65.8 | 67.6 |
| Northeast | 38.2 | 38.7 | 43.5 | 44.4 | 58.7 | 64.2 | 64.5 |
| Southeast | 44.0 | 48.9 | 57.0 | 57.0 | 64.5 | 67.5 | 68.8 |
| Infant mortality | | | | | | | |
| (per 1,000 | | | | | | | |
| births) | 158.3 | 144.7 | 118.1 | 116.0 | 69.2 | 47.1 | 36.1 |
| Northeast | 178.7 | 176.3 | 154.9 | 151.2 | 106.8 | 88.2 | n.a. |
| Southeast | 152.8 | 132.6 | 100.0 | 100.2 | 47.4 | 30.0 | n.a. |

Sources: *Estatísticas Históricas*, p. 50, and *Anuário Estatístico* (1994), pp. 2–53; for 1996, data reported on the Internet by the Ministry of Health.

n.a. Not available.

detriment of agriculture and of potential export markets.[17] Some critics regard the anti-inflation policies of the mid-1960s as unduly "orthodox," responsible for industrial recession and reduction in real wages; their defenders claim that less severe policies could not have broken inflationary expectations and laid a foundation for the high-growth "economic miracle" period of 1968–73. That period in turn is widely criticized for making income distribution in Brazil yet more uneven, one of the "worst" in the world. The frequent assertion that "the poor got poorer" during those years, however, is not correct; they became less poor while the rich became substantially richer.[18] Nonetheless, Brazil still has a huge residue of inadequately attended social needs by contemporary first world standards: in housing, health, education, urban services, and social insurance. Perhaps one-third of the population is "marginalized," not yet participating actively in any aspect of the modern economy. Brazil's Gini coefficient, a standard index of inequality in income distribution, stubbornly remains one of the worst in the world (see chapter 5).

On another front, occupying increasing public attention since the 1970s, there is growing concern about environmental deterioration, ranging from depletion of the Amazonian and coastal rain forests to air and water pollution in the overcrowded metropolitan centers. Since the restoration of

17. In chapter 2, I explain why the term "import substitution" is somewhat misleading in the Brazilian context.

18. See World Bank, *Brazil: Economic Memorandum* (Washington, 1984), pp. 126–36.

Figure 1-3. *Selected Social Indicators, 1950–98*

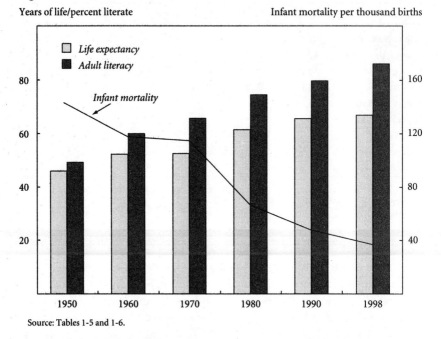

Source: Tables 1-5 and 1-6.

democratic rule in 1985, many nongovernmental organizations (NGOs) have been formed as political pressure groups on environmental protection, often cooperating with and actively supported by like-minded groups in first world countries.

Table 1-7. *Volume of Trade, 1938–99*
Millions of U.S. dollars, except as indicated

| Item | 1938 | 1950 | 1960 | 1970 | 1980 | 1990 | 1999 |
|---|---|---|---|---|---|---|---|
| Exports (fob)[a] | 296 | 1,355 | 1,269 | 2,739 | 20,133 | 31,414 | 48,011 |
| Imports (cif)[a] | 295 | 1,085 | 1,462 | 2,849 | 22,954 | 20,661 | 49,210 |
| Trade balance | 1 | 270 | −193 | −110 | −4,829 | 10,753 | −1,119 |
| GDP (billions) | 3.9 | 15.1 | 17.9 | 45.0 | 250.3 | 469.3 | 804.7 |
| Trade dependency[b] | | | | | | | |
| (percent) | 7.6 | 8.1 | 7.6 | 6.2 | 8.6 | 5.5 | 6.0 |

Sources: United Nations, *International Trade Statistics Yearbook* (various years).

a. fob = free on board; cif = cost, insurance, freight.

b. Trade dependency = (exports + imports)/2 as a percentage of GDP. Some authors use the sum of exports and imports rather than the average, thus doubling the result.

Table 1-8.  *Commodity Composition of Trade, 1938–95*
Percent

| Commodity[a] | 1938 | 1950 | 1970 | 1980 | 1995 |
|---|---|---|---|---|---|
| *Exports* | | | | | |
| Food and raw | | | | | |
| materials (0, 1, 2, 4) | 94.2 | 89.3 | 85.0 | 59.1 | 39.9 |
| Coffee | 45.0 | 63.9 | 35.9 | 13.8 | 5.3 |
| Iron ore | 0.4 | 4.9 | 7.7 | 8.6 | 5.5 |
| Cotton | 18.2 | 7.8 | 5.8 | 0.9 | 0.4 |
| Soybeans and oil | ... | ... | ... | 4.0 | 4.0 |
| Orange juice | ... | ... | ... | ... | 2.4 |
| Semimanufactures | | | | | |
| (5, 6) | ... | 2.1 | 9.1 | 16.6 | 31.8 |
| Machinery and transport | | | | | |
| equipment (7) | ... | ... | 3.5 | 16.9 | 19.0 |
| Automotive vehicles | | | | | |
| and parts | ... | ... | 0.3 | 5.2 | 5.7 |
| Aircraft | ... | ... | ... | 0.4 | 0.6 |
| Miscellaneous | | | | | |
| manufactures (8) | 0.1 | 0.6 | 0.8 | 4.3 | 6.3 |
| Shoes | ... | ... | 0.3 | 1.9 | 2.8 |
| Unspecified | 5.7 | 8.0 | ... | ... | ... |
| *Imports* | | | | | |
| Fuel and lubricants (3) | 10.8 | 13.4 | 12.4 | 43.1 | 8.7 |
| Food and raw | | | | | |
| materials | | | | | |
| (0, 1, 2, 4) | 17.0 | 18.3 | 13.5 | 12.4 | 12.1 |
| Semimanufactures | | | | | |
| (5, 6) | 5.9 | 3.6 | 33.4 | 22.5 | 26.4 |
| Machinery and | | | | | |
| transport | | | | | |
| equipment (7) | 29.1 | 32.9 | 35.2 | 19.5 | 39.1 |
| Aircraft and parts | ... | ... | 1.9 | 1.7 | 0.5 |
| Automotive vehicles | | | | | |
| and parts | 5.5 | 8.7 | 3.6 | 0.8 | 10.8 |
| Miscellaneous | | | | | |
| manufactures (8) | 12.2 | 9.6 | 4.7 | 2.4 | 7.3 |
| Unspecified | 25.0 | 22.2 | ... | ... | ... |

Sources: See table 1-7.
... Not applicable.
a. Major categories of the standard international trade classification (SITC) are in parentheses.

Table 1-9.  *Geographical Composition of Trade, 1938–99*

Percent

| Country | 1938 | 1950 | 1970 | 1995 | 1999 |
|---|---|---|---|---|---|
| *Exports* | | | | | |
| United States and Canada | 34.6 | 55.9 | 26.2 | 19.9 | 23.7 |
| Mercosur | 5.9 | 6.9 | 8.3 | 13.2 | 14.1 |
| Other Western Hemisphere | 0.2 | 1.1 | 3.4 | 9.9 | 7.7 |
| Western Europe | 45.4 | 30.9 | 37.1 | 27.8 | 28.6 |
| Other Europe | 1.6 | 0.7 | 4.5 | 2.9 | 2.5 |
| Japan | 4.6 | . . . | 5.3 | 6.7 | 4.6 |
| Other Asia | 0.5 | 0.8 | 3.5 | 10.9 | 7.4 |
| Africa | 0.5 | 0.7 | 3.3 | 2.5 | 2.8 |
| Middle East | . . . | 0.2 | 5.1 | 3.7 | 3.1 |
| Unspecified | 6.7 | 2.8 | 3.3 | 2.5 | 5.5 |
| *Imports* | | | | | |
| United States and Canada | 25.5 | 35.6 | 34.7 | 23.3 | 26.1 |
| Mercosur | 12.5 | 10.7 | 6.5 | 13.7 | 13.7 |
| Other Western Hemisphere | 3.7 | 12.8 | 5.6 | 6.8 | 5.5 |
| Western Europe | 51.3 | 38.0 | 31.5 | 27.5 | 30.5 |
| Other Europe | 1.8 | 0.8 | 2.1 | 2.2 | 1.4 |
| Japan | 1.3 | . . . | 6.3 | 6.6 | 5.2 |
| Other Asia | 1.0 | 0.4 | 5.7 | 9.9 | 7.9 |
| Africa | . . . | 0.3 | 2.2 | 2.5 | 4.5 |
| Middle East | . . . | 0.1 | 5.1 | 4.2 | 2.2 |
| Unspecified | 2.9 | 1.3 | 0.3 | 3.3 | 3.0 |

Source: For 1938–95, see table 1-7. For 1999, data from Brazil's Ministry of Development, Industry, and Commerce, by Internet.

Those issues apart, both the "miracle" years and the Real Plan period have been criticized intensely by the political left in Brazil for permitting too great participation by multinational corporations and other foreign investors. The political right, in turn, has criticized the excessive participation of state-owned enterprises. Moderate opinion on both left and right, however, would now agree that Brazilian industry should have been exposed to import competition well before 1990.

In the latter 1970s, there were sharply conflicting judgments on the wisdom of Brazil's external borrowing policy, designed to maintain rapid growth despite the pressure of high oil import prices on the balance of payments. And throughout these decades of modernization, up until the Real

Figure 1-4. *Export Destinations, 1950–99*

Percent

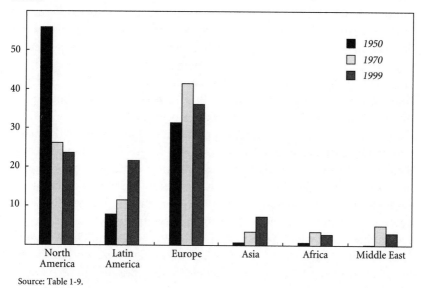

Source: Table 1-9.

Plan of 1994, Brazil failed to approximate price stability for more than a few months at a time. Inflation has been a chronic weakness and a source of unending technical and political dispute.

In later chapters, I assess the merits of many of these conflicting opinions and criticisms. It should be borne in mind that no country in the first world has reached its present stage of development without rough passages in its political and social evolution, least of all Victorian England, which inspired Karl Marx's revulsion against capitalism. For present purposes, the indisputable fact is that since the 1950s, Brazil has taken giant steps toward first world status on the economic side. There are sufficient parallels with American economic history to warrant a brief comparison.

## American Parallels?

On the surface, Brazil resembles the United States in many ways. They are both continental-size countries of similar dimensions. The natural resource bases differ in detail, with the United States possessing more arable land, easier physical access to its interior heartland, and a larger supply of fossil fuels. Yet Brazil also enjoys a generous natural endowment, including a subtropical climate permitting two or three crops a year. In both cases, the original European settlers easily subdued the relatively small and primitive native Indian populations, in contrast to the experiences in Mexico and Peru. The plantations of northeastern Brazil and the southern United States were both based on slaves imported from Africa, with emancipation coming peacefully to Brazil twenty-three years after the American Civil War. Industry, on the other hand, in São Paulo as in New England, was based from the start on free labor. So it is tempting to suppose that Brazil's development is following the American trajectory, but with a lag of a few decades.

Several quantitative indicators support that hypothesis. In 1991 Brazil's population reached the American figure for 1949. Brazil's per capita income matches the American level early in the twentieth century, as does agriculture's share of the labor force. The United States reached Brazil's present levels of electricity production only in 1941. The Brazilian highway network, however, lags much further behind the American, reflecting contrasting geographical settlement patterns and difficulties of terrain. On the side of public health, the United States had reduced infant mortality to present Brazilian levels by 1938, but did not achieve today's Brazilian life expectancy until 1944. Thus in broad brush terms, the Brazilian economy resembles the American of the 1920s, indicating a lag of about seven decades. The American economy in the period between the two world wars surely met the criteria of first world status.[19]

The question arises why there has been any lag at all, the topic of a celebrated study in the mid-1950s by Vianna Moog.[20] Moog rejected traditional explanations such as Brazil's tropical climate, racially mixed population, and geography. He gave somewhat greater weight to the effects of the Protestant ethic in America but focused primarily on psychological attitudes derived from the contrasting histories: the Portuguese coming simply to exploit and extract natural resources while the British and their early followers in North America sought permanent self-sustaining settlements. This analysis is still widely credited. But it is not a permanent obstacle to economic modernization, as demonstrated by Brazil's recent forced-pace industrialization. The alleged incompatibilities of Roman Catholicism with rapid economic devel-

---

19. Data for these comparisons are drawn from *Estatísticas Históricas; Anuário Estatístico 1994; The Europa Yearbook 1987;* and U.S. Department of Commerce, Bureau of the Census, *Historical Statistics of the United States, Colonial Times to 1970, Bicentennial Edition* (Government Printing Office, 1975).

20. Vianna Moog, *Bandeirantes e Pioneiros* (Rio de Janeiro: Editôra Globo, 1955), translated as *Bandeirantes and Pioneers* (New York: George Braziller, 1964).

opment are not persuasive in the face of recent experience in France, Italy, and the Iberian peninsula.

The Brazilian-American contrast in the timing of industrialization seems easily explainable by differences in geography and history. Brazil lacked coal to institute steel production when steel was the key material of the first industrial revolution. Brazil's early colonists came from unindustrialized Portugal whereas America's came from the birthplace of modern industry. The technological drive that inspired Britain's industrial revolution was carried intact to New England and Pennsylvania. Moreover, as Kuznets recognized, the holders of power in a highly oligarchical plantation society successfully exporting its tropical products had little incentive to promote industrial modernization.

The economic development literature diverges on the effects of being a "latecomer" to industrialization. One school holds that latecomers have an inherent advantage in being able to borrow technology and institutional models from the pioneers. The other argues that they face formidable hurdles in breaking into markets preempted by the early starters. Brazil's experience since the 1950s supports the former view, as does that of Southern Europe and the East Asian NICs. Moreover, "catching up" with the United States appears to have played a major part in the unusually high worldwide growth rates of the period 1948–73.[21]

The historical cultural differences between Brazil and the United States may be especially relevant to a second stage of modern economic growth in the first world. That is the shift from early monopoly capitalism, dominated by family-owned concerns and marked by a sharply differentiated class structure, to the more dynamic and competitive welfare capitalism of the mid–twentieth century, with its huge middle classes, high degree of social mobility, and widespread "safety nets," a more dynamic system that is also less prone to extreme economic depression. In bringing about that shift, America's stable democratic institutions played a major part, facilitating the reforms associated with Theodore Roosevelt, William Howard Taft, Woodrow Wilson, and above all Franklin Roosevelt's New Deal. There are counterparts in the political-economic histories of Canada, Australia, New Zealand, and Great Britain. By one route or another, including intervals of fascism, enemy occupation, and defeat in war, continental Europe and Japan have also achieved this second stage, which is still evolving. But in this

---

21. See Angus Maddison, "Growth and Slowdown in Advanced Capitalist Economies: Techniques of Quantitative Assessment," *Journal of Economic Literature*, vol. 25 (June 1987), pp. 649–98.

respect, there is no Brazilian parallel. It is on the political side that Brazil's readiness for first world status is most in question.

## Political Modernization

Stable pluralist political democracy, with respect for human rights and unconditional acceptance of the outcomes of free elections—the criteria defining the first world on the political side—has been the declared aspiration of a liberalizing element within the Brazilian elites for well over a century. But in contrast to its economic progress, Brazil's polity has not remotely achieved the democratic stability enjoyed by the United States well before the end of the nineteenth century. America's last—and only—stolen presidential election was in 1876, while Brazil was ruled by a one-man dictatorship from 1937 to 1945 and a military oligarchy from 1964 to 1985.

Brazil's Constitution of 1891 drew many features from the American, including the federal division of powers between the union and the states and the tripartite separation of powers (legislative, executive, and judicial) at both the national and state levels. But the underlying reality was entirely different. The Old Republic (1891–1930) was a loose federation with most authority at the state level. A limited franchise excluded the illiterate majority of the adult population, and few services were provided by government. The national Congress rarely disputed presidential authority, but state-level political machines and the military officer corps did so frequently. Instead of featuring two parties of national scope, Brazilian politics was essentially local or regional, highly personalistic, and based on the exchange of jobs and favors for votes, with large doses of petty and gross corruption and considerable organized violence. The closest American parallel was the city machine in the mold of Tammany Hall.

Before World War I, Brazil peacefully negotiated favorable boundary settlements all around its vast frontiers and played a leading role in forming the Pan-American Union. But these foreign policy accomplishments were not matched by national management of the domestic economy, which was totally dependent on the export of a few primary products—coffee, cacao, sugar, cotton, some minerals, and (for a brief period) rubber—and therefore highly vulnerable to fluctuations in export markets and in the terms of trade.

So there was fertile ground for popular unrest, regional use of force for parochial objectives, and mobilization movements against the established order. There were occasional clashes between the independent militias of some states. The armed forces were called in to deal with other episodes of violence: the notorious "rebellion in the backlands" in the late 1890s,[22] the short-lived but significant "lieutenants' revolt" in 1922, the Prestes Column of dissident junior officers in 1925–27. Military action was decisive in Getúlio Vargas's "revolution" of 1930, and military influence was never absent from the political scene, even under the able civilian presidents of the early twentieth century.

The era of Getúlio Vargas, including his second and legitimate presidency from 1950 to 1954, transformed the Brazilian state and many aspects of Brazilian society. It created full-fledged governmental institutions at the national level for the first time, including a rudimentary professional civil service. It ensured linguistic unity by requiring that elementary instruction be in the Portuguese language. It instituted—for good or for ill—a kind of embryonic developmental strategy based on state capitalism in basic industries: steel in the 1940s and petroleum in the 1950s. The corporative structure of labor unions and employer organizations, labor tribunals, and social security institutes remains to this day a significant element in Brazilian industrial relations. In a period of rapid urbanization and spreading literacy, which brought into being a substantial popular electorate, the Vargas era shaped the political parties of the Second Republic (1946–64).

The Second Republic can be considered Brazil's "first chance" to become firmly set on the road toward first world status, although not to its full achievement in a few years. Unfortunately, however, the political party structure of this fledgling new democracy was focused more on the pros and cons of the Vargas past than on the substantive issues of economic and social modernization. In the first decade, military intervention was frequently threatened. In 1952 it resulted in the ouster of the labor minister, João Goulart, and in 1954 to the suicide of Vargas himself under charges of corruption. Military threats were also leveled against the successor vice president, João Café Filho. After the election of 1955, elements in the armed forces conspired with anti-Vargas civilian circles against the inauguration of Juscelino Kubitschek, requiring a "preventive coup" against the outgoing interim president to ensure the succession.

During the late 1950s, however, with the major successes of Kubitschek's "developmentalism," it seemed that democratic institutions might finally be

---

22. This prolonged episode was the subject of *Os Sertões*, a sociological classic by Euclides da Cunha, published in 1902 and translated into English under the title *Rebellion in the Backlands* (University of Chicago Press, 1944). It was again the subject of a literary masterpiece in 1981 by Mario Vargas Llosa, *La Guerra del Fin del Mundo*, translated as *The War of the End of the World* (Farrar Straus Giroux, 1984).

on the way to consolidation, marked by the completely unruffled transfer of power to Jânio Quadros in 1960–61. The "first chance" failed in 1964 after the early resignation of Quadros and the ill-fated presidency of Goulart. Whether that failure was inevitable is explored in chapter 2. With the return to civilian rule in 1985 and the adoption in 1988 of a fully democratic constitution for the "New Republic," Brazil again faced the challenge of political modernization.

National euphoria after redemocratization was followed by a series of political disappointments, intensified by dismal economic performance. In 1985 Tancredo Neves, elected president by a quasi-democratic electoral college, became fatally ill on his scheduled inauguration day. He was succeeded by José Sarney, who enjoyed a brief period of immense popularity in the first few months of his Cruzado Plan, a heterodox "shock treatment" attempt to conquer inflation at one blow through a freeze on prices and wages. Lacking the necessary fiscal austerity, and doomed from the start by across-the-board wage increases, it lasted long enough to assist in electing a single party, Sarney's Party of the Brazilian Democratic Movement (PMDB), to a majority in Congress. By the end of 1986, however, the Cruzado Plan had become a total failure, leaving price stabilization an unmet goal through the rest of Sarney's term and beyond.

The election of 1989 was the first popular vote for the presidency since 1960. The electorate had been hugely enlarged by the increase in population, the enfranchisement of illiterates, and a lowering of the voting age. But the victor, Fernando Collor de Mello, was not an established national leader. He was the youthful and seemingly charismatic governor of the small and backward state of Alagoas, elected mainly for fear of his principal opponent, the metallurgical trade union leader Luís Inácio ("Lula") da Silva, whose supporters included the radical far left. As president, Collor presented a set of three economic policy objectives: price stabilization, opening of the economy to international competition, and privatization of state enterprises. Euphoria at his inauguration, however, was soon followed by disillusion with his package of shock treatment measures for economic stabilization and then with revulsion at the evidence of monumental corruption, which led to his impeachment by the Chamber of Deputies in September 1992 and resignation in December before a possible Senate trial. The reign of the succeeding vice president, Itamar Franco, was little more than a holding action, focused on warding off hyperinflation, until his appointment of Fernando Henrique Cardoso to the Finance Ministry in May 1993.

A former academic sociologist, elected senator from São Paulo and leader of the mildly left-of-center Brazilian Social Democratic Party

(PSDB), Cardoso formed a team of exceptionally able economists who formulated the Real Plan (Plano Real), a highly sophisticated program to overcome the inertial element in inflation without applying heterodox shock treatment.[23] Cardoso also extended the initiatives begun by Collor for opening Brazil to the world economy and further privatizations. Thus Brazil appeared to be following Chile, Mexico, and Argentina into a new era of macroeconomic policies for Latin America, sometimes known as the Washington consensus because of its support from the World Bank, the IMF, and the U.S. government.

The initial successes and critical trials of the Real Plan in its first five years are discussed in detail in chapter 7. Long-term success will require fiscal discipline on both expenditure and revenue sides, control of credit expansion without punitively high interest rates, and a more full-fledged integration into the world economy. Along with these macroeconomic measures, the economic criteria for first world membership require much fuller participation in the modern economy by hitherto marginalized segments of Brazilian society, a condition also likely to reduce the glaring inequalities in income distribution.

Returning to the political criterion, it cannot yet be said that Brazil possesses a fully stable and mature democratic system. The weaknesses in party structure and electoral arrangements are reviewed in detail in chapter 6. Civil society is only in the early stages of playing a substantial political role through nongovernmental organizations. While there is an elaborate legal system, with tenured judiciary and frequent recourse to litigation, many laws are flagrantly flouted and there are pressing needs for reform in the judicial system.

A large informal economic sector, motivated mainly by avoidance of taxes and of legal rules for hiring and firing, is estimated by some observers at one-third again of the recorded economy. Evasion of income taxes and dishonest bookkeeping are known to be widespread business practices. Official corruption is frequently uncovered but usually unpunished. Violence is endemic in urban slums, now often controlled by drug merchants, and in rural clashes between landless peasants and owners of large estates. Some portion of that violence is attributable to state-level military police forces, which are rarely held accountable. Automobile thievery and kidnappings for ransom are constant concerns for the middle- and upper-income groups. All these ills are less acute than in several other Latin American countries

23. The word "real" means both "real" as in English and "royal"; it had been a nineteenth-century monetary unit in both Portugal and Brazil.

and are certainly less acute than in early Victorian England, but they undermine the prospects for firm consolidation of democracy. These issues are
considered in chapter 5.

## Brazil and the Other NICs

On several fronts, Brazil enjoys great comparative advantage as a candidate
for first world status. Internationally, it is a completely satisfied power, with
no legacy (like Mexico's) of lost territory and no external threat (like South
Korea's) to its physical security. Although Brazilian blacks and mulattoes
suffer a great deal of de facto discrimination, the country has been spared
the vice of formal racial segregation. Unlike Mexico and the Andean nations,
Brazil has only a tiny Amerindian minority, and linguistic unity has been the
rule since the Vargas educational reforms. There is a very large marginalized
class of illiterate peasants and unskilled urban workers, but the class boundaries are softened by shared nationalism and by opportunities for upward
mobility for its more energetic members.

As between the middle and upper classes, mobility is especially striking.
Many of the leading figures in business and the professions come from
recent waves of European, Middle Eastern, or Japanese immigration. Only
a few political leaders descend from the old plantation-owning "aristocracy." The social patterns, in short, resemble those of North America more
closely than those of Brazil's Spanish American neighbors.

Among the NICs listed earlier, Brazil's most successful competitor is
South Korea. Notwithstanding the destruction of the civil war and the heavy
continuing budgetary and manpower drains of defense against the North,
Korea maintained a record of economic growth and industrial modernization and diversification through the 1970s on a scale similar to Brazil's; it has
subsequently moved well ahead. It has escaped debilitating inflation and
accommodated the oil shocks of the 1970s with extraordinary resiliency and
without excessive foreign borrowing. During the 1980s, its real per capita
incomes passed Brazil's, while its income distribution is much less uneven.
Korea's combination of export promotion and import substitution strategies have maintained a strong balance of payments position. The Asian crisis of 1997–99 revealed structural weaknesses in industrial organization and
the banking system, but they are not beyond redemption. Underlying
Korea's remarkable record are two salient features of its society, akin to
Japan's: the very high rates of savings and investment and the passion for
education. The novel experiment in constitutional democracy appears to be
taking firm root, completing Korea's claim to full first world membership.

## The Stakes

What are the consequences of success or failure in Brazil's quest for first world status? That it matters profoundly for Brazilians is self-evident: in terms of material prosperity, human rights and political liberties, and opportunity to make a distinctive mark as a great nation on the world scene. For the world at large, including the United States, the case is not so clear.

Perhaps in reaction to the excessively simplistic modernization models of the 1950s, one intellectual current in the 1980s and 1990s, achieving some vogue in both first world and third world quarters, raised doubts about the whole enterprise of economic and political development, at least as a goal for deliberate national planning and international cooperation.[24] These critics observed that economic modernization is often not the principal objective of leadership groups in the third world. In some cases, notably Iran, Western-style development has been violently rejected. There are still residues of Marxist objections to capitalism as the major vehicle of modernization, and nationalist politicians in the third world often object to the presence of multinational corporations based in the first world. Even though many development economists now argue that greater equality and higher growth rates are mutually supporting goals, there remains an underlying tension between those giving priority to a direct attack on basic poverty through the redistribution of income and wealth and those giving priority to growth along with improved income distribution.

Much of this critical reaction is essentially irrelevant to the Brazilian case. Although Marxist analytical frameworks continue to be used by large numbers of Brazilian (and other Latin American) intellectuals and some labor and student leaders, the Soviet methods of central planning have become totally discredited in the former second world and no longer serve as working models even for what remains of Brazil's far left. Cuba has conspicuously failed to provide an attractive model after thirty-five years of Communist rule.

Modernization has gone much too far to be replaced as a goal by some kind of nonmaterial objective, as in Iran. In culture and basic values, Brazil is fully and irrevocably part of the West. Nationalism is indeed a powerful force there, and versions of dependency theory, focused on resistance to

---

24. For examples, see John F. J. Toye, *Dilemmas of Development: Reflections on the Counter-Revolution in Development Theory and Policy* (Oxford: Blackwell, 1987); and "A World to Make: Development in Perspective," *Daedalus*, vol. 118 (January 1989). These analyses go further in questioning the goals than do the neoconservative criticisms of methods other than reliance on free market forces; see, for example, P. T. Bauer, *Equality, the Third World, and Economic Delusion* (Harvard University Press, 1981). A middle position is taken by Deepak Lal in *The Poverty of Development Economics* (London: Institute of Economic Affairs, 1983).

integration into the global economy, continue to enlist many supporters. But for both elites and mass publics, the essential tests of policy are pragmatic. Does it produce wider job opportunities and higher incomes? Does it overcome the historic national cancer of inflation? Does it incorporate successive segments of the marginalized? And, in relation to the world at large, does it provide a meaningful role for Brazil as a substantial actor in its own right?

Success in these terms could provide an example and a pole of attraction for most of Latin America. If the first world as a whole maintains an open system of trade, finance, and technological and cultural interchange, a Brazilian-led South America could make a major contribution to its further evolution. If the first world breaks up into regional trading blocs, the United States would benefit from South American affiliation with the rest of the Western Hemisphere, already a purported policy goal in both North and South America. In either event, there is ample ground for mutually beneficial relations. Brazilian success should be desired and encouraged by the United States, within the practical limits of its capacity to affect the outcome. The most likely alternative is a long period of economic decline and political instability, with the instability spilling over from Brazil to the rest of South America. That outcome would be a tragic missed opportunity.

# 2

## The First Chance: What Went Wrong?

As pointed out in chapter 1, the period of the Second Republic—the two decades following World War II—was Brazil's "first chance" to consolidate a movement toward first world status. More precisely, this prospect appeared at its clearest during the six years 1956–61, under the presidencies of Juscelino Kubitschek and Jânio Quadros. Although the earlier postwar years had also witnessed substantial economic growth, new qualitative features were introduced in the Kubitschek era. Until then, except for the nationalized steel and petroleum industries sponsored by President Vargas, industrialization had been mostly a spontaneous response to wartime cuts in imports or a shortage of foreign exchange. For Kubitschek and his supporters, however, accelerated economic development, focused on industrial modernization, was the key to national fulfillment. The Kubitschek slogan was "Fifty Years in Five."

During the early 1950s, a joint Brazil-U.S. economic commission had identified critical bottlenecks, notably in transportation and energy supplies. The National Bank for Economic Development (BNDE, subsequently BNDES to include "social" development) was established in 1952 to funnel capital into these critical areas. But Kubitschek's Goals Program (Programa de Metas) had a much broader compass, extending beyond infrastructure to major industries such as automobiles, shipbuilding, heavy chemicals, additional types of metalworking, machine tools, and other capital goods.

The whole span of the Second Republic is marked by significant contrasts (figures 2-1 and 2-2). Until 1957, growth rates fluctuated widely from year to year. But then came five consecutive years of high growth, averaging

Figure 2-1. *GDP Growth and Inflation, 1947–64*

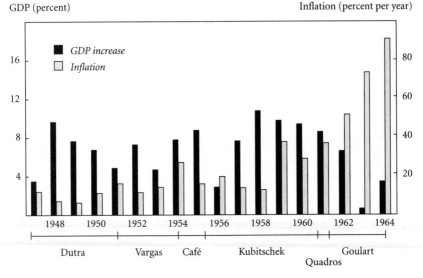

Source: Table 2-1, columns 1 and 7.

9.3 percent overall and 6.1 percent per capita (table 2-1, columns 1 and 2). At those rates, total output doubles in less than eight years and per capita output in twelve.

In that same five-year period, the share of the industrial sector in the rapidly growing national product rose from 26 to 32 percent (table 2-1,

Figure 2-2. *Increases in GDP and Electric Capacity, 1947–64*

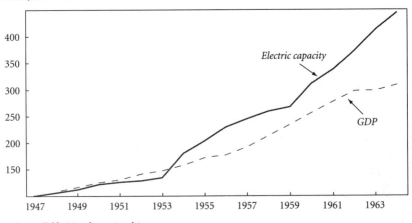

Source: Table 2-1, columns 1 and 4.

Table 2-1. *Economic Development under the Second Republic, 1947–64*

| President | Year | GDP percent | | 3. Industrial share | 4. Installed electric capacity (mW) | 5. Current balance of payments (millions of U.S. dollars) | 6. External indebtedness (millions of U.S. dollars) | 7. Change in general price level (percent) |
| | | 1. Increase | 2. Per capita increase | | | | | |
| --- | --- | --- | --- | --- | --- | --- | --- | --- |
| Dutra | 1947 | n.a. | n.a. | 25.2 | 1,534 | −151 | 625 | 11.8 |
| | 1948 | 9.7 | 7.1 | 24.2 | 1,625 | −2 | 597 | 7.0 |
| | 1949 | 7.7 | 5.1 | 24.7 | 1,735 | −82 | 601 | 6.8 |
| | 1950 | 6.8 | 4.3 | 24.1 | 1,883 | 140 | 559 | 11.5 |
| Vargas | 1951 | 4.9 | 1.8 | 25.1 | 1,940 | −403 | 571 | 16.5 |
| | 1952 | 7.3 | 4.2 | 24.2 | 1,985 | −624 | 638 | 11.8 |
| | 1953 | 4.7 | 1.6 | 25.4 | 2,089 | 55 | 1,159 | 14.5 |
| | 1954 | 7.8 | 4.7 | 25.8 | 2,805 | −195 | 1,317 | 27.2 |
| Cafe Filho | 1955 | 8.8 | 5.6 | 25.6 | 3,148 | 2 | 1,445 | 16.3 |
| Kubitschek | 1956 | 2.9 | −0.1 | 27.3 | 3,550 | 57 | 2,694 | 19.9 |
| | 1957 | 7.7 | 4.5 | 27.8 | 3,767 | −264 | 2,658 | 14.2 |
| | 1958 | 10.8 | 7.6 | 31.1 | 3,993 | −248 | 3,069 | 13.0 |
| | 1959 | 9.8 | 6.6 | 33.0 | 4,115 | −311 | 3,392 | 37.9 |
| | 1960 | 9.4 | 6.2 | 32.2 | 4,800 | −478 | 3,907 | 29.1 |
| Quadros | 1961 | 8.6 | 5.6 | 32.5 | 5,205 | −222 | 3,773 | 37.2 |
| Goulart | 1962 | 6.6 | 3.6 | 32.5 | 5,729 | −389 | 4,025 | 51.9 |
| | 1963 | 0.6 | −2.2 | 33.1 | 6,355 | −114 | 3,986 | 73.7 |
| | 1964 | 3.4 | 0.5 | 32.5 | 6,840 | 140 | 3,874 | 90.7 |

Source: *Estatísticas Históricas*. The basic data on GDP (in current cruzeiros) are in table 4.3 (consolidated national accounts), pp. 95–96. Columns 1 and 2 are from table 4.7 (total and per capita GDP, resident population, and implicit deflators), p. 111; column 3 from table 4.10 (GDP at factor cost by sectors and fields of economic activity), pp. 117–18; column 4 from table 9.1 (installed electric generating capacity), p. 447; column 5 from table 11.6 (balance of payments), line E, pp. 537–38; column 6 from table 11.8 (external indebtedness in dollars), p. 543; and column 7 from table 5.10 (general price index calculated by the Fundação Getúlio Vargas), pp. 189–94.

column 3). The expansion of electrical capacity (column 4 and figure 2-2) was made possible by the bottleneck-breaking efforts in basic infrastructure begun under Vargas and vastly expanded by Kubitschek. The excess of goods and services imports over exports (column 5) was largely financed by the inflow of direct private investments and development loans from international agencies and foreign governments (notably the U.S. Export-Import Bank). These transactions built up a considerable international indebtedness (column 6), but the debt-service ratio (interest and amortization payments as a fraction of export earnings) remained within comfortable limits.

The dark part of the picture, however, was the acceleration of inflation after 1958 (column 7), one of the central factors in the stagnation of the early 1960s and the collapse of democratic institutions in 1964. As seen in figure 2-1, growth and inflation showed no systematic correlation, either positive or negative, through 1958, but from 1959 to 1964 a dramatic explosion of inflation was combined with a sharp decline in growth rates. In that era, indexation of wages, rents, and asset values had not yet come into vogue and the double-digit *monthly* inflation rates of more recent times would have been inconceivable.

On the political side, there seemed to be a basic shift toward institutional consolidation. The early 1950s, climaxed by the Vargas suicide in 1954, had been far from stable. But the election of 1960 was wholly peaceful. The inauguration of Jânio Quadros in 1961 was a model of constitutional normality. To this day, analysts debate whether the death of the Second Republic resulted from an inescapable clash of underlying social forces or from the accidents of personalities and mismanagement. My own assessment favors the latter view and is spelled out later in this chapter.

## The Kubitschek Record: Successes and Failures

The outstanding feature of the Kubitschek era was its capacity to transcend historic Brazilian cleavages by securing broad support for developmentalism (*desenvolvimentismo*). A sense of national self-confidence and belief in unlimited horizons seemed to pervade all classes of society, putting an end to the tired old clichés depicting Brazil as a "sleeping giant." That mood applied to culture and sports as well as economics, as seen in the global popularity of Brazil's bossa nova and the 1958 victory in world soccer competition.

The gains of the great economic boom were not evenly distributed. In the grandiose—and initially popular—project for the new capital of Brasília, the regional gainers were the surrounding state of Goiás, along with São Paulo and the president's native state of Minas Gerais, which were the main suppliers of building materials. The losers were the old capital, Rio de Janeiro, and the Northeast. In the great drive for industrialization, led by the implantation of a substantial automotive industry, São Paulo was overwhelmingly the gainer. Agriculture in general, especially in the backward regions, fared much less well than industry, and exchange rate policy discriminated against exporters and potential exporters. A new class of skilled industrial workers reaped major benefits, as did businessmen and a growing middle group of service workers.

Despite these imbalances, however, the experience as a whole demonstrated the possibilities of positive-sum social relationships in an environment where rapid overall growth provides at least something for almost everyone. Those kinds of relationships are at the base of stable democratic politics in first world countries.

The softening of tensions also extended to the economic nationalism that has played a major role in Brazilian politics since the Great Depression of the 1930s. Nationalism reached a peak in Getúlio Vargas's campaign of the early 1950s for a state-owned petroleum monopoly under the slogan "The Oil Is Ours." It was reinforced by references in his 1954 suicide note to "decades of domination and plunder on the part of international economic and financial groups."[1] In its more extreme forms, sometimes known as "negative nationalism" and much in evidence in the constitutional assembly of 1987–88, some Brazilian writers and politicians regarded any kind of foreign economic relationship as inherently exploitative. Others believed that involvement in the world capitalist economy prevented Brazil from undertaking the radical domestic reforms they considered essential to social justice.

Yet in the Kubitschek era there was only muted objection to special exchange rate inducements for foreign private capital participating in Brazilian industrialization. European and American companies (plus a few Japanese) took the leading role in the new automotive and shipbuilding industries.[2] At the same time, these industries created markets for dozens of wholly Brazilian-owned companies supplying components and ancillary services, tempering the tensions between domestic and foreign entrepreneurs. Kubitschek was well aware of the political force of nationalist populism, as he demonstrated in 1959 in terminating negotiations with the

1. For the full text, see John W. F. Dulles, *Vargas of Brazil: A Political Biography* (University of Texas Press, 1967), pp. 334–35.

2. For a survey of attitudes of American manufacturing companies toward investment in Brazil in that period, see Lincoln Gordon and Engelbert Grommers, *United States Manufacturing Investment in Brazil, 1946–1960* (Harvard Business School, 1962).

International Monetary Fund. But for the most part he emphasized "positive nationalism," in which Brazilian greatness could be enhanced by the suitable use of foreign capital and technology.

This capacity to blunt social conflict and conciliate long-standing rivalries has proven perplexing to some historians and political analysts, especially those writing in the Marxist mode popular among Brazilian social scientists. The experience seemed to refute such doctrines as irreconcilable antagonism between rigidly defined socioeconomic classes and "inherent contradictions" in capitalist development, which were supposed to culminate in social revolution. One historian finds that the "success of Kubitschek's economic policy was a direct result of his success in maintaining political stability."[3] But the converse might equally well be argued: that political stability was made possible by economic success.[4]

The striking economic gains in quantitative terms reflected in table 2-1 tell only part of the story. Of even greater importance were the qualitative changes that transformed Brazil's industrial structure in those years. They seemed to go beyond Walt Rostow's "preconditions" into a full-fledged "take-off into sustained growth." The Brazilian economic historian (and later finance minister) Luiz Bresser Pereira—perhaps somewhat overstating the case—goes even further. After describing the Kubitschek era as "the golden period of national economic development," he writes: "In this period, the first phase of the Brazilian industrial revolution was consolidated, ending [that is, completing] the economic take-off."[5]

This phase of Brazilian development is often described as a classic example of "import-substituting industrialization." In the sense that additional types of goods previously imported now came to be manufactured at home, the description is accurate. But that kind of import substitution was already

3. Thomas E. Skidmore, *Politics in Brazil 1930–1964: An Experiment in Democracy* (Oxford University Press, 1967), pp. 163–70.

4. Kubitschek's concern with political stability was a noteworthy feature of his private conversations with me when I was in Rio de Janeiro as U.S. ambassador. On one occasion in 1962, he acknowledged the military uselessness to Brazil of the aircraft carrier *Minas Gerais,* which he had purchased secondhand from the British. "But you will recall," he said in substance, "that my own inauguration was almost frustrated by a naval rebellion. The carrier was the price of peace with the admirals. And you saw the result in my unruffled transfer of power to Jânio Quadros." In another conversation in early 1964, shortly before the military coup, he described repeated pleas at the end of 1960 by João Goulart (who had served as vice president during his own term and had just been reelected to serve under Quadros) that he, Kubitschek, precipitate an unconstitutional "self-coup" to keep himself in power. Kubitschek, who was aware of his own popularity and hoped to use it as a springboard for reelection in 1965, rejected this advice out of hand.

5. Luiz Bresser Pereira, *Development and Crisis in Brazil, 1930–1983,* translated by Marcia Van Dyke (Boulder, Colo.: Westview Press, 1984), p. 25.

an old story in Brazil, having started with simple consumer goods in the nineteenth century and progressing by the mid-1950s to include small electrical household appliances, other consumer durables, and even many of the simpler capital goods. The National Steel Company (1942) and Petrobrás's first oil refinery (1954) had initiated Brazil's entry into heavy industry. Under Kubitschek, the process was broadened, deepened, and accelerated. It went beyond mere import substitution, fostering a rapidly growing domestic market with the potential to become the principal engine of sustained further growth.

The exemplar of this qualitative change was the automotive industry. It was launched in 1956, with the announced aim of securing by 1960 domestic production of 90 to 95 percent by weight of all components, as well as final assembly, of some 170,000 vehicles per year. The longer-range goal was an annual capacity of 300,000. European and American automobile companies were given highly favorable exchange rates for importing manufacturing equipment and key components during the short transition period of progressive "Brazilianization." In turn, they had to accept rigorous schedules for the production of components in Brazil and undertake specific measures to secure local suppliers. For the more complex parts, the assembly companies often persuaded their own home component manufacturers to invest in joint ventures with promising Brazilian firms.[6]

Although the 1960 production target was not reached until 1962, the industry subsequently grew to major magnitudes, reaching 400,000 vehicles by 1970 and over 1 million by 1978. In 1994, it passed the 1.5 million mark, and in 1997 reached 2 million units, the world's eighth largest output that year.[7]

At the beginning, passenger car costs were well above those of hypothetical imports (actual imports were forbidden), but jeeps and commercial vehicles were competitive from an early stage. Exports became possible by the mid-1970s and in the 1980s accounted for almost one-quarter of total sales.[8] By then, Brazil's automotive industry ranked tenth, close in size to Britain's. The "ABC" suburbs of São Paulo (Santo André, São Bernardo do Campo, and São Caetano do Sul) had become a little Detroit. At the industry's start

6. For details on the incentive measures, see Gordon and Grommers, *United States Manufacturing Investment in Brazil,* chap. 4.

7. Data supplied by the National Association of Automotive Vehicle Manufacturers (ANFAVEA) are published regularly in *Conjuntura Econômica,* the monthly journal of the Fundação Getúlio Vargas (Rio de Janeiro).

8. Data on production, registrations, and exports are published annually in *Motor Vehicle Manufacturers Association of the United States, World Motor Vehicle Data* (Detroit: MVMA).

there were too many producers and far too many individual car and truck models, which later had to be shaken down. Yet the experience as a whole was a remarkable demonstration of successful infant-industry promotion.

As automotive production developed, its domestic market grew rapidly. The industry is famous among students of industrial structure for the variety of its backward and forward linkages to materials and component suppliers and to sales outlets and servicing. Skilled workers as well as managers in these activities soon became potential automobile owners. Imports of vehicles (including local assembly of imported sets of components) had averaged 60,540 units in the eight years 1947–54. In 1955 and 1956 they were restricted to less than 20,000 because of foreign exchange shortages. But by 1961 sales from domestic production came to 146,000, more than double the previous level of imports. In 1951 total registrations were 511,000, or one per 105 inhabitants; by 1962 registrations had grown to 1,339,000, and the vehicle density to 1 per 55. By the mid-1980s, registrations were almost 11.5 million and the density was 1 per 12 inhabitants. At the same time, the paved intercity road network was expanded from 2,000 to 11,000 miles (100,000 by 1990).

For better or worse, Brazil was becoming a full-fledged automotive society, with a corresponding network of repair shops, service stations, roadside motels, and restaurants. For the middle and upper classes, living and working and residential patterns shifted correspondingly toward those of the first world. "Import substitution" is far too narrow a term for this minirevolution. Rather, it resembles the broad tariff-protected industrialization fostered in the United States by Alexander Hamilton and later in Germany by the preachings of Friedrich List.

Other industries initiated during the late 1950s, such as shipbuilding and petrochemicals, were less spectacular but also important to rounded industrial modernization. The production of capital goods was already considerable by 1955, but in the Kubitschek era it underwent a quantum jump in both scale and complexity, reaching one-third of total manufacturing output by 1959. Qualitatively, it was moving from relatively simple equipment for sugar mills and coffee processing to a wide array of mechanical and electrical equipment and machine tools, produced at competitive costs to international technical standards.[9]

Entrepreneurship came partly from the newer European immigrant groups but also from scions of the traditional landowning families, many of

9. Nathaniel H. Leff, *The Brazilian Capital Goods Industry, 1929–1964* (Harvard University Press, 1968).

whom were shifting their main economic interests into industry. There was a parallel evolution in education, with engineering gaining space in universities alongside law, medicine, and the humanities, while a variety of technical and vocational training schools sprang up at the intermediate level. The middle classes and skilled workers began to play larger parts in political life. But these attitudinal and social changes were concentrated in São Paulo and the neighboring states of the Center-South, intensifying their polarization with the Northeast.

Against the Kubitschek record of dramatic developmental successes, there must be set a number of significant weaknesses. One was the exacerbation of regional differences, an issue attacked only toward the end of the period with the establishment of the Superintendency for Development of the Northeast (SUDENE). More serious was the almost total inattention to agriculture, leaving a large share of the population outside the modernizing revolution and failing to take advantage of Brazil's comparative advantage in that sector. The lost opportunities were demonstrated in later years, when soybean products and concentrated orange juice became major Brazilian exports. There was a similar disregard for export opportunities in minerals and in miscellaneous manufactures. The policymakers indulged the comforting illusion that import substitution, especially in capital goods, would free the nation from balance of payments constraints, making it unnecessary to promote exports beyond the traditional items of coffee, sugar, cotton, and cacao. In fact, however, each stage of import replacement was accompanied by new types of import requirements, so the balance of payments remained under pressure and by the early 1960s became a significant limitation on further economic growth. On the side of human capital, little was done to remedy the glaring weaknesses in elementary and secondary education or to build the foundations for comprehensive health care.

The fundamental weakness was irresponsibly inflationary financing, which led inexorably to the ending of the economic boom and played a major part in the subsequent collapse of constitutional democracy. The effect on price levels can be seen in the last column of table 2-1: from an annual average rise of 16 percent in the first three Kubitschek years (1956–58) to 35 percent in the following three, and then on up under Goulart, year by year, to 52, 74, and 91 percent in the fatal year 1964.

Inflation was not a deliberate objective of policy, although a good deal of the economic literature of the time considered it "structurally" unavoidable or positively welcomed it as a means of mobilizing capital via forced savings. Its immediate source was public budgetary deficits financed by the Bank of Brazil in its then partial role as central bank. Inflationary financing was used to conciliate a variety of interest groups. It was used in support payments for unrestricted coffee production, with surpluses then bought up and withheld from the world market; in increased subsidies for urban transport and utility services; in working capital loans to São Paulo industries at negative real interest rates; in exchange rate subsidies for imported wheat, petroleum, and newsprint; and in a host of other such measures.[10]

On top of all that came the building of the new capital of Brasília in a remote and vacant plain, the epitome of "pharaonic" projects (such as the Sphinx or the pyramids) that have been a periodic hallmark of Brazilian public policy in the postwar decades. At the time, the project for Brasília evoked mixed feelings. Most members of Congress and civil servants bemoaned the prospect of leaving the physical and social attractions of Rio de Janeiro, while many others, without giving much thought to the costs, gloried in the national symbolism of a super-modern capital attracting attention from urban planners and architects worldwide. Brasília even today has both enthusiasts and detractors, although disillusionment became widespread during the 1970s and 1980s.[11]

Whatever its political merits, the construction of Brasília was financed partly by increasing the fiscal deficit and partly by speculative profits on real estate sales, thus adding to the inflationary pressures of the time. The hurried schedule, aimed at inauguration while Kubitschek was still in office, made for very loose oversight of contractors, and rumors of corruption were commonplace. The president had also been misled by noneconomist advisers into the bizarre belief that budgetary deficits would not be inflationary if applied to investment rather than consumption. Hence his readiness in 1959 to terminate negotiations with the IMF, which might have brought the inflationary pressures under control.

### Stagnation and Inflation: Contending Diagnoses

After 1961, accelerating inflation became joined with a major economic slowdown. As table 2-2 (and figure 2-3) make clear, it was the industrial sec-

---

10. For a detailed exposition and somewhat sympathetic political-economic analysis of governmental financial practices in this period, see UN Economic Commission for Latin America, "Fifteen Years of Economic Policy in Brazil," *Economic Bulletin for Latin America*, vol. 9 (December 1964), pp. 153–214, especially pp. 172–73 and 180–84.

11. André Malraux and other international cultural stars were lavish in their praise. In conversation with me in 1962, Kubitschek himself acknowledged that it would have been more rational to open up the nation's interior first by building roads and railroads and encouraging migration, deferring the move of the capital. Politically, however, he was (probably correctly) convinced that the

Table 2-2. *Boom and Stagnation, by Major Sectors, 1955–65*
Annual growth rates of output (percent)

| Year | Agriculture | Industry | Services | Total GDP |
|------|-------------|----------|----------|-----------|
| 1955 | 7.0 | 9.5 | 11.7 | 8.8 |
| 1956 | −8.4 | 8.6 | 3.4 | 2.9 |
| 1957 | 4.6 | 9.9 | 8.3 | 7.7 |
| 1958 | −2.2 | 21.4 | 5.9 | 10.8 |
| 1959 | 2.1 | 16.0 | 8.1 | 9.8 |
| 1960 | 13.5 | 7.2 | 10.0 | 9.4 |
| 1961 | 5.7 | 11.6 | 11.7 | 8.6 |
| 1962 | 10.4 | 7.0 | 6.3 | 6.6 |
| 1963 | −8.1 | 2.6 | 2.4 | 0.6 |
| 1964 | 4.5 | 0.6 | 2.9 | 3.4 |
| 1965 | −1.0 | −0.1 | 3.6 | 2.4 |

Source: *Estatísticas Históricas.* Total GDP is from table 4.7 (indices of real product: annual percentage variation), p. 111. Sectoral figures are calculated from table 4.10 (GDP at factor cost by classes and sectors of economic activity, pp. 117–18), reducing the annual increases in current prices by the implicit GDP deflators shown in table 4.7, p. 111.

tor that led both the boom of the late 1950s and the stagnation of the early 1960s. Agriculture fluctuated randomly, depending on the vagaries of weather and export markets. Activity in the service sector was increasingly linked to conditions in industry. In judging the possibilities of success for the "first chance," therefore, a central question is whether, with different leadership and different policies, high rates of industrial growth could have been sustained.

Counterfactual alternatives are by definition hypothetical and somewhat artificial, so it is tempting for social scientists to argue that whatever happens is the inescapable result of deep underlying forces. Journalists watching contemporary events, on the other hand, and some schools of historians, give much more weight to the accidents of personality and immediate circumstances, attributing substantial degrees of freedom to decisionmakers even though the consequences may often be inadvertent. The strong Marxist current in the formation of Latin American social scientists pushed most of them in this period toward historical determinism, in opposition to the more empirical, inductive, antidoctrinaire Anglo-American tradition, not only in economics but also in political science and sociology. This contrast

move would have been deferred permanently and he continued to take great pride in his role as "creator of Brasília."

Figure 2-3. *Boom and Stagnation by Sectors, 1955–65*

Annual growth (percent)

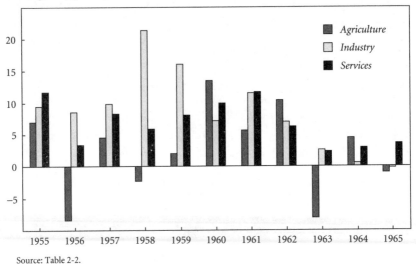

Source: Table 2-2.

is clearly visible in the contending diagnoses of the Brazilian stagnation cum inflation of the early 1960s.

The determinist analysis focused on "structural" constraints on economic growth and causes for inflation. Following a line of thought first developed at the UN Economic Commission for Latin America (ECLA), the critical limitation on growth was said to be the capacity to import capital goods and raw materials not available domestically. Import capacity, moreover, was supposed to be limited by a continuous shift in the terms of trade against primary-product producers in the "periphery" of the world economy (third world) and in favor of industrial exporters in the "center" (first world). The solution would be found through import substitution industrialization (ISI), starting with the simpler nondurable consumer goods and working upstream through durable consumer goods to capital goods, eventually achieving a fully rounded industrial economy.

Brazil's experience in the 1950s appeared to confirm that analysis. It soon became clear, however, that replacing imports of consumer goods might entail new import requirements for raw materials, components, and production equipment, thus re-creating the foreign exchange bottleneck in a new guise. The remedy would appear to be still further import substitution, such as occurred during the Kubitschek boom. At some point, however, contended the structuralists, the opportunities for import substitution became exhausted, partly because of a badly skewed income distribution and "dual economy," which limited the market for the kinds of consumer products Brazil could produce at reasonable costs, even if not fully competitive. To make matters worse, Brazil's terms of trade turned more unfavorable after 1955, leading to excessive short-term foreign borrowing and aggravating the foreign exchange constraint on continued growth.[12]

The empiricists, in contrast, considered the availability of capital to be the key to economic growth, capital that might in part be mobilized domestically and in part imported by borrowing from abroad or by direct foreign investment. They joined the structuralists in supporting protection for infant-industry industrialization, following the classic examples of the United States and Germany. But they believed that a foreign exchange bottleneck could be avoided by diversifying exports: first making use of Brazil's vast mineral resources in addition to the traditional agricultural items and then adding successive categories of manufactured goods.[13] Their advice was rejected mainly on nationalist grounds. Having secured political independence from Portugal in 1822, their opponents argued, Brazil had become a commercial colony of Great Britain in the later nineteenth century and should not now become an industrial colony of the United States. This was an early version of the "dependency theory" elaborated by many Latin American social scientists in the 1970s.[14] During the Goulart period (1961–64), nationalism of this kind dominated Brazilian policymaking.

Both sides in these disputes concurred that accelerating inflation was a major factor in the economic stagnation of the early 1960s. But they differed fundamentally on inflation's causes and cures. The structuralists' analysis on this front was closely related to their diagnosis of growth and stagnation.

---

12. The best-known exposition along these lines available in English translation is in Celso Furtado, *Diagnosis of the Brazilian Crisis* (University of California Press, 1965), esp. chap. 8, pp. 96–114. A detailed quantitative review appeared under the title "The Growth and Decline of Import Substitution in Brazil," in Economic Commission for Latin America, *Economic Bulletin for Latin America*, vol. 9 (March 1964), pp. 1–59. This article was complemented nine months later by an extended analysis of policies and policy instruments: "Fifteen Years of Economic Policy in Brazil," *Economic Bulletin for Latin America*, vol. 9 (December 1964), pp. 153–214. For a later analysis displaying the complexities of import substitution, see Richard Weisskopf, "The Growth and Decline of Import Substitution in Brazil—Revisited," *World Development*, vol. 8 (September 1980), pp. 647–75.

13. This school of thought was dominant in the Instituto Brasileiro de Economia (IBRE), a unit established in 1951 within the Fundação Getúlio Vargas to assemble basic economic statistics that also initiated the systematic study of economics in modern Brazil. The institute's founder and leading figure for several decades was Eugênio Gudin; its most articulate spokesmen included Octávio Bulhões, Roberto Campos, and Mário Henrique Simonsen, key economic policymakers in the mid-1960s and 1970s.

14. A brief exposition and criticism of dependency theory appears in chapter 3.

Their opponents were generally called "monetarists," although the views of many fell far short of extreme monetarism as advocated by Milton Friedman. There was considerable overlapping of analysis. Brazilian monetarists recognized that successful development would have to entail major changes in economic structure. The structuralists acknowledged that open-ended budget deficits and credit creation could intensify inflation beyond any possible useful limits. But until the end of the 1950s, when annual price increases soared to nearly 40 percent, the cleavage generated polar opposition on all aspects of macroeconomic policy: fiscal (budgetary), monetary (credit and interest rates), and international (exchange rates, controls over trade and capital movements, foreign investment, and borrowing from abroad).

Structuralists argued that in the conditions of the peripheral Latin American economies, satisfactory rates of development were impossible without substantial inflation and that up to some point (perhaps 20 or 25 percent a year) inflation positively aided economic growth.[15] The impulses to inflation were said to include (a) inadequate expansion of food supplies by a tradition-bound agricultural sector in a dual economy; (b) rising governmental costs for urban services for which tax revenues could not easily be secured; (c) the import capacity constraint already mentioned, including constantly worsening terms of trade for countries exporting primary products; (d) relatively high costs for domestic-manufactured products in the early stages of import substitution; and (e) labor market rigidities, requiring high wages for the new industrial skills. At the same time, they argued, inflation served as a means of mobilizing capital: it transferred purchasing power to would-be entrepreneurs and also, on Keynesian principles, ensured full use of economic capacity.

The monetarists conceded that a rapidly changing economic structure would almost certainly involve some inflation, since relative prices must be changed and it is always hard to lower nominal prices or wages. But they wanted to keep the rate of inflation as low as possible to avoid its distorting effects on investment decisions and income distribution and to preclude its acceleration into an open-ended wage-price spiral. To this end, they recommended the conventional instruments of first world stabilization policies: avoidance of budget deficits, realistic foreign exchange rates, with-

15. In addition to Celso Furtado, the names most frequently cited in this connection were Oswaldo Sunkel and Dudley Seers, both associated with the UN Economic Commission for Latin America, together with ECLA's secretary-general, Raul Prebisch. For a summary review with extensive bibliography, see Werner Baer, "The Inflation Controversy in Latin America: A Survey," *Latin American Research Review*, vol. 2, no. 2 (1967), pp. 3–25.

drawal of subsidies distorting the connection between prices and costs, limits to protection against import competition, and strict control of monetary expansion. These were also the main lines of policy advice from the IMF. By the 1990s, the intellectual dispute on inflation control had been won by the monetarists. Nevertheless, controversy and basic uncertainty remain on the related policy questions: how best to secure growth without undue inflation and how to promote an equitable distribution of the fruits of growth.

In hindsight, the structuralist analysis of both stagnation and inflation seems largely invalid. Although it certainly contained some plausible elements and had some basis in the experience of other Latin American countries, it simply did not fit the facts of Brazil in the period 1959–63. Subsequent empirical studies demonstrate conclusively that food supplies kept up with growth in population and incomes, that urbanization did not impose major new pressures on government budgets, that the terms of trade did not turn sharply unfavorable, and that labor supplies were ample and quickly responsive to demand. There were indeed pressures on the balance of payments, but they arose mainly from chronically overvalued exchange rates, coffee policies that greatly reduced Brazil's share in world markets, and an almost systematic discouragement of exports of minerals and manufactured goods.[16]

In short, the slide toward "galloping" inflation by 1959 cannot be blamed on inherent structural causes. It resulted from an array of unwise policies, some going back to the late Vargas years and others adopted under Kubitschek. In addition to the loose fiscal and credit practices already noted, they included excessive periodic increases in the minimum wage and in civil and military government salaries and pensions, going well beyond increases in the cost of living. There was gross overstaffing of the bureaucracy and especially of state-owned enterprises. There were periods of badly overval-

---

16. The most extensive book-length analysis of these issues is Raouf Kahil, *Inflation and Economic Development in Brazil: 1946–63* (Oxford: Clarendon Press, 1973). See also Albert Fishlow, "Some Reflections on Post-1964 Brazilian Economic Policy," in Alfred Stepan, ed., *Authoritarian Brazil: Origins, Policies, and Future* (Yale University Press, 1973), pp. 69–113; and Samuel A. Morley, "Inflation and Stagnation in Brazil," *Economic Development and Cultural Change*, vol. 19 (January 1971), pp. 184–203. In early 1963, I published an analysis of the terms of trade and of relatively easy opportunities for additional exports; see Lincoln Gordon, "Terms of Trade and the Brazilian Balance of Payments," *Department of State Bulletin*, vol. 48 (February 25, 1963), pp. 284–93. It is noteworthy that Celso Furtado himself, in the celebrated Plano Trienal (Three-Year Plan) prepared under his direction as special minister for planning in the Goulart government, said nothing about exhaustion of import substitution possibilities and recommended (without success) policies largely in the monetarist mode. See Estados Unidos do Brasil, *Presidência da República, Three-Year Plan for Economic and Social Development, 1963–65* (Brasília, December 1962).

ued foreign exchange rates. There was a chronic failure to integrate fiscal and monetary policies, aggravated by institutional weaknesses in the budgetary mechanisms and in the absence, until 1965, of a central bank.

Whether these errors were an inescapable product of Brazil's sociopolitical structure is considered below. They can be summarized as concessions to a variety of individual and group interests whose claims added up to totals far larger than the real resources available. For a few years, the strong growth record of the Kubitschek era seemed to justify the structuralist tolerance toward inflation. Unfortunately, their intellectual rationalizations also helped persuade the president against disciplining his populist political instincts. The consequence was an acceleration of inflation to a level that even the most devoted structuralists judged counterproductive and dangerous. In Celso Furtado's words, "In its totally sterile phase, inflation is no longer harmful merely to the community as a whole and the working class in particular, but becomes harmful also to the class that originally benefitted from it."[17]

The legacy bequeathed to Jânio Quadros was thus a mixed bag. It included a greatly strengthened and diversified industrial capacity, with a far more adequate infrastructure in energy and transportation, bases for the Brazilian "economic miracle" of 1968–74. But it also required immediate priority for curbing inflation and improving the external balances of trade and payments, a challenge that proved to be beyond the new president's capacity, or his will, or both.

## The Politics of Frustration: Contending Diagnoses

On the political side, the divergent analyses also divide structuralists from empiricists. In this field, however, in contrast to the diagnosis of inflation, the empiricists have no doctrine corresponding to neoclassical or monetarist economics. The main historical facts are clear and readily summarized.[18] Quadros won the three-cornered presidential campaign of 1960 by a large plurality, two points short of an absolute majority. Although not a long-standing party member, he had been nominated by the National Democratic Union (UDN), the grouping based on opposition to the Vargas tradition. As governor of the state of São Paulo, he had presided over a progressive and well-administered program of development. He was expected to do the same at the national level, carrying economic development forward while

17. Furtado, *Diagnosis of the Brazilian Crisis*, p. 107.
18. The best running account in English is in Skidmore, *Politics in Brazil, 1930–1964*, chaps. 6 through 8.

curbing the inflationary excesses of Kubitschek and also giving greater attention to education, health, and other social needs. His peaceful inauguration on January 31, 1961, seemed to epitomize the consolidation of democracy under the 1946 Constitution. But he stunned the country and the world by resigning the presidency on August 25, after less than seven months in office.

João Goulart had been elected vice president under the Brazilian Labor Party (PTB) label in a separate three-cornered race, with a plurality of only about 100,000 over his UDN rival, in contrast to the Quadros plurality of more than 2 million. Earlier in August, Quadros sent him on a trade mission to the People's Republic of China, with which Brazil then had no diplomatic relations. On August 25, he was still in Singapore. Ranking officers of the Brazilian military had long regarded Goulart as closely and dangerously associated with communist elements in the trade unions; in 1954 they had forced Vargas to dismiss him as minister of labor. Many of them considered Communist China a potentially more threatening source of subversion than the Soviet Union.

On the heels of the Quadros resignation, the three military ministers (army, navy, and air force) declared that they would not permit Goulart to return to Brazil to take office as president. There followed a two-week constitutional crisis. Goulart's brother-in-law, Leonel Brizola (then governor of the southernmost state of Rio Grande do Sul), organized a network of radio stations as the "chain of legality" to argue in favor of the Goulart succession. The military became divided and there were genuine fears of outright civil war. The crisis was resolved by an ingenious compromise fashioned by the Congress in Brasília. Through the so-called Additional Act, passed twice in two successive days, they converted the 1946 Constitution into a parliamentary system, incorporating many of the provisions pioneered in the German Federal Republic and designed to ensure governmental stability. Goulart pretended to accept the resulting vast reduction in presidential powers and was inaugurated on Independence Day, September 7. He nominated as prime minister a widely respected centrist political figure, Tancredo Neves, the man elected twenty-four years later to serve as the first civilian president in a newly demilitarized Brazil, but who became mortally ill before he could take office.

Institutional stability was never fully restored during the two and one-half years of government under Goulart. After nine months of relative calm, he maneuvered to shake up the cabinet as the first step in an agitated campaign to restore full presidential powers. That goal was accomplished through a plebiscite in January 1963. A second period of relative calm followed, in which able ministers of finance and of planning undertook serious efforts to control the accelerating inflation and to cope with the balance of payments deficit. In mid-1963, however, the president decided to discontinue support for these efforts.

Toward the end of that year, as economic conditions deteriorated, strikes multiplied, and other indications of social unrest grew apace, Goulart decided to radicalize the situation through a campaign for "basic reforms." In my judgment as a witness at first hand, it was not a serious reform program but a thin disguise for an effort to assume dictatorial power as a populist in the mold of Vargas before the war or Juan Perón in Argentina.[19]

Goulart's efforts were resisted by centrist and conservative leaders in Congress, governors of several major states, and elements in the military officer corps. On March 13, 1964, a huge "reformist" rally in Rio de Janeiro was addressed by Goulart, Brizola, and others, with overt threats against the Congress and the announcement of executive decrees of questionable legality for partial land reform and expropriation of the remaining private oil refineries. In the following week there was a large, conservative counter-rally in São Paulo. Then matters came to a head with a mutiny of navy petty officers, which was given moral support in a nationally broadcast speech by Goulart on March 30. That threat to basic principles of military hierarchy and discipline was intolerable to a pivotal group of army officers, led by Chief of Staff Humberto Castello Branco, who had by then organized a defensive conspiracy to keep presidential action within constitutional bounds. The military centrists, or constitutionalists, were thus added to the rightist group that had long sought the president's ouster.

An anti-Goulart military movement, backed by Governor Magalhães Pinto of Minas Gerais, commenced at dawn on March 31. By the afternoon

19. As an interim measure, he sought at one time to launch a campaign for a plebiscite to support his immediate reelection, which was not permissible under the 1946 Constitution. For an extended account of my personal observations as American ambassador during this period, see U.S. Senate, Committee on Foreign Relations, Hearing on Nomination of Lincoln Gordon to be Assistant Secretary of State for Inter-American Affairs (GPO, February 7, 1966). My interpretation of Goulart's motives was supported by Samuel Wainer, publisher of the Goulart-favoring newspaper chain *Ultima Hora* and an intimate associate of the president. In addition to many personal conversations in 1963 and 1964, see Samuel Wainer, *Minha Razão de Viver: Memórias de um Repórter* (My Reason for Being: Memoirs of a Reporter) (Rio de Janeiro: Editora Record, 1987), chap. 33. It is also shared by Jacob Gorender, a former member of the Brazilian Communist Party politburo. See *Combate nas Trevas: A Esquerda Brasileira: Das Ilusões Perdidas à Luta Armada* (Fighting in the Dark: The Brazilian Left: From Lost Illusions to Armed Struggle) (São Paulo: Editora Ática, 1987). See also Moniz Bandeira, *O Governo João Goulart: As Lutas Sociais no Brasil, 1961–1964* (The João Goulart Government: Social Struggles in Brazil, 1961–64) (Rio de Janeiro: Editora Civilização Brasileira, 1977); and Hélio Silva, *1964: Golpe ou Contragolpe,* 2d ed. (1964: Coup or Countercoup) (Porto Alegre: L&PM Editoras Ltda., 1978).

of April 1, Goulart had flown from Rio to Brasília to explore whether support for him could be reassembled. Finding that impossible, he flew on to Porto Alegre, capital of his native state of Rio Grande do Sul. Being unable to muster significant military backing there, he acknowledged defeat, went into hiding on a ranch in the countryside, and opened negotiations for asylum in Uruguay.

Although lacking proper constitutional sanction for his action, the president of the Senate then declared the presidency vacant and escorted the constitutional successor—Ranieri Mazzilli, the speaker of the lower house— to an improvised ceremony in the Supreme Court building where Mazzilli was sworn in as acting president by the chief justice. There was virtually no organized opposition to the coup d'état. On April 2, this brusque ending of the Second Republic was greeted with broad popular acclaim, reflecting relief from the tension of crisis. At that moment, what might follow was unclear to anyone, although no one would have predicted twenty-one years of military rule.[20]

## The Quadros Resignation: Structural or Adventitious?

These developments can be viewed either as nearly inescapable consequences of Brazil's social and political structure in the 1960s or as adventitious, almost accidental, happenings resulting from individual personalities and their errors of judgment. The conflict between structural and empirical diagnoses is focused on two critical events: the resignation of Quadros and the fall of Goulart.

Consider first the Quadros resignation. The structural analysis begins with Brazil's population growth, regional migrations, industrialization, and urbanization since Vargas first assumed power in 1930. It then argues along the following lines. The economic and social changes left the old landowning and coffee-exporting elites in charge of the political system but greatly accentuated the dualism of Brazilian society and laid the basis for conflict

20. My own (erroneous) expectation in April 1964 was that there would be a period of arbitrary military rule, perhaps lasting through the remainder of the original Quadros term, that is, to the end of 1965. During that period, there might be substantial purging of elements viewed as "subversive" from all branches of government at all levels, and from trade unions, university faculties, and student organizations. Some changes in the 1946 Constitution might be adopted, but civilian constitutional rule would be restored with the election of a new president—most likely Juscelino Kubitschek again—on schedule in October 1965. This appears to have been Castello Branco's own expectation, but it was frustrated by a "hard-line" victory in a political struggle within the military in late 1964. In fact, the first civilian president took office only in 1985, after an indirect election, and the first direct presidential election of a civilian was delayed until November 1989.

with a new class of industrial entrepreneurs and a new urban proletariat. Vargas had kept the tensions within bounds by his populist nationalism and Kubitschek by his charismatic developmentalism. But the structural distortions remained, finding their main expression in inflationary pressures. At the start, Quadros sought to combat inflation only through orthodox economic remedies favored by the old elites. When he found those policies insufficient to maintain a mass political following, his own variant of developmentalism, coupled with neutralist initiatives in foreign policy, was so hotly resisted by defenders of the status quo that (in Hélio Jaguaribe's words), "he chose ... to opt out rather than be ousted from power."[21]

In the perspective of three decades, however, the adventitious factors, including Quadros's unstable personality, seem clearly dominant. It is true that by mid-1961 he had become the target of tirades by Guanabara governor Carlos Lacerda, who had helped bring Vargas to his suicide in 1954. But Quadros was never the object of serious military opposition. It is also true that some of his inquiries into corruption under previous administrations were antagonizing important congressmen, but there was no initiative whatever toward impeachment.

A review of his few months in office does show growing tension between Quadros and the Congress, even though there was no record of sustained effort on his part to enact a legislative program against congressional resistance. Quadros was overtly disdainful of the legislators, bypassing their traditional role as intermediaries by establishing direct political relations with state governments. Congress itself was divided and rudderless, incapable of generating a substantive program of its own. There was mutual mistrust, exacerbated by a stream of almost whimsical presidential memoranda on trivial matters such as the morality of bathing costumes on the beaches of Rio or gambling and horseracing on weekends. Quadros also alienated his original UDN sponsors by initiatives toward an "independent" foreign policy, slanted toward affirmative relations with the communist and third world nations in place of Brazil's traditional associations with the United States and Western Europe. That policy reached a symbolic peak in mid-August, when the president personally pinned a high national decoration on visiting Cuban Che Guevara.

---

21. Hélio Jaguaribe, *Economic and Political Development: A Theoretical Approach and a Brazilian Case Study* (Harvard University Press, 1968), p. 185. References to powerful forces and formidable pressures arrayed against Quadros also appear in two essays in Riordan Roett, ed., *Brazil in the Sixties* (Vanderbilt University Press, 1972). They are Douglas A. Chalmers, "Political Groups and Authority in Brazil: Some Continuities in a Decade of Confusion and Change," pp. 51–76, at p. 71; and Werner Baer and Isaac Kerstenetzky, "The Brazilian Economy," pp. 105–45, at p. 114.

Quadros began his term with a widely respected finance minister and a fairly orthodox approach to economic stabilization. By mid-1961, however, he was drawing away from accepting even a short period of genuine austerity. Congress, unclear as to where he was seeking to move and increasingly mistrustful of his motives, delayed action on his few proposals rather than opposing him outright. As the respected newsweekly *Visão* put it in an article a few weeks after the resignation, the president found it "impossible to dialogue with the people through the valid and traditional political intermediaries. Jânio shifted toward monologue. The country heard him in silence, and JQ was acting like a free force, separated from the natural gearing mechanisms of the constitutional order and the political party system."[22]

Quadros never supplied a credible explanation for his resignation, either at the time, a year later when he returned to Brazil from voluntary exile, or twenty-five years later when he had been reelected mayor of the city of São Paulo. The consensus of his contemporaries from all parties was that the move was a bid for greater presidential powers, which he supposed might be accorded by a Congress fearful of a crisis flowing from Goulart's possible succession.[23] It was, in short, a gross error of political judgment, neither forced nor justified by governmental impasse.

The resignation came as a total surprise to both colleagues and opponents. Quadros had sufficiently antagonized Congress, and raised enough doubts about his own psychological stability, to preclude any movement to reject the resignation, and the constitution had no requirement for formal congressional acceptance. The step was an adventitious personal decision, but it was to have profound consequences for the nation's future.

## Political Forces and Personalistic Politics: The Goulart Disaster

The fall of Goulart, and with him the Second Republic, is a less clear-cut case, since it was not a deliberate act on Goulart's part. Looking back from the early 1970s, historian Thomas Skidmore described the 1946 Constitution as "an interlude between authoritarian governments," destined to fail-

22. *Visão*, September 22, 1961, p. 23; my informal translation.
23. See interviews in *Folha de S. Paulo*, August 24, 1986. The same hypothesis was stated to me in 1961 by several former cabinet colleagues of Quadros. It is substantially confirmed by the publication in 1996, after the author's death, of notes written in 1961 by Carlos Castello Branco (not related to the president), a highly respected political commentator who was serving as Quadros's press assistant and who accompanied him on the flight to São Paulo. See Carlos Castello Branco, *A Renúncia de Jânio* (The Resignation of Jânio) (Rio de Janeiro: Revan, 1996). More recently Quadros's own grandson has stated that Quadros himself admitted as much in a deathbed confession.

ure because of inherent pressures of nation-building and economic development. In his view, polarization of the political elites between leftist revolutionaries and conservative military officers resulted from "class or sectoral tensions inherent in the process of economic development." Inflation and balance of payments pressures had created an economic challenge "too great for any government that could have been elected in the deeply divided political atmosphere of early 1964."[24]

Writing a few years closer to the event, on the other hand, political sociologist Hélio Jaguaribe divided the period of Goulart's full presidential powers (after January 1963) into two sharply contrasting phases: a "positive left" experiment in "national laborism," led by Finance and Planning Ministers San Tiago Dantas and Celso Furtado, and—after July 1963—an effort by Goulart "to promote a social revolution from above." Jaguaribe believed the first to be a viable course of action, while the second was frustrated by the military coup. But he did not attribute the abandonment of the first to unyielding resistance from conservative political elites. It was rather Goulart's own doing as an individual, with motives "ranging from personal resentment to [his] fear of losing the struggle for supreme leadership of the masses to his rival ..., Leonel Brizola."[25]

My own opinion, based on close firsthand observation of that period, including frequent and wide-ranging one-on-one discussions with Goulart, became—and remains—that his change of course in the second half of 1963 was not a genuine effort at "basic reforms." There is compelling evidence that Goulart had decided to overthrow the constitutional order in favor of a personal populist dictatorship, copying the course of his mentor Vargas in the 1930s and aiming at ultimate ratification by plebiscite.[26]

In addition, bearing in mind the evident weaknesses in Goulart's personality compared with that of Vargas, I was fearful, as were many Brazilians at the time, that a "coup from above" (which I christened "superversion") might be followed by a more radical hard left assumption of power, such as Egypt experienced with Mohammed Naguib and Gamal Abdel Nasser. During my interviews in 1988 and 1990, several men who had been radical student leaders in the 1960s stated that they had hoped for and expected just such an outcome, since they regarded Goulart as an inherently

---

24. Thomas E. Skidmore, "Politics and Economic Policy Making in Authoritarian Brazil, 1937–71," in Alfred Stepan, ed., *Authoritarian Brazil: Origins, Policies, and Future* (Yale University Press, 1973), pp. 3–5.

25. Jaguaribe, *Economic and Political Development*, pp. 185–87.

26. See Peter Flynn, *Brazil: A Political Analysis* (Boulder, Colo.: Westview Press, 1978), pp. 308–09.

weak and ineffectual leader. On that speculative hypothesis, Communist Party influence might easily have become dominant, in the extreme case aligning Brazil with Cuba and the Soviet Union. In the geopolitical framework of the time, that would have been a huge setback to the interests of the United States and its European allies and of liberal democracy more broadly.[27]

There was, of course, an adventitious aspect in Goulart's incumbency in the presidential palace from the start. At several critical points, a very slight change of circumstances would have kept him out. He owed the succession to Quadros's gross error of judgment in resigning. He was never a sufficiently respected political figure to have been elected to the presidency on his own. In Brazil in 1960, the broad current of opinion that supported Quadros was opposed to Goulart, whose small margin of victory resulted from different party constellations in the separate three-cornered contests for president and vice president. Moreover, had his brother-in-law (Brizola) not been a state governor in August 1961, the military ultimatum against Goulart's return from China would probably have succeeded. Nevertheless, once that succession crisis passed, Goulart was accepted by the vast majority of the political establishment, including the military. And the plebiscite of January 1963, restoring full presidential powers, could well be construed as a kind of popular mandate.

The central question, therefore, is whether the situation Goulart confronted in 1963–64 was inherently unmanageable through democratic institutions or whether the president's contempt for those institutions brought about his own overthrow. As with Quadros, the immediate economic issues were the accelerating inflation and the balance of payments. The longer-term issues concerned the restoration of economic growth and the tackling of Brazil's basic problems of regional and social inequalities, obsolete agrarian structure in the Northeast, urban hypertrophy in São Paulo, Rio, and

27. Looking back from the 1980s, Skidmore concludes that the "patchwork on the left was hardly the base for a serious attack on Brazil's established order" (*The Politics of Military Rule in Brazil, 1964–85* [Oxford University Press, 1988], p. 16). But that was certainly not the view of the left itself at the time. Gorender rejects it categorically, describing the early months of 1964 as a "prerevolutionary situation," with real chances for victory (*Combate nas Trevas*, pp. 66–67). Note also the doctrinal disputes within the Brazilian Communist Party, summarized in Dulce Chaves Pandolfi, "Os Comunistas e o Golpe," in Gláucio Ary Dillon Soares and Maria Celina D'Araujo, *21 Anos de Regime Militar* (Twenty-One Years of Military Rule) (Rio de Janeiro: Fundaçao Getúlio Vargas, 1994), pp. 71–88. The Skidmore view also underestimates the vast weight of opportunism. Once it became clear in April 1964 that the military was united against Goulart, there was almost no overt opposition to the coup. But if Goulart had prevailed, as many observers thought possible even on the evening of March 31, he would also have been supported by a large body of uncommitted opportunists and even former opponents.

Recife, and glaring weaknesses in education, public health, environmental protection, and institutional modernization.

It would certainly be wrong to underestimate the severity of those problems, either for the short term or long. Inflation was a chronic Brazilian malady, not mastered even by the "heroic" stabilization measures of the military regime. In the 1980s and early 1990s, it once again soared to dizzying heights before successful stabilization under the Real Plan of 1994. Given the centrality of organized labor in his political support, it would have been extremely difficult for Goulart to endorse a policy of substantial wage compression along the lines applied in 1965–66. But a number of serious analysts have concluded that wage compression in the early years of the military regime went unnecessarily far and was not a major factor in the stabilization achieved in that period.[28] Whatever Goulart's motives in putting forward Celso Furtado's Three-Year Plan, its analysis of inflationary pressures was serious and the remedial measures might have been politically acceptable if given genuine presidential backing.[29]

On the balance of payments side, the case is even clearer. The deficits were serious, but on a very modest scale compared with those of the 1980s. Easy opportunities to expand exports were simply disregarded. Foreign investment was almost completely dried up by severe limitations on remittance of profits, enacted in 1962 and approved by Goulart against the advice of his then ministers of finance and foreign affairs. The U.S. government was eager to provide help through the Alliance for Progress and to that end offered substantial balance of payments relief in the agreements negotiated in April 1963 between Finance Minister San Tiago Dantas and U.S. Agency for International Development (AID) administrator David Bell, contingent on a serious effort at inflation control. At my initiative, moreover, Dantas's successor as finance minister was educated on the possibilities of debt rescheduling through the "Paris Club" of governmental creditors, following the then recent precedents of Colombia and Turkey. But in November, when the Inter-American Economic and Social Council held its annual review of the Alliance for Progress in São Paulo, Goulart made it clear that he had no interest in using those opportunities. The extreme forms of "negative nationalism," which he had decided to exploit as part of his quest for extraconstitutional power, simply ruled out systematic cooperation with "Yankee imperialism."

28. For example, see Fishlow, "Some Reflections on Post-1964 Brazilian Economic Policy."
29. Gorender believes that the plan was simply a gambit to secure conservative and centrist support in the January 1963 plebiscite. *Combate nas Trevas*, p. 55.

The longer-term structural issues were certainly fundamental to the political polarization of that era. Their roots lay in centuries of Brazilian history and Luso-Brazilian culture. In the Marxist-Leninist diagnosis, they could be effectively tackled only through a social revolution under the political leadership of the "vanguard" Communist Party. Cuba was supposed to be pointing the way. In contrast, the philosophy of the Alliance for Progress sought solutions through institutional reforms within a democratic framework, facilitated by economic growth.[30] The transformations already achieved in Brazil since the 1920s seemed to augur well for the success of such reforms, which were enlisting considerable intellectual and political support at the time. In his two "moderate" phases (September 1961 to June 1962 and January to July of 1963), Goulart himself appeared to endorse them. But by late 1963, he had opted for the disastrous course of seeking absolute power.

Even then, however, the resilience of Brazilian society and reluctance of the bulk of the officer corps to violate legality might have held the constitutional structure together. In its positive aspects, Brazilian nationalism implies a faith that positive-sum outcomes to class conflict can be found. Although a number of high-ranking officers, including the generals and admirals who had opposed Goulart's return in 1961, began plotting his removal from the beginning, the controlling majority believed that Brazil was too advanced a society to be indulging in coups d'état of the kind a Central American republiqueta ("banana republic") might experience. Even in the increasingly polarized atmosphere of early 1964, and perhaps as late as March 30, a modest retreat by Goulart could have saved his presidency and the constitution.[31]

If Goulart would not accept constitutional constraints, why was he not impeached rather than deposed illegally? That course was in fact advocated by several conservative members of Congress. In practice it was ruled out,

30. My principal speeches in Brazil in 1961–62 were intended as a systematic exposition of that philosophy. They were delivered in Portuguese, but the original versions in English were published in *A New Deal for Latin America: The Alliance for Progress* (Harvard University Press, 1963).

31. In the final days of the crisis, he was urged by several close associates, both civilian and military, to make a declaration on three points: (1) to renounce support from the Brazilian Communist Party, which had been technically illegal since 1948; (2) to dissolve the so-called Central Workers' Command, which was an illegal labor confederation under the then prevailing labor legislation; and (3) to affirm his intention to respect the constitution during the remainder of his term, which was scheduled to end in January 1966. In all likelihood, his acceptance would have nullified any prospect of a coup against him or resulted in its failure. Instead, in a critical overestimate of the strength of his military and trade union "machines" (*dispositivos*), he plunged ahead in the speeches of March 13 and March 30 that led directly to his downfall.

both by the party constellation in Congress and by the threat of military intimidation from the loyalist garrison in the isolated environment of Brasília. Given Goulart's obstinacy, Brazil no longer faced a choice between coup d'état and maintenance of constitutional legitimacy. It had become a choice between populist coup from the top down and preventive counter-coup from the mainstream military. The latter prevailed.

## Lessons of the Failure

Thus ended a sad and unnecessary chapter in Brazil's postwar history. But it was not an end to economic modernization or structural change. Nor was it an end to the democratic aspirations of most Brazilians, never abandoned and felt with growing force after 1975. The failure of the Quadros-Goulart period showed all too clearly the ease of destroying a constitutional consensus compared with the difficulty of building a new one. On the economic side, it demonstrated the counterproductive force of negative nationalism. And it reflected a paucity of able leadership in the political sphere in contrast to Brazilian dynamism in entrepreneurship, culture, and sports. The long period of Vargas hegemony no doubt contributed to that weakness, which continued to plague the nation a generation later, long after the restoration of democracy and civilian government.

## Addendum: The United States and the 1964 Coup d'Etat

Because of the large official American presence in Brazil in that period and the undisguised enthusiasm with which Goulart's overthrow was received in Washington, there is a considerable literature of allegations that the United States government took an active part in engendering or executing the coup d'état. As American ambassador throughout the Goulart regime, I can state with assurance that these charges are unfounded. A full study by unbiased historians of the documents of the period, now publicly available, will demonstrate that fact.[32]

U.S. participation or support has been charged in three respects:

—The claim that from mid-1963 on, the United States manipulated its economic and aid policies to intensify the Goulart regime's macroeconomic difficulties and to strengthen state-level regimes led by governors hostile to Goulart.

---

32. Some of the issues are dealt with in Lincoln Gordon, "U.S.-Brazilian Reprise," *Journal of Interamerican Studies,* vol. 32 (Summer 1990), pp. 165–78.

—The claim that American officials participated with Brazilian plotters in detailed planning for the coup.

—The claim that the U.S. government was directly involved in the military movement against Goulart, beginning on Tuesday, March 31, 1964, which eventuated in his flight from Brasília and de facto abandonment of the presidency on the afternoon of April 1.

I review each of these briefly.

## Alleged Economic Pressures against Goulart

In my testimony to the Senate Foreign Relations Committee on appointment as assistant secretary of state for inter-American affairs in February 1966, I summarized the course of Brazilian-American relations during the Goulart presidency in four phases.[33] During the first, the parliamentary period under Prime Minister Tancredo Neves from October 1961 until June 1962, relations were generally cordial, except for conflicting policies toward Cuba. A good start was made on initiating projects under the Alliance for Progress, most with the federal government but some also with Brazil's states and with SUDENE, the Northeast Regional Development Agency. That phase included the seemingly successful Goulart state visit to Washington, with an address to Congress promising amicably negotiated Brazilian purchases of foreign-owned electric power and telephone companies. I called it a positive phase.

The second phase ran from the forced dismissal of the Tancredo Neves cabinet in June 1962 until the plebiscite of January 1963, which terminated the parliamentary experiment and restored full presidential powers to Goulart. The prime ministers (Brochado da Rocha and Hermes Lima) were well to the left of Tancredo Neves. This was a clearly negative phase, including many expressions by senior officials of overt hostility to the United States. Congress passed a very restrictive law on remittance of profits by foreign investors, and the foreign minister's promise of an item veto on the most harsh clauses went unfulfilled by Goulart. Some Washington officials at that time and some American business groups recommended a suspension of economic aid, but the Kennedy administration accepted my recommendation to avoid an outright break in the hope that a better relationship could be restored after Goulart won back full presidential powers. Kennedy did postpone the presidential return visit then scheduled for August 1962. As acknowledged publicly many years ago, I also supported the proposal to

33. See U.S. Senate, Hearing on Nomination of Lincoln Gordon, pp. 31–43.

provide some financial assistance through the Central Intelligence Agency (CIA) to congressional candidates friendly to the United States.

In the Cuban missile crisis, Goulart's initial reaction was very favorable to Kennedy's naval quarantine. Believing that Goulart had not yet decided on his basic economic and foreign policy positions for 1963, we arranged for a personal visit in mid-December by Attorney General Robert Kennedy. His presentation to Goulart pointed to the anti-American views of many Brazilian high officials, the failure to work toward genuine cooperation under the Alliance for Progress, and Brazil's macroeconomic deterioration. There were no threats. Goulart's response was bland, with promises of less anti-Americanism under the restored presidential regime and a more salutary macroeconomic policy under the Three-Year Plan prepared by Celso Furtado, who joined the party at lunch. Goulart also urged an early return visit to Brazil by President Kennedy.[34]

The third, and seemingly positive, phase began in January 1963 with the restoration of full presidential powers. Goulart appointed a fresh cabinet, dominated by San Tiago Dantas as finance minister and Celso Furtado as planning minister. We were on the whole favorably impressed by the Three-Year Plan, which appeared to promise a genuine effort at containing inflationary pressures and getting the balance of payments under control. It became the basis for a comprehensive long-term aid negotiation in Washington in April 1963, led by Dantas in several meetings chaired by David Bell, then director of AID. The resulting Dantas-Bell agreement appeared to lay the foundation for macroeconomic support from the United States through "program loans" and microeconomic support through "project loans," coupled with Brazilian commitments on anti-inflationary fiscal policies and a variety of social reforms. Joint reviews of performance were scheduled for each calendar quarter. The first installment of American funds was released immediately.

Soon after Dantas's return to Brazil, however, both he and Furtado were dismissed by Goulart. The Three-Year Plan was abandoned. The new finance minister was Carlos Alberto Carvalho Pinto, who had succeeded Jânio Quadros as governor of São Paulo and had supervised a very effective state-level development program there. He failed to persuade Goulart to maintain the fiscal stringency provided in Furtado's program and in the Dantas-Bell agreement. In September, the annual ministerial-level review of the Alliance for Progress was held in São Paulo, but Goulart's opening speech was sharply critical rather than supportive. By October, fiscal strin-

---

34. A full account is in Embassy Airgram A-710, dated December 19, 1962, declassified in 1988.

gency had been thrown to the winds, and macroeconomic program lending had to be suspended. Mid-1963 therefore began the fourth and final phase of U.S. relations with Brazil under Goulart, ending with the military coup of March 31/April 1, 1964.

Contrary to many published allegations, the U.S. government did not then seek to weaken the Goulart regime by putting it under economic pressure.[35] By late August, as reflected in a long telegram to Washington, I had become convinced "that Goulart's personal aim is to perpetuate himself in power through repetition of Vargas's 1937 coup, looking toward Peronist type regime of extreme anti-American nationalism, fortified by privileged labor unions exerting general strike threats and by personal military *dispositivo* [support machine]." I then expressed the concern that, once having assumed dictatorial powers, Goulart's incompetence might easily lead to his being "pushed aside, like General Naguib in Egypt, to make way for some communist Nasser."[36] The immediate picture seemed to me very unstable, with great hostility to Goulart in the congressional majority, but no realistic likelihood of impeachment. I wrote that "oppositionist golpistas seem even weaker than a few months ago." My policy conclusion was as follows:

> In these circumstances, our aim should be to help frustrate [Goulart's] authoritarian proclivities and maintain prospects for genuine election in 1965, keeping most favorable possible image U.S. and Brazilian-American relations, countering or delaying antagonistic action. At minimum, this would increase likelihood of break in constitutional continuity taking form favorable to our interests. To do this will require great improvements in some of our current operating methods, for example in rapid action on aid projects where they can be turned to our political advantage. Recent delays on CHEVAP and Fortaleza generators are typical of serious failure in Washington to appreciate nature political circumstances here and urgency moving rapidly and affirmatively where we are going to move. But our great card in this game is presidential visit.

The Kennedy visit was rescheduled for November but once again postponed because of growing political instability in Brazil, exemplified by Goulart's unsuccessful request to Congress for martial law and indications that he would have used that authority to "intervene" in two key states, dismissing their governors in favor of his own appointees.

---

35. Thomas Skidmore's comment on this issue in his generally excellent book published in 1967, *Politics in Brazil, 1930–1964*, p. 324, is wrong by almost 180 degrees.

36. Rio telegram EMBTEL 373 to State, August 21, 1963, declassified in 1976.

In subsequent months, I reiterated the advice that we take special efforts to ensure that, if Brazil's political crisis came to a head, leading to civil war or an attempted coup or countercoup, the issues at stake be exclusively domestic and Brazilian, not involving the United States. To that end, I sought to maintain as much of the Alliance for Progress as possible, even though program assistance had to be ruled out. I was also very reluctant to shut down the Alliance, which had been the basis for my appointment and was making genuine contributions to Brazil's economic development. Those concerns led to my proposal for identifying "islands of administrative sanity," where project lending could be maintained. Contrary to many allegations, it was not limited to state governors hostile to Goulart; it included projects in Goiás, Bahia, and other states where the governors were neutral or pro-Goulart, and also federal highway and power projects where standard lending conditions were agreeable to both sides. I meant "administrative sanity" literally, and did not equate it with political hostility to Goulart.

More important, as the interest charges on foreign indebtedness were posing increasing burdens on Brazil's balance of payments, I secured Washington's approval to educate Finance Minister Carvalho Pinto on the possibilities of consensual debt renegotiation through the Paris and London "clubs" of international creditors. He had been totally uninformed on those procedures, so we translated into Portuguese the recent documents on debt renegotiations for Colombia and Turkey.[37] Negotiations were started by Brazil but not completed at the time of the coup; they were successfully concluded later by the military regime.

In short, far from bringing economic pressures to bear to weaken the Goulart regime, our policy was to sustain economic assistance where it could be effective.

## Alleged U.S. Participation in Planning of the Coup

There have been many reports over the years of the direct involvement of American officials, either military officers or CIA personnel, in planning for the coup by Brazilian officers. On this score, Skidmore was correct when he

---

37. Carvalho Pinto was so appreciative that he urged me to accompany him to Washington, where an informal meeting of Paris Club creditors would take up the Brazilian case for the first time. I did so, but his visit was cut short by the news from Brasília that Goulart was requesting Congress to grant him martial law powers ("state of siege," or *estado de sitio* in Portuguese), with rumors that they would be used to depose the governors of Guanabara and Pernambuco.

wrote that "there is no evidence to support the claim that the military con-spirators were sponsored or directed by the United States government."[38]

As the economic conditions and signs of political instability worsened during the second half of 1963, embassy officers were occasionally approached by civilian or military coup plotters. Except for emergency gaso-line and jet fuel supplies, I do not recall any cases of requests for assistance or participation.[39] My instructions were to maintain enough contact to keep informed on these movements.

The critical literature often points to Colonel Vernon ("Dick") Walters as a possible channel for covert U.S. military participation in coup plotting.[40] He was on excellent terms with many Brazilian Army officers who had fought in Italy in World War II, notably including Castello Branco. I have sometimes been asked whether he might have been engaged in a "Track B" operation behind my back, similar to the experience of our ambassador in Chile years later in the coup against Salvador Allende. That idea seems implausible. Walters reported to me regularly on his conversations with Brazilians and showed me his dispatches in draft. If there were a "Track B" operation, it was successfully concealed at the time, and I have never since seen any evidence of it. Nor is any such activity mentioned in the many pub-lished memoirs of Brazilian military participants in the 1964 coup.[41]

38. Skidmore, *Politics in Brazil, 1930–1964*, pp. 324–25.

39. Early in my tenure, in November 1961, I had been approached by Admiral Silvio Heck, navy minister under Quadros and therefore one of the signers of the ultimatum in August 1961 oppos-ing Goulart's assumption of the presidency after Quadros's resignation. He said that Goulart was an outright Communist Party member and that a vast military conspiracy to overthrow him was being organized. They neither wanted nor needed help from the United States, but he was inform-ing me of the plan in the hope that "when it takes place, your government will understand the rea-sons for it." I requested the appropriate embassy officers to confirm the story and was told that it was a gross exaggeration and that coup plotters were only small minorities within the officer corps of the three military services, many of them retired.

40. I had become acquainted with Walters in 1948 when we were both in Paris on the staff of Ambassador Averell Harriman, special representative in Europe for the Marshall Plan. I learned then that he spoke fluent Portuguese and had been liaison officer for the U.S. Fifth Army commander with the Brazilian Expeditionary Force in the World War II Italian campaign of 1944–45. In July 1962, after the postponement of President Kennedy's scheduled visit to Brazil, the president had asked me to report to him personally in Washington on political conditions there. In the confused situation, with elements of political instability, he surmised that the Brazilian military might take some active part and felt it important that our defense attaché be well informed on any such move-ments. Walters was the obvious choice, although he was very reluctant to leave his post in Rome.

41. Nonreaders of Portuguese will find a detailed and informative account of the often confusing and overlapping military conspiracies in John W. F. Dulles, *Castello Branco: The Making of a Brazil-ian President* (Texas A&M University Press, 1978), chaps. 8–11.

## Alleged U.S. Military Involvement in the Coup Itself

Here the allegations are mainly based on the naval task force, code-named "Brother Sam," consisting of an aircraft carrier and escorting destroyers, which departed the Caribbean headed toward Brazil on March 31, 1964. Its existence became publicly known with the declassification of relevant telegrams in the Johnson presidential library in the late 1970s and the publication of Phyllis Parker's doctoral dissertation, "U.S. Policy Prior to the Coup of 1964."[42] No Brazilians, either military or civilian, were aware of the formation of that task force at the time. It was organized on my recommendation to respond to the contingency that a regime crisis might develop into a civil war situation, with the armed forces, including state militia, divided geographically between pro- and anti-Goulart elements. By 1964, most state governors could be classified into pro- or anti-Goulart camps, and they often had great influence with military commanders and garrisons in their states. I knew from history that a near civil war situation had occurred in São Paulo's "constitutionalist revolution" of 1932 against Vargas. More recently, a direct confrontation of army units had seemed a real possibility after the military ultimatum against Goulart's return to Brazil in August 1961.

In that kind of event, I believed that a "showing of the American flag" might serve two purposes: (1) to exert psychological pressure in favor of the anti-Goulart side and (2) to assist in the evacuation of the thousands of U.S. civilians living in or visiting all regions of Brazil. Washington endorsed the proposal, and the U.S. military's Southern Command, based in the Panama Canal Zone, developed detailed plans. In the closing days of March 1964, as the crisis in Brazil was reaching its climax, Washington also made contingency plans for the supply of light weapons and ammunition, which could be shipped by air in contrast to the eleven days of sailing time for the naval task force to reach southern Brazil.

There were no plans for active participation by American troops. In mid-March, as political instability mounted and the media speculated on possibilities of violence, we also acceded to a request from an anti-Goulart businessman to load three tankers with petroleum supplies, for delivery in

---

42. The first publication of the dissertation was a Portuguese translation under the title *1964: O Papel dos Estados Unidos no Golpe de Estado de 31 de Março* (1964: The Role of the United States in the Coup d'Etat of March 31) (Rio de Janeiro: Editora Civilização Brasileira, 1977). In 1979 the original version in English was published under the title *Brazil and the Quiet Intervention, 1964* (University of Texas Press, 1979).

case of sabotage of oil pipelines in the São Paulo region.[43] The naval vessels and tankers were loaded in the Caribbean and started toward Brazil on March 31 but were turned around on my advice long before reaching Brazilian waters.

Fortunately, the contingency of civil war did not materialize. The task force was not equipped for military intervention and was still ten days' sailing time away when Goulart abandoned the presidency. In spite of Parker's thoroughly documented account of these events, published more than twenty years ago, and the ample publication and translation of declassified messages between Washington and Rio, some elements in the Brazilian press and public seem unwilling to recognize that the overthrow of Goulart was accomplished by the Brazilian military without assistance or advice from the United States.

Most recently, a new set of misunderstandings has arisen from the revelation that President Johnson was making tapes of his telephone conversations, some of which were published in 1997 in a book covering the years 1963 and 1964.[44] The book contains only three brief references to Brazil. The first, dated March 30, 1964, at 9:35 P.M. (Texas time), is only three lines long, with Johnson at his ranch telling his press assistant, George Reedy, that "if it blows tonight" they may have to return to Washington on Tuesday rather than Wednesday. The book's editor prefaces this excerpt with a note in small type, which reads: "The CIA has warned Johnson that a military coup it is supporting against the government of Brazil is imminent." I was puzzled by that note, since on that Monday evening, we in the embassy in Rio did not know that military action would begin in Minas Gerais the next morning. I was at home, watching on television Goulart's speech at the Automobile Club supporting the navy mutineers. At about 10 P.M. (7 P.M. Texas time), Secretary of State Dean Rusk telephoned to ask whether Goulart had finished speaking and whether he was endorsing the mutiny or supporting military hierarchy and discipline. I replied that he was still speaking, but up to that point showed no sign of support for military discipline.

Now, with the declassification and release of LBJ Library Tape No. WH6403.19 (available to the public for U.S.$5.00), it becomes clear that

43. For a vivid contemporaneous account of the public atmosphere of the time, see Alberto Dínes and others, *Os Idos de Março e a Queda em Abril* (The Ides of March and the Fall in April) (Rio de Janeiro: José Álvaro, 1964).

44. Michael R. Beschloss, ed., *Taking Charge: The Johnson White House Tapes, 1963–1964* (Simon and Schuster, 1997).

Johnson's call to Reedy was not inspired by a CIA report but rather by a call from Rusk, made immediately after Rusk's talk with me. In his call to President Johnson, Rusk said: "The crisis is coming to a head in the next day or two, perhaps even overnight. There's a snowballing of resistance to Goulart and therefore the thing may break at any moment. The armed forces, the governors—particularly in the populated states of the east coast—seem to be building up real resistance there." There is no reference to inside knowledge of a military movement the next day.

Rusk continued by reading a long draft telegram to me, noteworthy for its emphasis on the need for legitimacy in any anti-Goulart movement to which we might provide military support. That telegram was received by me the next morning, March 31, but was overtaken by events. (The full text, along with my reply, is transcribed at the end of this addendum.) Early that day we learned, as did all Brazilians, that a military movement from Juiz de Fora toward Rio de Janeiro had begun. That evening, I sought out former president Kubitschek to urge that he use his great influence with Congress to preserve a maximum of constitutional continuity if Goulart were forced out of office. By April 1, Goulart had given up any idea of resistance and House Speaker Ranieri Mazzilli had been sworn in as acting president.

Both the Rusk-Johnson conversation and one the next afternoon, March 31, between Johnson and Under Secretary George Ball (on the same tape) demonstrate that there was no coordinated military planning with the anti-Goulart elements in the Brazilian military. The task force was only set on its way on March 31, and in Ball's words, "It couldn't get into the area before April 10."

There was in fact no joint planning with the golpistas in the Brazilian armed forces. They knew nothing whatever about the "Brother Sam" task force. It was a contingency plan, unknown to Brazilians, based on a hypothetical civil war that never even came close to materializing. That we welcomed the overthrow of Goulart is well known. But there was no American participation in his removal by military force. These were the facts that permitted me to testify to the Senate that the coup was "100 percent, not 99.44 percent, Brazilian."

## Telegrams

Text of State Department telegram 1296 to American Embassy, Rio de Janeiro, dated March 30, 1964, 9:52 P.M. (Washington time):

FOR AMBASSADOR FROM SECRETARY.

US policy toward Brazil is based upon our determination to support in every possible way maintenance of representative and constitutional government in Brazil free from continuing threat of dictatorship from the left erected through a Goulart/Brizola manipulation. It is of great importance that there be a preemption of the position of legitimacy by those who will oppose communist and other extremist influences. It is highly desirable, therefore, that if action is taken by the armed forces such action be preceded or accompanied by a clear demonstration of unconstitutional actions on the part of Goulart or his colleagues or that legitimacy be confirmed by acts of the Congress (if it is free to act) or by expressions of the key governors or by some other means which gives substantial claim to legitimacy.

With respect to US support capabilities, we can act promptly on financial and economic measures. With regard to military assistance, logistic factors are important. Surface vessels loaded with arms and ammunition could not reach southern Brazil before at least ten days. Airlift could be provided promptly if an intermediate field at Recife, or other airfield in northern Brazil capable of handling large jet transports, is secure and made available. In ambiguous situation it may be difficult for us to obtain permission for intermediate stops from other countries such as Peru.

You should ask your own service attaches, without consulting Brazilian authorities just yet, to prepare recommendations on types of arms and ammunition most likely to be required in light of their knowledge of the situation.

In fast moving situation we are asking all of our posts in Brazil to feed Washington continual flow of information on significant developments [in] their areas and to stay on 24-hour alert.

At this particular moment it is important that US Government not put itself in position which would be deeply embarrassing if Goulart, Mazzilli, Congressional leaders and armed forces leadership reach accommodation in next few hours which would leave us branded with an awkward attempt at intervention. However, every disposition here is to be ready to support those elements who would move to prevent Brazil from falling under an authentic dictatorship of the left heavily infiltrated or controlled by the communists. Obviously in a country of over 75 million people, larger than continental United States, this is not a job for a handful of United States Marines. A major determination by the authentic leadership of Brazil and a preemption of the position of legitimacy are [of] the greatest possible importance. We will not, however, be paralyzed by theoretical niceties if the options are clearly between the genuinely democratic forces of Brazil and a communist dominated dictatorship.

As we see [the] problem tonight, the greatest danger may well be that Goulart will be able to pull back enough within next day or two to confuse situation, blunt edge of key incipient conservative military action, and gain more time to paralyze those elements who could resist a Communist infiltrated authoritarian regime. Fragmentary reports reaching here tonight suggest that anti-Goulart forces may be developing a certain momentum. Our big problem is to determine whether this presents an opportunity which might not be repeated. In this case we would wish to make a major decision as to whether and by what means we might give additional impetus to forces now in motion consistent with considerations expressed above. No judgment you have been required to make will compare to this in earning the pay of an underpaid Ambassador.

Text of Rio Embassy Telegram 2125 to Department of State, dated March 31, 1964, 1 P.M. (Rio time):

FOR SECRETARY FROM AMBASSADOR Re Deptel 1296.

1. I warmly welcome Reftel [reference telegram]. Things moving very quickly with apparently reliable reports military movements in Minas Gerais fully backed by Governor Magalhães Pinto and State Police. As of noon, no clear indications corresponding action São Paulo or other states.

2. I have taken action to get to key governors [a] message on vital importance color of legitimacy, stressing desirability political coverage by majority Congress if that humanly possible. My intermediaries are inquiring how governors' group proposes handle critical question [of] mantle of legitimacy and position as defenders of constitution, both in immediate and in subsequent actions, if Congressional coverage not available.

3. Most urgent logistical problem is motor and aviation gasoline in event normal supplies become unavailable to friendly forces. Local ESSO contact states only avgas [aviation gasoline] tanker en route is Petrobrás vessel, and he knows of no mogas [motor gasoline] in South Atlantic. Immediate action [to] set this in motion is in order. [Three tankers loaded with gasoline and jet fuel were departing the Caribbean for Brazil at the time this telegram was drafted.] We are developing recommendations on possible arms and ammunition requirements.

4. Goulart's Monday night speech to [mutineering] sergeants, which was ending when you telephoned, looks like last straw. He made appropriate verbal bows to constitution and legality, to Church, and to green and yellow [Brazilian national colors] nationalism rather than red models, but this was

transparent disguise for active support of subversion in NCO's [noncommissioned officers] and psychological warfare against officer corps, as well as Congress, press, and foreign and domestic business groups. While dictating this, I received reliable report that Kubitschek phoned Goulart this morning to declare his open opposition and has so stated to [the] press.

5. After deducting sixty-four dollars from my pay [a facetious comment on his reference to "an underpaid Ambassador"], my present judgment is that this might not be last opportunity, but well might be last good opportunity to support action by anti-Goulart group which still occupies large proportion strategic military commands and direction state-level forces in cohesive region [of] states accounting for over half [of] population and all industry. I believe your major decision should be in affirmative and will be preparing [to] recommend means [of] giving resistance forces additional impetus.

6. Your background briefing statement supplementing House Committee Report was very well played here in [the] press and serves immediate purpose desired by my recommendations for some public expression [of] interest and concern. [This paragraph refers to a congressional report on communist activities in Brazil.]

# 3

## Structural Change under the Military Republic

B razil's twenty-one years of military governance (1964–85) were a traumatic experience for the nation and its people, which neither civilian nor military leaders of the new millennium would like to see repeated. This chapter focuses on structural change during that period, the factors altering the basic features of the Brazilian polity, economy, and society.[1] In major respects, post-military Brazil came closer to typical first world patterns, but sizable gaps remain, as discussed in chapters 4–6.

1. The course of the military period as a whole is amply treated in the literature. On the political side, the most comprehensive sources in English are Thomas E. Skidmore, *The Politics of Military Rule in Brazil, 1964–85* (Oxford University Press, 1988); and Ronald M. Schneider, *"Order and Progress": A Political History of Brazil* (Boulder, Colo.: Westview Press, 1991). Both books include extensive bibliographical references in Portuguese as well as English. Scholarly essays on all aspects of the military regime are in Gláucio Ary Dillon Soares and Maria Celina D'Araujo, organizers, *21 Anos de Regime Militar* (Twenty-One Years of Military Rule) (Rio de Janeiro: Fundação Getúlio Vargas, 1994). On the economic side, see Werner Baer, *The Brazilian Economy: Growth and Development*, 3d ed. (New York: Praeger, 1989). Source materials on the crisis years after 1980 are given in chapter 7 in this volume. A broad chronological review of economic developments also appears in Marcelo de Paiva Abreu, organizer and ed., *A Ordem do Progresso: Cem Anos de Política Econômica Republicana, 1889–1989* (The Order of Progress: One Hundred Years of Political Economy under the Republic, 1889–1989) (Rio de Janeiro: Editora Campus, 1990). An account based on extensive interviews with a wide range of participants from both government and opposition, with particular emphasis on the reopening to democracy, is in Ronaldo Costa Couto, *História Indiscreta da Ditadura e da Abertura—Brasil: 1964–1985* (Indiscreet History of the Dictatorship and the Opening—Brazil: 1964–1985) (Rio de Janeiro: Editora Record, 1998).

## The Political Framework

Much of the Brazilian and foreign commentary on the military regime, both contemporary and retrospective, grossly oversimplifies its character. It has been pictured as fascist-reactionary, brutally oppressing the rural and urban masses to favor the interests of the military establishment and a small civilian elite allied with foreign-based (mainly American) multinational corporations. In the 1970s, even sophisticated analysts found it hard to believe that many generals might genuinely intend to restore constitutional democracy.[2]

In the same vein, the regime's enthusiasm for economic development has often been attributed to a narrow desire to maintain military rule. That view disregards the more obvious motive, belief by the rulers that successful development could help meet both a collective desire for enhanced national stature and the individual desires of most Brazilians. The concept of trusteeship for the national interest had long been a central feature of the training and indoctrination of military officers, even though their interpretation of national interest might be questioned and their assumption of the right to be its interpreters was obviously undemocratic.

In reality, the entire period was marked by dispute and dissension within the military concerning broad policies, programs, and personalities. The sharpest cleavage, though not the only one, was between the followers of Castello Branco, known as the Sorbonne group, and the more authoritarian officers of the *linha dura,* or hard line. The former always anticipated a fairly early return to some kind of civilian constitutional regime based on pluralist democracy, if possible freed from what were considered distortions in the Second Republic. Some of the hard-liners, by contrast, favored permanent military rule, as envisaged by Pinochet in Chile or various juntas in Argentina. For both groups, however, the dominant sentiment was against one-man dictatorship (*caudilhismo*), against extended terms in office (*continuismo*), and against establishing a single-party system like that of Mexico.

The Sorbonne group strategists, led by General Golbery do Couto e Silva, repeatedly rejected the one-party concept as inherently antidemocratic. They certainly hoped that Arena (the Aliança Renovadora Nacional) might

---

2. Two especially interesting examples are the essays by Philippe Schmitter and Juan Linz in Alfred Stepan, ed., *Authoritarian Brazil: Origins, Policies, and Future* (Yale University Press, 1973), chaps. 6 and 7. Schmitter predicted "Portugalization," meaning a semipermanent Salazar- or Franco-like regime, a prediction soon to be proven faulty. Linz was correct in diagnosing the elements of instability and impermanence but also wrong in his forecast of the ultimate outcome. Within a year of the book's publication, dismantling of the authoritarian structure was under way. Many other studies also illustrate the hazards of trying to fit Brazilian experience into generalized social science categories.

become a broadly based political party in support of their policy goals, if possible with long-term predominance like that of the Liberal Democratic Party in Japan, the Christian Democratic Party in Italy, or the Social Democratic Party in Sweden. During the 1970s and early 1980s the government manipulated the constitutional and electoral arrangements extensively to that end through a series of Institutional Acts. But the excesses of repression, especially in the years 1968–73, alienated more and more sectors of the public, including large elements of the middle classes and professional groups that had enthusiastically welcomed the ouster of Goulart in 1964. Noteworthy examples include the Bar Association (Ordem dos Advogados do Brasil), various journalists and newspaper publishers, and most middle-of-the-road Catholic bishops and priests, in addition to the narrow circle of radical "liberation theology" supporters. The main opposition political grouping, the Movimento Democrático Brasileiro (MDB), increasingly incorporated centrist and even right-of-center elements. From 1974 on, the MDB regularly demonstrated its capacity to win majorities in genuinely open elections, even with illiterates still denied the vote.

At the start, political repression and human rights abuse were substantial, even though less severe than in neighboring countries or Brazil itself after 1968. The main action was the "cassation" of several hundred high officials, including members of Congress and high-court judges, which meant removal from office and deprivation of political rights for ten years. There were many voluntary exiles, along with arrests and interrogations of supposed extreme leftists. The curve of arbitrary action rose steeply in the late 1960s, culminating in the suspension of Congress by the Fifth Institutional Act (IA-5) in December 1968. Repression began to subside with President Ernesto Geisel's policy of *distensão* (relaxation) in 1974, including the repeal of IA-5 in 1978, an amnesty permitting the return of political exiles in 1979, and President João Batista Figueiredo's policy of *abertura* (opening) after 1980. The path of declining rigor was by no means smooth, being marked by several false starts and reversals, but the underlying trend was steady.

On the human rights side, the "dirty war" instituted by President Emílio Garrastazú Médici against urban and rural guerrillas in the early 1970s appeared to institutionalize torture and included some 333 "disappearances." There is little comfort in the fact that the scale of disappearances was only one-tenth of Uruguay's and one-hundredth or less of Argentina's.[3] But the relatively small scale did facilitate the acceptance in 1979 by all parties of

3. See Alfred Stepan, *Rethinking Military Politics: Brazil and the Southern Cone* (Princeton University Press, 1988), pp. 69–72; and Skidmore, *The Politics of Military Rule in Brazil, 1964–85*, p. 269.

an amnesty applying both to left-wing terrorism and to abuses by police and military officers. However unjust to the victims of repression, the amnesty law has had the advantage of avoiding the unending recriminations that bedeviled political life in postwar France and continue to do so in Chile and much of Eastern Europe.[4] In postmilitary Brazil, there is no apparent political liability either in having been *cassado* by the military regime or in having occupied high office during those two decades.

With the adoption of the 1988 Constitution and the direct presidential election of 1989, Brazil completed its transition to pluralist democracy under civilian control. In form, the political system, like that of the 1950s, is presidential and federal, with separation of powers among the three branches and division of responsibilities between center and states broadly as in the United States. In content, however, Brazilian politics under the new constitution are substantially different from the conditions of 1946–64. The electorate has been enormously enlarged, now including illiterates and youth of sixteen, so that 82 million were eligible to vote in 1989 compared with the 12 million who voted in 1960. Television has become the overwhelmingly dominant medium of political communication. Since 1995, presidents, state governors, and mayors have been permitted to run for a second consecutive term. The two-turn voting system, requiring a runoff between the top two if no candidate receives an absolute majority on the initial ballot, has potential consequences for reshaping party structures and coalitions that have not yet been fully explored. There is widespread dissatisfaction with the party structures, the electoral system, relations among the three branches of government, and the workings of federalism. The continuing problems of political modernization and democratic consolidation are explored in detail in chapter 6.

## The Economic Transformation

The principal indicators of macroeconomic development during the military period are summarized in table 3-1 and figure 3-1. The four phases indicated there were not sharply separated by calendar years and included subphases not reflected in annual summary figures. Each of them, however, had salient features that left durable marks on the structure and performance of the Brazilian economy.

---

4. In the late 1990s, the government sponsored a program of financial compensation to victims of severe repression during the military period, with special attention to families of the "disappeared."

Table 3-1. *Economic Development under the Military Regime, 1964–85*
Percent, except as indicated

| Phase | Year | GDP | | 3. Gross savings ratio | 4. Current balance of payments (millions of U.S. dollars) | 5. External debt (millions of U.S. dollars) | 6. Debt-to-GDP ratio | 7. Change in general price level |
|---|---|---|---|---|---|---|---|---|
| | | 1. Increase | 2. Per capita increase | | | | | |
| Stabilization and reform | 1964 | 3.4 | 0.5 | 19.6 | 140 | 3,874 | 18.5 | 90.7 |
| | 1965 | 2.4 | -0.5 | 22.8 | 368 | 4,758 | 21.2 | 57.1 |
| | 1966 | 6.7 | 3.6 | 21.8 | 54 | 5,196 | 18.4 | 38.5 |
| | 1967 | 4.2 | 1.3 | 17.9 | -237 | 3,281 | 10.6 | 28.6 |
| "Economic miracle" | 1968 | 9.8 | 6.7 | 20.7 | -508 | 3,780 | 11.1 | 24.2 |
| | 1969 | 9.5 | 6.4 | 25.4 | -281 | 4,403 | 11.9 | 20.1 |
| | 1970 | 10.4 | 7.2 | 22.9 | -562 | 5,295 | 12.5 | 19.5 |
| | 1971 | 11.3 | 8.6 | 21.7 | -1,307 | 6,622 | 13.3 | 20.3 |
| | 1972 | 12.1 | 9.4 | 21.9 | -1,489 | 9,521 | 16.3 | 17.3 |
| | 1973 | 14.0 | 11.3 | 24.7 | -1,688 | 12,572 | 15.9 | 14.9 |
| Adjustment to external shocks | 1974 | 9.0 | 6.5 | 21.5 | -7,122 | 17,166 | 16.3 | 28.7 |
| | 1975 | 5.2 | 2.8 | 24.3 | -6,700 | 21,171 | 17.1 | 27.9 |
| | 1976 | 9.8 | 7.2 | 21.8 | -6,017 | 25,985 | 17.0 | 41.2 |
| | 1977 | 4.6 | 2.2 | 22.5 | -4,037 | 32,037 | 18.2 | 42.7 |
| | 1978 | 4.8 | 2.4 | 22.0 | -6,990 | 43,511 | 21.7 | 38.7 |
| | 1979 | 7.2 | 4.8 | 20.1 | -10,742 | 49,904 | 22.2 | 54.0 |
| | 1980 | 9.1 | 6.7 | 19.4 | -12,807 | 53,848 | 22.5 | 100.2 |

| Debt crisis and | 1981 | -3.1 | -5.3 | 18.6 | -11,734 | 61,411 | 23.3 | 109.9 |
| stagflation | 1982 | 1.1 | -1.2 | 15.6 | -16,310 | 70,198 | 25.8 | 95.5 |
| | 1983 | -2.8 | -5.0 | 12.7 | -6,837 | 81,319 | 39.4 | 154.5 |
| | 1984 | 5.7 | 3.4 | 17.0 | 45 | 91,091 | 43.1 | 220.6 |
| | 1985 | 8.4 | 6.1 | 18.2 | 268 | 95,857 | 41.9 | 225.5 |

Sources: All data are reported in or calculated from *Estatísticas Históricas*, using national accounts revisions for 1970–86 from *Indicadores* (IBGE, June 1988), pp. 95–104. Columns 1 and 2 are from *Estatísticas Históricas*, table 4.7, pp. 111–12; column 3 from table 4.4, line 2.3, pp. 100–02; column 4 from table 11.6, line E, pp. 537–39; columns 5 and 6 from tables 11.8 and 11.9, pp. 543–44 (for column 6, GDP data in Brazilian currency were converted into U.S. dollars using average annual market exchange rates as shown in International Monetary Fund, *International Financial Statistics Yearbook, 1982*, line rf, and subsequent monthly issues of *International Financial Statistics*); and column 7 from table 5.10, pp. 194–99.

Figure 3-1.  *GDP Growth and Inflation, 1964–85*

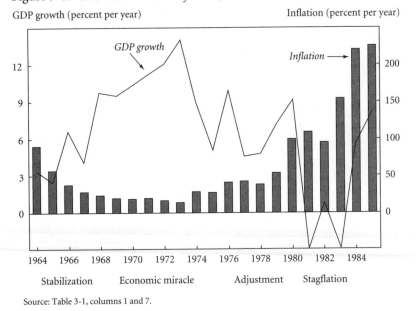

GDP growth (percent per year)                                    Inflation (percent per year)

Stabilization        Economic miracle            Adjustment        Stagflation

Source: Table 3-1, columns 1 and 7.

Stabilization efforts began almost immediately after the military coup and the installation of President Humberto Castello Branco. The short-term policies, introduced by Finance Minister Octávio Bulhões and Planning Minister Roberto Campos, focused on inflation control through reduced budgetary deficits, limits on monetary expansion, realistic foreign exchange rates, and restraints on wage increases. These austere policies were broadly in line with "orthodox" remedies for inflation prescribed by the International Monetary Fund, although they were more gradual in their application than the IMF ideal of that era.

The measures were denounced in populist quarters and among theorists of "structural" causes of inflation. Much of the business community considered them overly restrictive. On the more conservative side, the austerity measures were criticized by the monetarist school as being too "gradualist" and permitting too much "corrective inflation" to remove distortions in the price structure. In any event, as seen in figure 3-1 and column 7 of table 3-1, the rate of inflation was cut by three-quarters, returning it by 1968 to the order of magnitude Brazil had experienced in the 1950s.

More important for the longer term were major reforms in the nation's economic institutions, following first world practice and providing the foundations for a new phase of intensive growth. A genuine Central Bank was established, replacing the unsound confusion of commercial and central banking functions within the Banco do Brasil.[5] Basic statistical services were expanded and improved, providing a modern system of national accounts and annual household surveys on key indicators. Taxation was made more rational and collection efficiency improved. Domestic capital was mobilized, partly voluntarily and partly as forced savings, and applied through new institutions to key sectors such as housing and agriculture and to the distressed Northeast region. "Monetary correction," or "indexation," was introduced for long-term debt instruments, such as government bonds and private mortgages and for rental contracts. This innovation greatly facilitated private saving and investment, although it came to be regretted in later years as a major factor in sustaining "inertial inflation." Steps were taken to expand the primitive stock exchanges of Rio de Janeiro and São Paulo and to establish the equivalent of a Securities and Exchange Commission.[6]

On the external side, promotion of exports was given equal priority with import substitution, for the first time since 1930. Debts to foreign governments were rescheduled through the Paris Club of creditor nations, and relations were restored with the IMF and the World Bank. Private foreign investment was again made welcome. Out of concern that foreigners might acquire too large a share of strategic Brazilian industries, a tripartite concept was introduced in which the ownership of major companies (for example, in the petrochemical industry) was divided in approximately equal one-thirds among the Brazilian national government, foreign private investors, and Brazilian private investors, thus ensuring majority control for Brazilians but avoiding majority control in government hands.

The second major phase, which came to be known as the economic miracle, began in 1967 with the succession as president of General Artur Costa e Silva and the appointment of Antônio Delfim Netto as finance minister, later associated with João Paulo dos Reis Velloso as planning minister. The policy hallmark of this new economic team was expansive liberalization of credit in the private sector. It was based on the somewhat dubious hypotheses that monetary austerity was by now perpetuating industrial recession

5. In his memoir published in 1994, however, Roberto Campos expressed regret that when Castello Branco was succeeded as president by General Costa e Silva, the Banco Central was unable to retain the full independence originally intended for it. See Roberto Campos, *A Lanterna na Popa—Memórias* (The Lantern on the Stern—Memoirs) (Rio de Janeiro: Topbooks, 1994), pp. 669–74.

6. For a well-informed and sympathetic but critical exposition and analysis of these reforms, see Donald E. Syvrud, *Foundations of Brazilian Economic Growth* (Stanford, Calif.: Hoover Institution, 1974).

without further reducing inflation and that high interest rates were themselves an inflationary factor. The continuing inflationary pressures were attributed mainly to supply-side limitations. In keeping with the more relaxed attitude toward inflation, the policymakers enlarged the scope of indexation and introduced a crawling-peg exchange rate, with frequent mini-devaluations to prevent domestic price increases from overvaluing the currency and thus hampering exports.

As shown in columns 1, 2, and 7 of table 3-1, the policy gamble paid off handsomely. During the next six years, overall economic growth averaged 11.2 percent a year and per capita growth 8.3 percent. At those rates, unmatched elsewhere in Latin America and paralleled only by Japan and the Asian "tigers," the total output of the economy was being doubled in six and one-half years and average per capita incomes in less than nine years. At the same time, far from experiencing a new inflationary upsurge, price levels were increasing at less than 20 percent annually for the first time since 1958.

The economic miracle years coincided with the political phase of brutal repression of dissent and consequent political polarization. There has been much dispute about whether this was mere coincidence or involved a causal connection in which political repression was required for economic success. The coincidence has also skewed the critical analysis of the period, since opponents of the military regime (a group that by 1973 had come to include a very large proportion of Brazilian intellectuals and interested outsiders) were reluctant to believe that anything good could emerge where human rights were being so widely abused.

In fact, however, there was little direct connection between the technocratic makers of economic policy and the abuses committed by the military-police apparatus. The anti-inflationary wage compression was certainly facilitated by a discouragement of strikes, but torture was not needed for that purpose. The extreme abuses were motivated by military and police hostility to left-wing persons and organizations, not by economics. The abusers and the technocrats were working in separate worlds.

The more serious critical issues concerning the Brazilian economic miracle can be stated succinctly:

—Was there really any miracle at all, or merely a making up for time lost in the slow growth years of the earlier 1960s?

—Were the miracle levels of growth simply the result of an abnormal coincidence of favorable (and inherently short-lived) external circumstances, bound to be followed by a new balance of payments crisis?

—Was the miracle self-limiting because it concentrated on consumer durable goods for the upper classes and would necessarily exhaust the possibilities of import substitution in a nation sharply divided between a small well-to-do elite and an impoverished mass?

—Did the policies of the period expand foreign ownership of the Brazilian economy to a level threatening permanent denationalization and second-class status in the world?

—Did policy on wages intensify the already severe inequalities in Brazil's income distribution?

This list excludes the more radical socialist criticisms seeking an entirely different kind of economic and political order. Since most of these questions also pertain to the later 1970s, they are reviewed in the next section of this chapter.

How long the miracle could have been sustained in the absence of external shocks can never be known with certainty. Even before September 1973 there were signs of increasing inflationary pressures, while debt-servicing costs to sustain the surge in foreign borrowing were rising ominously. Imports were already expanding in response to an overvalued exchange rate and the full utilization of domestic production capacity. Then the first oil shock—a fourfold rise in world prices engendered by the Organization of Petroleum Exporting Countries (OPEC)—suddenly increased Brazil's annual oil import costs by over $2 billion, raising them from 13 to 22 percent of total imports. This oil shock was the setting for the third major phase, under Presidents Geisel and Figueiredo, in which balance of payments management perforce became the main focus of economic policy. At the same time, their commitments to political relaxation and an ultimate return to civilian rule made both of these presidents intent on maintaining as much economic growth as feasible.

The inherent conflict between short-term stabilization and continued growth, intensified by the worsening external economic environment, produced an alternation of macroeconomic stop-and-go policies.[7] On taking office in March 1974, Geisel's new team, led by Finance Minister Mário Henrique Simonsen with Reis Velloso continuing as planning minister, first relied mainly on monetary restraint to contain inflationary pressures. On the external side, the team decided to avoid major import cuts and general economic slowdown as means for offsetting the vastly increased oil import

7. For a well-informed year-by-year exposition and critical analysis of the economic policies and experience of the period 1971 to 1984, see Albert Fishlow, "A Tale of Two Presidents: The Political Economy of Crisis Management," in Alfred Stepan, ed., *Democratizing Brazil: Problems of Transition and Consolidation* (Oxford University Press, 1989), pp. 83–119. For a more detailed macroeconomic analysis, see Donald V. Coes, *Macroeconomic Crises, Policies, and Growth in Brazil, 1964–90* (Washington: World Bank, 1995).

costs, choosing instead the inherently risky policy of increased foreign bor-rowing, together with major new programs for import substitution in the sectors of capital and intermediate goods.

For a while, this gamble seemed to pay off. While growth rates declined from the miracle era, they averaged a very respectable 8.0 percent from 1974 to 1976. Brazil had no trouble covering its current balance of payments deficits through direct private investments and especially through loans from U.S. and European banks awash with "petro-dollar" funds from the Middle East, even though the size of those deficits was surging from less than $2 billion to more than $6 billion a year (table 3-1, column 4). A drive for exports, based partly on new kinds of subsidies, also proved successful, rais-ing their value from less than $3 billion a year in 1969–72 to almost $15 bil-lion in 1976–79.[8] Measures were taken to expand domestic oil production, to increase hydroelectric output, and later to begin an ambitious (but unsuc-cessful) nuclear energy program with West German help and an effective (but very costly) drive for partial replacement of gasoline by alcohol distilled from sugar cane.

From 1976 on, as seen in table 3-1, columns 5, 6, and 7, danger signs became increasingly evident in the disproportionate increase in foreign debt and in accelerating inflation. After the second oil shock in 1979, these con-cerns became serious constraints on macroeconomic policy. Then in the early 1980s, constraint shifted to sharp reversal, since much higher world interest rates were imposed by U.S. anti-inflation policies, a global recession reduced the imports of all industrial countries, and Mexico's threatened default on foreign loans undermined the credit standing of Latin America as a whole.

Thus began the "lost decade," a phase of debt crisis and stagflation and economic decline for Latin America as a whole. Brazil's experience in the 1980s was not as bad as most of its neighbors', when annual growth for all Latin America averaged 1.3 percent compared with Brazil's 2.8 percent. Nevertheless, that was a major decline from the preceding thirty years, and it was accompanied by constantly worsening and seemingly incurable infla-tion. Brazil's policy responses were often short-term improvisations to ward off exhaustion of foreign exchange reserves or the immediate threat of unre-strained hyperinflation. Commitments in "letters of intent" to the IMF were repeatedly unfulfilled. Almost continuous negotiations with foreign gov-ernmental and commercial bank creditors, occasionally punctuated by

8. For annual figures from 1945 through 1985, see *Estatísticas Históricas*, p. 525.

defaults on interest payments, failed to arrive at a durable settlement of the accumulated external debt, whose monetization and partial servicing became a major factor in the inflationary process.

Successive efforts at inflation control through "heterodox shock packages," beginning with the Cruzado Plan of 1986, proved ineffectual, with each failure increasing public skepticism of the workability of direct price and wage controls. Yet a return to orthodoxy of the 1964–66 type, accepting prolonged recession along with the pain of "corrective inflation," seemed politically unmanageable. This unhappy phase spanned the transition from military to civilian rule. It is analyzed in chapter 7.

## The Growth Period in Retrospect

The voluminous literature on the Brazilian economy of the late 1960s and 1970s includes a great deal of high-quality analysis. Yet much of it is also marked by doctrinal rigidity and dogmatic rivalries among competing schools of thought. Here are some eclectic reflections on the critical issues already noted, with the advantage in perspective from distance in both space and time.

1. *Was there really an economic miracle?* The principal argument to the contrary is that high growth in 1968–74 was merely the upswing in a long postwar cyclical pattern, made possible by the low growth years 1961–67.[9] In support of that position, it is clear that the very high rates of industrial growth in the early miracle years were made possible in part by the large volume of unused production capacity in 1967. In the later years, on the other hand, much of the high growth was flowing from new investment. It is also clear that by 1973 production levels were pressing hard on available capacity so that, regardless of the oil shock, it would not have been possible to prolong that year's phenomenal growth rate of 14 percent.

Nevertheless, the policymakers surely deserve credit for getting the unused capacity to work and then substantially enlarging capacity through incentives to both Brazilian and foreign investors. The "cyclical upswing"

9. See, for example, Edmar L. Bacha, "Issues and Evidence on Recent Brazilian Economic Growth," *World Development*, vol. 5, no. 1/2 (1977), pp. 47–67; also included in Lance Taylor, Edmar L. Bacha, Eliana A. Cardoso, and Frank J. Lysy, *Models of Growth and Distribution for Brazil* (Oxford University Press, 1980), chap. 2. A similar argument, but giving more weight to policy influences, was made in Pedro S. Malan and Regis Bonelli, "The Brazilian Economy in the Seventies: Old and New Developments," *World Development*, vol. 5, no. 1-2 (1977), pp. 19–45, where the authors consistently refer to "the so-called Brazilian 'miracle.'"

was no more automatic or inevitable than the high rates of growth under Kubitschek in the late 1950s.

The critics were no doubt reacting against the boastful claims of some officials that they had found a miraculous formula for maintaining double-digit annual growth rates indefinitely while keeping inflation and the balance of payments under adequate control. By that definition of miracle, the Brazilian performance certainly fell short. Yet those seven years of sustained growth, along with only moderate inflation, made major contributions to the structural modernization of the Brazilian economy. More recent policy-makers would have been delighted to repeat the experience.

2. *Were the high growth levels due mainly to favorable external circumstances?* This argument points to several factors: (a) high growth rates in the industrial world, facilitating exports from Brazil and other developing countries; (b) a favorable turn in Brazil's terms of trade (prices of exports in relation to imports); (c) substantial assistance from the international financial institutions (World Bank, Inter-American Development Bank, and IMF) and from friendly governments (especially the United States through the Agency for International Development and the Export-Import Bank); and (d) the ready availability of private foreign capital for direct equity investment and portfolio lending. Even with these advantages, it is claimed, the strategy was creating undue strains on the balance of payments prior to the oil shocks and became completely unsustainable in the face of those shocks.

In longer-term perspective, these points seem only partly persuasive, as can be seen by comparing conditions in the six growth years (1968–73) with the six previous years (1962–67). For the industrial world as a whole (members of the OECD), average annual growth of real gross domestic product (GDP) in 1968–73 was 5.0 percent, slightly below the prior period's 5.1 percent. There was indeed a surge in industrial country imports, which in dollar value (undeflated for price changes) rose by 108 percent between the two periods, but Brazil's overall exports fared even better, rising by 122 percent. The terms of trade for Brazil averaged 113.7 for the later period compared with 105.1 for the earlier (based on 1975 = 100), a gain of 8 percent, which can be considered significant but hardly spectacular.[10]

---

10. Malan and Bonelli, in "The Brazilian Economy in the Seventies," give the figure of 20 percent for the improvement between 1967 and 1973, but that was for only a single year. The industrial country growth data in the text are calculated from *OECD Economic Outlook*, no. 31 (July 1982), p. 142. The data on industrial country imports, Brazilian exports, and terms of trade are calculated from International Monetary Fund, *International Financial Statistics: Supplement on Trade Statistics*, Supplement Series 4 (Washington, 1982), pp. 130–31, 120–21, and 158–59, respectively.

Nor did Brazil's export performance worsen during the mid-1970s, even though industrial country growth was sharply retarded by the oil shock of 1974. As shown in table 3-2, export growth became slower than during the miracle years but was still substantial through 1981, even after correcting for inflation. But the import bill rose much more rapidly, while the debt-service ratio (interest plus amortization payments as a proportion of export earnings) entered the alarming range of 40 to 70 percent, as seen in table 3-2 and in figure 3-2. The policymakers had clearly overestimated the gains to the balance of payments from their drive toward import substitution in capital and intermediate goods. They had also encouraged state-owned industries to borrow heavily from foreign commercial banks at variable rates tied to the London interbank borrowing rate (LIBOR), a policy that helped keep inflation down for a few years but proved enormously costly when world interest rates soared and Brazil's credit standing was undermined by the Mexican financial crisis of 1982. In retrospect, it would have been far wiser to avoid excessive indebtedness by accepting import reductions and lower growth rates for a few years, the road taken by South Korea.[11] In that event, Brazil might have been spared a full decade of near stagnation.

3. *Was the miracle self-limiting because of the concentration on luxury goods for a narrow upper-class market?* This "underconsumptionist" hypothesis was advanced in the early 1960s by the well-known economist Celso Furtado and widely accepted among Brazilian intellectuals. It argued that import-substituting industrialization was applied mainly to consumer durable items, notably automobiles, affordable only by an elite measuring 5 or 10 percent of the population, whose absorptive capacity would soon be exhausted. In addition, it claimed that the policy contributed to Brazil's highly unequal income distribution and required constantly intensified inequality for any economic growth to continue. The empirical evidence of the 1970s, however, shows unequivocally that it was wrong on both counts.[12]

11. An alternative school of thought holds that Brazil could have shifted in the mid-1970s to export-led growth based on realistic exchange rates and enforcement of competition, anticipating the astounding records of Korea and the other East Asian "tigers." That kind of policy, however, would have been strongly resisted by the "industrial establishment," both in the São Paulo–based private sector and in the large state-owned sector. At the time, the business community was focused on the large domestic market, a possibility not open to the smaller economies of East Asia.

12. The hypothesis was set forth frequently in Furtado's prolific writings. For examples, see *Subdesenvolvimento e Estagnação na America Latina* (Underdevelopment and Stagnation in Latin America) (Rio de Janeiro: Civilisação Brasileira, 1967); *Análise do Modelo Brasileiro* (Analysis of the Brazilian Model) (Rio de Janeiro: Civilisação Brasileira, 1972). The most detailed summary of the empirical evidence to the contrary is in John Wells, "The Diffusion of Durables in Brazil and Its Implications for Recent Controversies Concerning Brazilian Development," *Cambridge Journal of Economics,* vol. 1 (September 1977), pp. 259–79.

Table 3-2. *Merchandise Trade and Debt Servicing, 1960–89*
Millions of U.S. dollars, except as indicated

| | | | Debt-servicing payments | | | 6. Debt service |
| | | | 3. Interest | | | ratio |
| | | | and | 4. Amorti- | 5. Total | (percent) |
| Year | 1. Exports | 2. Imports | dividends | zation | (3+4) | (5/1) |
|---|---|---|---|---|---|---|
| 1960 | 1,269 | 1,462 | 134 | 370 | 504 | 39.7 |
| 1961 | 1,403 | 1,460 | 123 | 307 | 430 | 30.6 |
| 1962 | 1,214 | 1,475 | 120 | 265 | 385 | 31.7 |
| 1963 | 1,406 | 1,487 | 87 | 219 | 306 | 21.8 |
| 1964 | 1,430 | 1,263 | 132 | 185 | 317 | 22.2 |
| 1965 | 1,596 | 1,096 | 156 | 274 | 430 | 26.9 |
| 1966 | 1,741 | 1,496 | 157 | 298 | 455 | 26.1 |
| 1967 | 1,654 | 1,667 | 186 | 382 | 568 | 34.3 |
| 1968 | 1,881 | 2,129 | 146 | 394 | 540 | 28.7 |
| 1969 | 2,311 | 2,263 | 184 | 439 | 623 | 27.0 |
| 1970 | 2,739 | 2,845 | 242 | 479 | 721 | 26.3 |
| 1971 | 2,904 | 3,696 | 329 | 572 | 901 | 31.0 |
| 1972 | 3,991 | 4,776 | 413 | 1,271 | 1,684 | 42.2 |
| 1973 | 6,199 | 6,992 | 582 | 1,676 | 2,258 | 36.4 |
| 1974 | 7,951 | 14,163 | 730 | 1,929 | 2,659 | 33.4 |
| 1975 | 8,670 | 13,578 | 1,497 | 2,190 | 3,687 | 42.5 |
| 1976 | 10,128 | 13,714 | 1,809 | 3,014 | 4,823 | 47.6 |
| 1977 | 12,120 | 13,254 | 2,102 | 4,125 | 6,227 | 51.4 |
| 1978 | 12,659 | 15,016 | 2,694 | 5,263 | 7,957 | 62.9 |
| 1979 | 15,244 | 19,731 | 4,102 | 6,558 | 10,660 | 69.9 |
| 1980 | 20,132 | 24,949 | 7,456 | 6,677 | 14,133 | 70.2 |
| 1981 | 23,292 | 24,073 | 10,306 | 7,442 | 17,748 | 76.2 |
| 1982 | 20,173 | 21,061 | 12,550 | 8,109 | 20,659 | 102.4 |
| 1983 | 21,898 | 17,233 | 10,267 | 10,167 | 20,434 | 93.3 |
| 1984 | 27,005 | 15,209 | 11,449 | 16,186 | 27,635 | 102.3 |
| 1985 | 25,639 | 14,329 | 11,092 | 16,795 | 27,887 | 108.8 |
| 1986 | 22,382 | 15,555 | 10,054 | 13,923 | 23,977 | 107.1 |
| 1987 | 26,229 | 16,578 | 8,971 | 15,135 | 24,106 | 91.9 |
| 1988 | 33,788 | 16,054 | 10,408 | 17,096 | 27,504 | 81.4 |
| 1989 | 34,379 | 19,857 | 9,633 | 14,549 | 24,182 | 70.3 |

Sources: Trade data for 1960–62 are from *Estatísticas Históricas*, p. 525, and for 1963–89 from World Bank, *World Development Indicators, 1999* (CD-ROM). Other data are from annual balance of payments statements published in Banco Central do Brasil, *Boletim Mensal* (Monthly Bulletin), and tabulated in more convenient form in International Monetary Fund, *Balance of Payments Statistics*, and United Nations Economic and Social Commission for Latin America and the Caribbean (CEPAL), *Statistical Yearbook* (Santiago, Chile). This table uses CEPAL for 1960–80, IMF for 1981–88, and Banco Central for 1989.

Figure 3-2. *Exports and Debt Servicing, 1960–89*

Exports and debt service (billions of U.S. dollars)          Debt service ratio (percent)

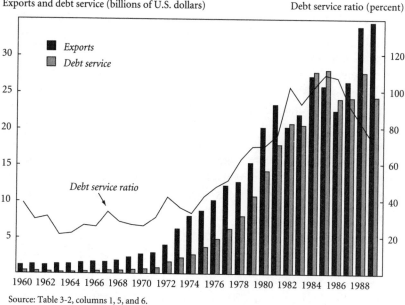

Source: Table 3-2, columns 1, 5, and 6.

As early as 1972, items like radios, refrigerators, and gas and electric stoves were owned by 30 to 53 percent of all Brazilian households. There was no sharp discontinuity between owning and nonowning income groups. By 1980 even automobiles were owned by 22 percent of all households (28 percent of urban households) and television by 55 percent. Market saturation was not an important factor in the recessions of the early 1960s or the early 1980s. If aggravated income inequality had any effect on demand for consumer durables, it was probably depressant rather than stimulative. As electrification became the norm in urban households and began its spread to rural areas, simple electro-domestic appliances were widely diffused.

In retrospect, the underconsumptionist hypothesis reflected two basic misconceptions. On the demand side, it assumed a cleavage between two sharply defined classes, rather than a gradation through a variety of middle classes, with substantial social mobility into and among them. And on the supply side, it assumed that producers—especially affiliates of multinational companies—would concentrate exclusively on "high-end" goods affordable only as conspicuous consumption. The prevalence of Marxist and extreme nationalist doctrines undoubtedly contributed to these misconceptions.

4. *Was there an intensification of foreign ownership of the Brazilian economy, so great as to threaten permanent denationalization and second-class status in the world?* In judging this issue, one must bear in mind the enormous vogue in Brazil during the military period of the theories of *dependência* ("dependency" or "dependent development").

Dependency theorists were not a single school; they were a congeries of social scientists with substantial differences among them and considerable change in their thinking over time. Most were hostile to capitalism in general and favored a shift to some kind of "socialism," generally not well defined. None of them advocated autarky as an alternative to dependency and their preferred mode of development was rarely specified. Those in the classic Marxist tradition still considered capitalism a necessary historical stage en route to socialism. The neo-Marxists believed that socialism could be achieved directly through revolutionary means, while the non-Marxists saw possibilities of a more gradual and peaceful transformation. All were influenced by the concepts of "center" and "periphery" developed by Raúl Prebisch and his colleagues at the UN Economic Commission for Latin America in Santiago, Chile, concepts that played a major role in the creation in 1964 of the UN Conference on Trade and Development (UNCTAD) and the subsequent campaign for a "new international economic order."[13]

Most of the dependency theories converged on two critical points, one negative and the other positive. They challenged the idea that today's underdeveloped countries might simply follow the paths of nineteenth-century Germany and United States (or twentieth-century Japan and Italy) into comprehensive industrial and technological modernization and self-sustaining economic growth, the path foreseen by neoclassical economic

13. For expositions of the variety of "dependency" theories and their decline, see Magnus Blomstrom and Bjorn Hettne, *Development Theory in Transition: The Dependency Debate and Beyond: Third World Responses* (London: Zed Books, 1984); and Robert A. Packenham, *The Dependency Movement: Scholarship and Politics in Development Studies* (Harvard University Press, 1992). A briefer treatment appears in Charles P. Oman and Ganeshan Wignaraja, *The Postwar Evolution of Development Thinking* (New York: St. Martin's Press, 1991), chap. 5, "Structuralism and Dependency." An oft-cited article in 1975 by an Indian economist questioned whether the concept was not so fluid as to be either operationally meaningless or a mere synonym for underdevelopment without any useful explanatory content (Sanjaya Lall, "Is 'Dependence' a Useful Concept in Analysing Underdevelopment?" *World Development*, vol. 3, nos. 11 and 12 [1975], pp. 799–810). One of the best-known Brazilian dependency theorists, Fernando Henrique Cardoso, was never on the extremes but in recent years has substantially abandoned the entire line of thought while becoming an important leader in national politics and rising to the presidency in 1994. His best-known writing in the field, widely available in translation, is Fernando Henrique Cardoso and Enzo Faletto, *Dependency and Development in Latin America* (University of California Press, 1979).

theorists in the western mainstream and by such historians as Kuznets and Rostow. In the view of the *dependentistas*, today's poorer countries are not merely latecomers but are symbiotically connected with the advanced industrial countries in ways that make their own rounded development impossible. Either they will endure permanent poverty, technological backwardness, and imperialist exploitation, or at best they may experience a distorted kind of growth into dual societies in which their oligarchical elites become mere extensions of the center, sharing its interests and consumption patterns, while the masses are marginalized in traditional agriculture or as urban slum dwellers without regular employment.

In political terms, these analyses had great appeal. Poverty and backwardness (along with inflation) could be blamed on distant wealthy countries rather than on policy mismanagement and insufficient capital formation at home. Nationalist sentiment could be invoked against foreign investors and their local allies. (Americans will recognize the same appeal in their own politicians' widespread indulgence in "Japan-bashing" when large tracts of Hawaiian land and Rockefeller Center in New York were acquired by Japanese nationals.)

A central point of convergence among dependency theorists concerned the growing role in Latin American industrialization of multinational corporations (MNCs), in that period mostly based in the United States. The MNCs were considered the cardinal instruments of dependency, commonly described in Brazilian left-wing circles as "suction pumps on the national body." Their defenders, in contrast, pointed to their positive effects as sources of capital, technology, and advanced management methods, providers of high-wage employment, and leaders in export marketing earning foreign exchange for Brazil's chronically hard-pressed balance of payments. Dependency theory apart, however, the multinationals were also objects of suspicion in the more chauvinistic military circles. They were naturally opposed by local businessmen fearful of competition in any form, especially when it came from companies with superior technological and financial resources. Concerns about denationalization did not end in the 1970s. They were reflected in the "informatics" policy of the 1980s and in several highly restrictive provisions in the 1988 Constitution. They are still a substantial element in the arsenal of Brazilian politics, especially on the left.

In the controversial atmosphere surrounding these issues, it is not easy to form an objective judgment on their merits. Foreign direct investment certainly played a major part in the industrial expansion of the military era, perhaps amounting to over one-third of total manufacturing investment, compared with 28 percent in the Kubitschek years.[14] Much of that investment, however, was in import-substitution lines for which domestic entrepreneurs were wholly unprepared. During the recession of the mid-1960s, on the other hand, there was a considerable wave of foreign takeovers of economically distressed Brazilian companies caught in the anti-inflationary domestic credit squeeze.[15] Political reaction against this trend led the government to reserve for the state itself a large ownership share in such expanding sectors as steel, nonferrous metals, and petrochemicals, alongside the established Petrobrás monopoly in oil. The desired pattern, as already noted, was equal thirds for public holdings, domestic private investors, and foreign multinationals, but in many cases it proved impossible to raise the full domestic private quota; then the gap was filled by the government. In the last years of the military period, government shares were often increased further to rescue ailing firms from insolvency. It was these policies, rather than any ideological inclination toward socialism as such, that led to the large state industrial sector of the 1980s, including many of the major candidates for privatization in the 1990s.

Lacking a consistent statistical base, one cannot confidently define the precise role of foreign ownership in the Brazilian economy or its trends over time. One careful estimate for 1971 put the foreign share of assets in manufacturing industry at about 34 percent and the share of sales at 45 percent, up from 33 percent in 1967.[16] By 1985, however, the foreign proportion of assets and sales was falling in almost all industrial sectors, although automobile assembly and pharmaceuticals remained almost exclusively foreign controlled.[17] In the 1970s, joint ventures with Brazilian participation became the rule rather than the exception, and Brazilianization of local management was almost universal. Some anecdotal evidence, such as a case study of the Usiminas steel mill (the first enterprise to be privatized in 1991), also indicates Brazilianization of some aspects of technology, even where the foreign

---

14. See Winston Fritsch and Gustavo Franco, *Foreign Direct Investment in Brazil: Its Impact on Industrial Restructuring* (Paris: OECD Development Centre, 1991), table 1.2, p. 23.

15. See Richard S. Newfarmer and Willard F. Mueller, *Multinational Corporations in Brazil and Mexico: Structural Sources of Economic and Noneconomic Power*, Report to the Senate Subcommittee on Multinational Corporations of the Committee on Foreign Relations (GPO, 1975), chaps. 5 and 6.

16. William G. Tyler, *Manufactured Export Expansion and Industrialization in Brazil* (Tübingen: J. C. B. Mohr, 1976), pp. 51–54.

17. See the surveys in 1971 and 1985 reported by the magazine *Visão* in April 1972 and August 1986.

investor was Japanese.[18] In a world of growing industrial interdependence, in which a large share of trade in manufactured goods involves specialized components exchanged within industries and even within firms and large corporations are owned by shareholders of many nationalities, the very meaning of "denationalization" becomes obscure.

More significant is the extent to which a country's nationals secure employment, income, and capital returns from the international complex as a whole. That depends less on formal ownership shares than on levels of productivity and contributions to technological advance, factors in which Brazil's performance remains well below first world standards. In retrospect, the charges that multinational companies were "controlling" the Brazilian economy in the 1970s were not well founded. As one close observer wrote at the time: "Certainly the argument that foreign firms exercise undue influence in LDC [less developed country] policy formulation is mitigated in the case of a powerful, far-reaching, and effective government. Such is the case with Brazil, where the government has emerged as the dominant single force in the economy."[19]

The other principal charges against the multinationals were a distortion of consumption patterns and the use of inappropriate technology, employing too much capital and too little labor. The effect, it was asserted, was to provide first world standards for a small elite segment, including a new aristocracy of skilled labor, but without contributing to economic welfare for the masses. The issue of appropriate technology has been widely studied, without clear-cut conclusions. In some fields, such as petrochemicals, the central manufacturing processes provide little latitude for varying ratios of labor to capital, although ancillary processes such as materials handling and shipping may be more or less labor intensive. Overall, more man-hours are generally spent in Brazil per unit of product than in advanced industrial countries, indicating—as would be expected—some business responsiveness to relative costs of labor and capital.

As to the type of goods produced for domestic consumption, the multinationals, like their Brazilian counterparts, were responding to market demands. Those demands, in turn, reflected the extremely unequal distribution of wealth and incomes that have characterized Brazil before, during, and after the era of intensive economic growth. As already pointed out,

18. See Carl J. Dahlman and Fernando Valadares Fonseca, "From Technological Dependence to Technological Development: The Case of the USIMINAS Steel Plant in Brazil," in Jorge M. Katz, ed., *Technology Generation in Latin American Manufacturing Industries* (New York: St. Martin's Press, 1987), chap. 6, pp. 154–74.

19. Tyler, *Manufactured Export Expansion and Industrialization in Brazil*, pp. 57–58.

many of the consumer durable goods were not limited to high-income luxury consumers. In the second phase of multinational expansion, focused on intermediate products and capital goods, the ultimate destination was often in export markets and, in any case, the demand for those products, such as petrochemicals, has no systematic relationship to income groupings. The relevant issue here has little to do with foreign investment; it is whether public policies exacerbated the distributional inequalities.

5. *Did policy on wages needlessly intensify the already severe inequality in Brazil's income distribution?* This is the most sensitive and controversial issue in the economic policy record of the military governments. The question was precipitated by evidence in the 1970 census that, compared with 1960, shares in the distribution of national income had moved markedly toward the top two deciles at the expense of the lower- and middle-income earners. Since restraint of wage increases had been a cardinal feature of Castello Branco's stabilization program, including a deliberate 20 percent reduction in the minimum wage along with the removal of militant trade union leaders, many critics attributed the intensified inequality directly to the government's labor policies.[20] Those policies were only slightly relaxed under Costa e Silva during the economic miracle. Although the professional analysts never claimed a worsening of absolute (in contrast to relative) income levels in the poorer classes, both Brazilian and foreign critics of the military regime soon misused their findings to charge that the regime's policies for stabilization and growth were "making the rich richer and the poor poorer."[21]

20. The most frequently cited critic in this vein was the American economist Albert Fishlow, an exceptionally well-informed Brazilianist at the University of California. His articles in the early 1970s made professional circles aware of the facts of increasing inequalities in Brazil's income distribution. The articles were for the most part strictly analytical, but with occasional polemical passages, one of which described the priorities of the Castello Branco administration as "destruction of the urban proletariat as a political threat, and reestablishment of an economic order geared to private capital accumulation." See "Brazilian Size Distribution of Income," *American Economic Review*, vol. 62 (May 1972), p. 400. See also "Some Reflections on Post-1964 Brazilian Economic Policy," chap. 3 in Stepan, ed., *Authoritarian Brazil*, pp. 69–118, esp. pp. 84–97.

21. Thus Sylvia Ann Hewlett stated: "The hallmark of contemporary Brazilian development has been the coexistence of great and growing wealth with deepening poverty and political repression" (*The Cruel Dilemmas of Development: Twentieth-Century Brazil* [Basic Books, 1980], p. 31). In fact, the central concern of her analysis was with increasing inequality rather than deepening poverty. The book's appendix table 13 showed a 35 percent gain between 1960 and 1976 in absolute income levels for the lowest decile among income groups and an average gain for the lowest three deciles of 109 percent (that is, more than a doubling of actual incomes—an annual growth rate of 4.7 percent). For the rapid growth period of 1970–76, although the ratios were not calculated, the book's data reveal a 52 percent gain in six years for the lowest decile and a 70 percent average for the lowest three deciles, more than 9 percent a year. For the top decile, the corresponding figures were 221 percent for 1960–76 and 106 percent for 1970–76. The book also made questionable generalizations

The World Bank's president singled out Brazil for explicit mention as an example of inequitable growth, signaling a shift of that institution's interests toward greater concern with overcoming poverty and giving equal priority to redistribution along with economic growth.[22]

It is beyond question that the overall distribution of income in Brazil became increasingly unequal during the military period. The basic data are summarized in table 3-3, which also gives comparable figures for the United States. On the other hand, it will be noted that the intensification of inequality was considerably slowed after 1970 and slightly reversed in favor of the middle groups during the early 1980s. In the high-growth decade of the 1970s, in fact, there were large income improvements for every group, the lowest decile gaining 50 percent and the lowest three deciles 48 percent, compared with 53 percent for the top decile and 50 percent for the top three.[23]

The literature on economic growth during the military period, however, contains heated dispute on two issues: (a) whether governmental wage policies during the stabilization phase were a major factor in increasing inequality, and (b) whether poverty was substantially alleviated during the periods of high growth. On the first question, the penetrating study by Samuel Morley, based on extensive work in Brazil in the late 1970s, provided an unequivocal negative.[24] His analysis included regional and sectoral differentials in income and educational levels, along with the massive labor force migrations of those decades from rural to urban and from Northeast to Center-South and also the indications of social mobility within regions. He took into account the large fractions of the population earning much less than the urban minimum wage. His central finding was that, when starting with a dual economy including a large surplus agricultural labor force living at the margin of subsistence, almost any successful industrialization effort would make the income distribution more unequal, up to the "turning point" where rural labor is no longer in surplus. The Brazilian experience conformed to the patterns found earlier by Simon Kuznets in the historical experience of Europe and North America.

---

concerning limited social mobility and wrongly anticipated a very long prolongation of authoritarian government.

22. See the book coauthored by the Bank's chief economist of that period: Hollis B. Chenery and others, *Redistribution with Growth* (Oxford University Press, 1974).

23. See David Denslow Jr. and William Tyler, "Perspectives on Poverty and Income Inequality in Brazil," *World Development*, vol. 12 (October 1984), p. 1023.

24. Samuel A. Morley, *Labor Markets and Inequitable Growth: The Case of Authoritarian Capitalism in Brazil* (Cambridge University Press, 1982).

Table 3-3.  *Income Distribution of the Economically Active Population,*
*Brazil and the United States, 1960–87*
Percentage share

| | Brazil | | | | United States |
|---|---|---|---|---|---|
| Income group | 1960 | 1970 | 1980 | 1985 | 1987 |
| Lowest 10% | 1.9 | 1.2 | 1.1 | 0.9 | n.a. |
| Lowest 20% | 3.9 | 3.4 | 3.0 | 2.7 | 4.6 |
| Lowest 40% | 11.3 | 10.0 | 8.8 | 8.7 | 15.4 |
| Middle 40% | 33.9 | 28.1 | 25.1 | 27.1 | 41.0 |
| Highest 20% | 54.8 | 61.9 | 66.1 | 64.2 | 43.7 |
| Highest 10% | 39.6 | 46.7 | 51.0 | 47.7 | n.a. |

Sources: Brazilian data for 1960, 1970, and 1980, based on censuses, are reported in *Estatísticas Históricas*, table 3.6, p. 75; data for 1985, based on National Household Surveys, are reported in *Anuário Estatístico* (1986), p. 435. U.S. data for 1987 (tabulated in quintiles rather than deciles) are from *Statistical Abstract of the United States, 1989*, p. 446.

n.a.  Not available.

Contrasting the cases of South Korea and Taiwan, where rapid growth over the same period was not "disequalizing," Morley noted the drastic land redistributions made possible in those countries by the removal of Japanese landlords, together with their societies' vigorous dedication to primary and secondary education and their focus on labor-intensive exports. As to wage policy, both those countries refrained from establishing urban minima, thereby maximizing the industrial employment of migrants from the country-side. In Brazil, Morley concluded that policy on minimum wages had little effect on income distribution. Instead, he wrote:

> It mainly determines the fraction of the unskilled labor force that works in formal-sector jobs earning the legal minimum wage, not the average wage earned by all the unskilled.... The point is that the basic problem of poverty in Brazil is not solvable by wage policy. Poverty occurs because the society is not rich and productive enough to provide everyone with a job at a decent wage. As long as there is surplus labor, there will be a pool of workers and families earning less than the poverty wage. Poverty can only be eliminated by eliminating surplus labor.[25]

The wage policy of the mid-1960s, however, did have relevance to the effort to overcome inflation. The dissenters did not deny that connection

25. Morley, *Labor Markets and Inequitable Growth,* p. 289.

but contended that the Bulhões-Campos team gave too great a priority to stabilization and too little to restoring growth and attacking poverty. Looking back on that dispute, one notes that more recent experience in many developing countries, and also in Eastern Europe, suggests that bringing annual inflation rates (without indexation) down to 20 percent or less is an indispensable prerequisite to sustained growth and broadly distributed economic welfare.

By the late 1970s, Morley's "turning point" seemed to have been reached, with increasing fractions of the labor force earning more than the legal minimum and a slowdown in rural-to-urban migration. Boom conditions also increased family incomes by employing more household members. In principle, that should have been followed by a gradual trend toward greater equality. After the time of his study, unfortunately, the stagnation of the 1980s and early 1990s regenerated labor surpluses and their depressing effects on real wages, once again intensifying inequality as well as poverty (see chapter 5).

On poverty alleviation during the economic miracle, the favorable evidence is even more compelling. Over the 1960s, Morley's analysis estimated income gains of 57 percent for the "base-period poor" (that is, those who were poor in 1960), in contrast to the 28 percent increase for the lowest deciles in 1960 and 1970. Migration out of the rural sector and from the Northeast to Center-South helped make this possible, along with a surprising degree of interclass social mobility, in contradiction to widely accepted stereotypes about the rigidity of Brazil's social structure.[26]

For the 1970s, the decennial censuses permitted a direct comparison of proportions of "absolute poverty." Taking as the poverty line a family income of one minimum wage (as defined for Rio de Janeiro in 1980), the data are shown by regions in table 3-4.

Thus the share of the population below the poverty line had been cut in half by 1980 and the amount of income transfer needed to bring the poor-

---

26. Morley, *Labor Markets and Inequitable Growth*, pp. 79–80. Regarding social mobility, special census bureau tabulations in 1973 made possible a pathbreaking study by Professor José Pastore of São Paulo that demonstrated degrees of intergenerational mobility (downward as well as upward) greater than in Western Europe and only slightly less than in the United States. See Pastore, *Desigualdade e Mobilidade Social no Brasil* (São Paulo: Editora Queiroz, 1979), translated into English as *Inequality and Social Mobility in Brazil* (University of Wisconsin Press, 1982). Within the top group (of six stratified groups) in 1973, the fathers of only 17 percent had come from their own group, compared with 18 percent from the bottom group and 35 percent from the lowest three groups. The total mobility between fathers and sons was 58 percent. (See *Inequality and Social Mobility in Brazil*, pp. 32–33).

Table 3-4.  *Absolute Poverty, by Region, 1970 and 1980*
Percent

| Region | Proportion of families below poverty line | | Poverty gap in relation to total family income | |
|---|---|---|---|---|
| | 1970 | 1980 | 1970 | 1980 |
| North | 45.3 | 21.8 | 8.7 | 2.5 |
| Northeast | 68.2 | 43.9 | 26.5 | 7.3 |
| Southeast | 27.1 | 11.5 | 3.4 | 0.8 |
| South | 35.9 | 16.1 | 6.2 | 1.4 |
| Center-West | 46.2 | 20.2 | 8.8 | 1.7 |
| Urban total | n.a. | 13.5 | n.a. | 1.0 |
| Rural total | n.a. | 42.1 | n.a. | 8.0 |
| Brazil total | 42.2 | 21.9 | 7.7 | 1.9 |

Source: Calculations by Rodolfo Hoffman, reported in Helga Hoffman, "Pobreza e propriedade no Brasil: O que está mudando?" (Poverty and Property in Brazil: What Is Changing?) in Edmar Bacha and Herbert S. Klein, eds., *A Transição Incompleta: Brasil desde 1945* (The Uncompleted Transition: Brazil since 1945), vol. 2 (São Paulo: Paz e Terra, 1986), pp. 87–88.

n.a. Not available.

est group up to the poverty line had been cut by three-quarters. Rural areas in general and the Northeast in particular continued to stand out as huge pockets of poverty. But that record was very far from "immiseration" or mere trickle-down. There had been ample participation in income gains by the poorest as well as the upper and middle classes.

This experience does not justify complacency concerning income distribution in Brazil, which again became more unequal during the stop-and-go era of 1981–95, along with a large increase in urban poverty.[27] As chapter 5 suggests, it points to deeper historical causes than these recent decades, including a grossly uneven distribution of land ownership and of corporate capital and other forms of urban wealth, matters not covered by official statistics. Early in the military period, comprehensive land reform legislation, based on moderate taxation of potential output, was enacted, but it was never effectively implemented. On the human capital side, a major project for improved elementary and secondary education was planned by the Castello Branco government jointly with the U.S.-sponsored Alliance for Progress, only to be frustrated by nationalist hostility and populist student demon-

27. See M. Louise Fox and Samuel A. Morley, "Who Paid the Bill? Adjustment and Poverty in Brazil, 1980–1995," Working Paper for World Bank, *World Development Report 1990* (February 23, 1990), mimeo.

strations against "educational imperialism." After the restoration of civilian rule, opponents of land reform showed exceptional strength in the democratically elected constitutional convention of 1988 and in the Congresses elected in 1990 and 1994. Thus reforms that might work in the direction of a broader distribution of both human and physical capital, leading in turn to a more equal distribution of income, remain among the major unfinished business of Brazilian society (see chapter 5).

## The Military Republic's Economic Legacy

What, then, was the condition of the Brazilian economy bequeathed in 1985 to the first civilian government in twenty-one years? In macroeconomic terms, it was a mixed bag, as will be recalled from table 3-1. The deep recession of 1981–83 had been followed by a healthy recovery of production. A huge surge in exports had closed the gap in the current balance of payments, slowing the growth in external indebtedness. But that debt now amounted to almost $100 billion and debt management was to become the priority concern of the new policymakers. At the same time, fiscal discipline had been relaxed. The central bank's purchases of foreign exchange for debt servicing placed huge additional strains on monetary policy, and the annual rate of inflation in both 1984 and 1985 passed the 200 percent mark for the first time in Brazilian history.

On the political side, the sense of legitimacy of the new administration was gravely weakened by the fatal illness of president-elect Tancredo Neves. His personal popularity and broadly based support did not extend to Vice President José Sarney, who had led a dissenting faction out of the military government's preferred party to join the successful coalition in the transitional electoral college.

The failure of the Sarney administration (1985–90) to resolve the interrelated problems of external debt, internal debt, and accelerating inflation is relevant here because it postponed any effective further development in Brazil's economic and political structures. On the economic side, however, those structures had been fundamentally altered during the military era, moving the country into the category of "newly industrializing nations" differing in almost all respects from typical third world conditions. Before considering how close Brazil has come to full first world status, we review briefly the major changes between 1964 and 1985.

Population had grown from 80 million to 135 million, but the rate of annual increase was slowing from over 3 to about 2 percent. Urbanization had risen from less than one-half to almost three-quarters of the total. The

Northeast was still a huge pocket of poverty and illiteracy, with birthrates well above the national norm. Out-migration had reduced its share in the total population from 31 to 28 percent, still too large to end its role as a source of surplus labor for agriculture within the region and for unskilled urban work in all regions. At the other extreme, not only the city of São Paulo, but the entire state, with one-fifth of the nation's population and half its industry, had reached the living standards of southern Europe in the 1960s, with a similar structure of social classes. New frontiers of settlement had been opened in sparsely settled northern and western regions.

As noted in chapter 1, the labor force had shifted massively out of agriculture and into both industry and services. There was a large increase in the participation of women. The most striking changes were in the industrial sector, which now accounted for about 40 percent of GDP. In 1985, the volume of industrial output was more than 3.6 times that of 1962. As shown in table 3-5, the character of industry had shifted from traditional soft consumer goods to consumer durables, intermediates, and capital goods.

Although not easily quantifiable, there had also been a quantum jump in technological sophistication, exemplified by sales of Brazilian aircraft, military hardware, and automobiles in highly competitive export markets. A large proportion of industrial machinery and equipment was being supplied from domestic sources. Engineers, geologists, accountants, and professional business managers, trained at both high school and university levels, were now available in substantial numbers, and the local affiliates of foreign companies were staffed mainly or entirely by Brazilians.

These developments made possible a dramatic shift in the volume and composition of Brazilian exports. Their total rose from $1.4 billion in 1963 to $25.6 billion in 1985, an elevenfold expansion in real terms, while the industrial share in those exports was increasing from 15 to almost 60 percent.[28] Thus the old commercial hegemony of coffee, sugar, cacao, and cotton had taken a minor position alongside manufactured goods, steel, iron ore, soybeans and derivatives, and orange juice, making for a highly diversified trading pattern. There was also more geographical diversity. In 1963 the United States accounted for 38 percent of Brazil's exports and 31 per-

28. Calculated from data in World Bank, *Brazil: Industrial Policies and Manufactured Exports,* Country Study (Washington, 1983), supplemented by the *Estatísticas Históricas* and the *Anuário Estatístico,* 1986. See also Werner Baer, Manuel A. R. da Fonseca, and Joaquim J. A. Guilhoto, "Structural Changes in Brazil's Industrial Economy, 1960–80," *World Development,* vol. 15, no. 2 (1987), pp. 275–86.

Table 3-5. *Distribution of Value of Production, by Industry, 1962 and 1985*
Percent

| Industry | 1962 | 1985 |
|---|---|---|
| Traditional | 49.2 | 34.0 |
| Wood | 2.0 | 2.1 |
| Furniture | 1.7 | 1.5 |
| Leather | 1.2 | 0.5 |
| Textiles | 14.3 | 6.2 |
| Apparel | 3.3 | 3.9 |
| Food | 20.0 | 15.0 |
| Beverages | 2.2 | 1.0 |
| Tobacco | 1.3 | 0.7 |
| Publishing and printing | 1.9 | 1.6 |
| Miscellaneous | 1.3 | 1.5 |
| Other | 50.8 | 66.0 |
| Nonmetallic minerals | 4.3 | 3.5 |
| Metallurgy | 10.7 | 13.3 |
| Machinery | 2.9 | 5.8 |
| Electrical and communications | | |
| equipment | 4.8 | 5.0 |
| Transportation equipment | 9.6 | 6.5 |
| Paper | 2.7 | 3.2 |
| Rubber | 1.9 | 1.5 |
| Chemical products | 9.8 | 23.2 |
| Pharmaceuticals | 2.0 | 1.2 |
| Perfumes | 1.0 | 1.0 |
| Plastic products | 1.2 | 1.9 |

Sources: Data are based on quinquennial industrial censuses and annual sample censuses of the IBGE. Data for 1962 are from World Bank, *Brazil: Industrial Policies and Manufactured Exports* (Washington, 1983), p. 9. Data for 1985 are calculated from 1980 census as reported in *Anuário Estatístico* (1986), p. 311, and adjusted to 1985 by applying the annual indexes for industrial production (1981 = 100) from *Estatísticas Históricas*, p. 360.

cent of imports; in 1985 these shares were down to 27 and 20 percent. The European share was also down, the gainers being Japan, the Middle East, Africa, and neighboring Latin America. The sources of foreign investment were also more varied, with North America yielding shares to Western Europe and Japan.

Although less dramatic than the industrial transformation, there were also important changes in Brazilian agriculture, which continues to employ almost one-quarter of the national labor force. Growth rates of production in this sector were only half those in industry, but still substantially above population growth. They resulted mainly from opening up new lands in the Center-West and Northwest (not much in Amazônia proper), applying new technology to the relatively infertile central plain (the *cerrado*), and shifting land use to crops of higher value. Much of the new frontier was developed by capital-intensive commercial methods like those of the United States, Canada, and Australia, in contrast to the traditional plantation-type sugar *fazendas* of the Northeast. Government policies toward agriculture were a complex mixture of penalties (in effect favoring industry) and incentives. The latter included large volumes of highly subsidized credit, an important contributor to fiscal deficits and inflationary pressures. Some of the new crops, notably soybeans and orange juice, were spectacular successes. On the other hand, the well-known Pro-Alcohol program, expanding sugar lands to produce alcohol as a substitute for gasoline, was a very questionable use of scarce resources, with unit costs at least double those of imported oil, even in the oil shock era.[29]

As in the Italian *mezzogiorno*, agriculture in Brazil's Northeast has been highly resistant to change and a breeding ground for deep discontent in the peasantry. In the economic recessions of the 1980s, migration to cities ceased to be a major source of relief. While lacking the seeming potential for violent revolution feared by many in the 1960s, this aspect of the military era's socioeconomic legacy was a continuing challenge for the civilian governments that followed.

In the services sector, the most spectacular structural changes lay in the financial field. The central bank became a sophisticated and competently staffed institution, without which the fiscal indiscipline of recent years would long since have led to outright hyperinflation. In the environment of accelerating inflation, the commercial banking sector became grossly over-built and careless in its lending standards, but highly sophisticated in its techniques. The stock exchanges of Rio and São Paulo, with their regulatory agency (Comissão de Valores Mobiliários) modeled after the American Securities and Exchange Commission, showed promise of becoming significant institutions for the mobilization of private capital, including foreign

---

29. On changes in agricultural structures and related governmental policies, see William C. Thiesenhusen and Jolyne Melmed-Sanjak, "Brazil's Agrarian Structure: Changes from 1970 through 1980," *World Development*, vol. 18, no. 3 (1990), pp. 393–415; and José L. Carvalho, "Agriculture, Industrialization, and the Macroeconomic Environment in Brazil," *Food Policy*, vol. 16 (February 1991), pp. 48–57. On comparative costs of alcohol and petroleum, see Victor Yang and Sergio C. Trindade, "The Brazilian Fuel Alcohol Program," in *Chemical Engineering Progress*, April 17, 1979, p. 17.

investors. If and when a new era of economic growth materializes, the finan-cial sector, which underwent a major shakedown in the 1990s, is well equipped to assist it. In this respect, Brazil enjoys enormous advantages over the newly democratized countries of central and eastern Europe.

This mainly favorable assessment of structural change should not be mis-read as praise for all the economic policies of the military era. At the macro-economic level, those policies were very deficient, at least after the second oil shock. At the microeconomic level, they clearly should have done much more to strengthen primary and secondary education and to encourage more labor-intensive industrialization, thus working toward a reduction of income inequalities.[30] Much of industry remained grossly overprotected from foreign competition and little exposed to domestic competition. The "social debt"—in education, health care, and equalization of opportunity—was widely recognized, but the political structure was not yet ready to cope with it.

There had also been major blunders, partly reflecting a kind of chauvin-istic grandiosity, in pharaonic projects such as the Brazilian-German nuclear energy program and the vain effort at major agricultural coloniza-tion in the Amazon. The widespread neglect of environmental concerns until well into the 1970s may prove costly in the long run, even though many of the journalistic allegations of deforestation in the Amazon were grossly exaggerated. The effort to create a domestic "informatics" industry through measures of extreme protectionism was ill-advised when Brazil was simply unequipped to match the leaders in this area of dynamic technological advance.

Taken on balance, however, Brazil's economic structure in 1985 con-tained most of the modernizing elements needed for a final push into the community of advanced industrial nations. The political structure, in con-trast, was still largely inchoate. The electorate had been vastly enlarged since 1964, but too many ill-defined parties were competing for its attention and support. Many of the prominent political figures were from the premilitary generation, still debating issues of the 1950s and 1960s with little relevance to the challenges ahead. Military rule had inoculated the body politic against any early recrudescence of authoritarianism, wanted neither by the public nor by the great majority of the officer corps, but stable and effective plu-ralist democracy was not yet assured. Nor had Brazil redefined its desired place in the economic and political fabric of a rapidly changing world con-

---

30. See Peter T. Knight, "Brazilian Socioeconomic Development: Issues for the Eighties," *World Development*, vol. 9, no. 11/12 (1981), pp. 1063–82.

text. These defects left the country ill-prepared to cope with the debt and inflation crises that disfigured the lost decade of 1981–95, as discussed in detail in chapter 7. The intervening chapters analyze more precisely the shortfalls between the Brazil of the late 1990s and the goals set forth in chapter 1.

# 4

## The Incomplete Transformation: Economic Structures

This chapter assesses Brazil's progress toward first world status in the economic dimension. It draws on quantitative data where available, supplemented by qualitative judgments. Chapters 5 and 6 provide similar assessments in the less tangible but equally important social and political dimensions. In all three aspects—economic, social, and political—the goal of first world status is not static but undergoes continuous evolution.

### Production Levels

The initial measurements refer to overall economic output. Where available, they include comparisons for the first world as a whole, using the World Bank's category of "high-income" countries. In most cases, however, Spain and Italy are shown as representative first world nations with strong cultural affinities to Brazil and records of economic success and political stability in recent decades. Data are also included for Mexico and South Korea, the two semi-industrialized countries that have been Brazil's leading competitors for full modernization, and India, which is a prototypical large third world economy. India is by no means stagnant, in contrast to much of sub-Saharan Africa. It has a substantial cadre of well-educated personnel skilled in modern technologies. In the 1990s India introduced far-reaching market-oriented reforms in its macroeconomic policies, with dramatic early results. Yet it is still in the early stages of industrialization and structural change, with the mass of its rural population remaining at near-subsistence living standards.

Table 4-1, illustrated by figure 4-1, shows per capita output for this group of countries from 1955 to 1998 using purchasing power parity (PPP) exchange rates and 1998 price levels throughout. Brazil's level in 1998 was more than three times India's but still only one-third of the Spanish-Italian average and one-quarter of the high-income group as a whole. Note that Spain and Italy have been rapidly moving targets. Brazil today is almost equal to southern Europe in 1965, and today's shortfall, while large, is by no means unbridgeable if given ten to fifteen years of sustained high growth.

Korea's recent experience demonstrates that possibility vividly, as shown in figure 4-2, comparing the performance of Mexico, Brazil, Korea, and India in relation to one another and to the Spanish-Italian average. During the 1965–75 decade, Brazil and Korea were both advancing rapidly in relation to Spain and Italy, while Mexico and India were declining. Then came the "lost decade" of the 1980s for Latin America. As noted in chapter 7, Brazil's per capita output from 1980 to 1993 was falling by 0.7 percent a year, while Korea maintained a prodigious annual growth rate of 6.8 percent, raising the output level beyond two-thirds of Southern Europe's. Between 1975 and 1998, Korea advanced from one-third behind Brazil to 100 percent ahead. Brazil had reached one-half of Spain's standing by 1980 but then fell back to 40 percent during the lost decade. These data are also a reminder that first world status is itself a moving target, with Spain and Italy among the faster movers in Europe.

Per capita output levels and rates of growth are not by themselves adequate indicators of economic modernization or of human welfare. GDP figures provide no information on distribution of incomes or noneconomic elements in well-being. A number of scholars and development practitioners have sought to create an alternative index that might incorporate a wider array of factors. The most ambitious such attempt has been the human development index of the United Nations Development Programme (UNDP).[1] In my view the objective is praiseworthy but the results inherently arbitrary because no rational basis can be found for the proper weighting of components as diverse as economic output, health, and education. I would prefer to recognize that development involves much more than growth in economic output and then to examine relevant indicators seriatim rather

1. See United Nations Development Programme, *Human Development Report*, published annually since 1990 by Oxford University Press. Chapter 5 of the 1994 report (pp. 90–108) discusses in some detail the rationale of the human development index and the evolution of thinking about its composition and the weighting of its various components. The 1999 report opens with a review of the effort (pp. 1–23), including an essay by Nobel laureate Amartya Sen indicating how and why his own initial skepticism has been overcome.

Table 4-1.  *Real GDP per Capita, Selected Countries, 1955–98*
1998 U.S. dollars, except as indicated[a]

| Country | 1955 | 1965 | 1975 | 1985 | 1998 | Annual growth rate (percent) 1955–75 | 1975–98 |
|---|---|---|---|---|---|---|---|
| Brazil | 2,075 | 2,560 | 4,820 | 5,488 | 6,460 | 4.3 | 1.3 |
| India | 814 | 895 | 995 | 1,249 | 2,060 | 1.0 | 3.2 |
| Mexico | 3,457 | 4,612 | 6,444 | 7,347 | 7,450 | 3.2 | 0.6 |
| Korea | 1,224 | 1,470 | 3,248 | 5,927 | 13,286 | 5.0 | 6.3 |
| Spain | 3,707 | 6,517 | 10,264 | 10,483 | 15,960 | 5.2 | 1.9 |
| Italy | 5,063 | 8,008 | 11,604 | 15,134 | 20,365 | 4.2 | 2.5 |
| High-income | n.a. | n.a. | n.a. | n.a. | 23,420 | n.a. | n.a. |

Sources: For 1955–85, data diskette provided by the World Bank socioeconomic data staff, based on the Penn World Tables Mark 5 prepared by Robert Summers and Alan Heston (University of Pennsylvania) for the UN International Comparison Programme. For 1998, World Bank, *World Development Indicators, 2000* (Washington, 2000), table 1-1.

n.a. Not available.

a. Dollar values calculated on a purchasing power parity basis. Data for 1955 through 1985 originally in 1985 prices have been converted to 1998 prices using the U.S. GDP implicit price deflators reported in *Economic Report of the President, 2000*, p. 310.

than seek a single index that suffers from inescapable technical flaws. It should be emphasized, moreover, that while growth in per capita output alone is not a sufficient index of progress toward first world status, it is most decidedly a necessary prerequisite.

## Production Structure

Table 4-2, on the broad structure of production, confirms Brazil's intermediate position in transformation toward the first world. The shift from agriculture to industry, with its correlative urbanization, is the classic element in the historical studies of development noted in chapter 1. Brazil was already well along that road by 1965, but even in 1998 the agricultural sector still accounted for 8 percent of total output, compared with 3 percent for Italy (likewise Canada and Australia). By 1998 Brazil was moving toward the subsequent stage, as seen in the Italian case, in which modern kinds of services gain on both agriculture and industry.

Table 4-3 again confirms Brazil's intermediate position. Urbanization appears on a par with the high-income countries but may be somewhat overstated because of an unusually broad definition. In commercial energy

Figure 4-1. *International Comparisons, GDP per Capita, 1955–98*

1998 U.S. dollars

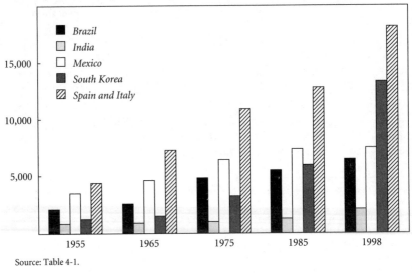

Source: Table 4-1.

Figure 4-2. *Per Capita Incomes Relative to Those of Spain and Italy, 1955–98*

Percent

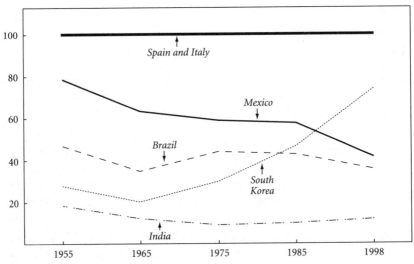

Source: Calculated from data in table 4-1.

Table 4-2.  *Structure of Production, Selected Countries, 1965 and 1998*[a]
Percent

| Country | Agriculture 1965 | Agriculture 1998 | Industry 1965 | Industry 1998 | Manufacturing 1965 | Manufacturing 1998 | Services and other 1965 | Services and other 1998 |
|---|---|---|---|---|---|---|---|---|
| Brazil | 19 | 8 | 33 | 29 | 26 | 23 | 48 | 63 |
| India | 44 | 29 | 22 | 25 | 15 | 16 | 34 | 46 |
| Mexico | 14 | 5 | 27 | 27 | 20 | 20 | 59 | 68 |
| Korea | 37 | 5 | 24 | 44 | 18 | 31 | 37 | 52 |
| Spain | n.a. | n.a. | n.a. | n.a. | n.a. | 25 | n.a. | n.a. |
| Italy | 8[b] | 3 | 41[b] | 30 | 27[b] | 20 | 51[b] | 67 |
| High-income | 5 | 2 | 43 | 30 | 32 | 21 | 52 | 68 |

Sources: World Bank, *World Development Report* (Oxford University Press, 1996), statistical appendices, table 3; World Bank, *World Development Indicators, 2000*, table 4.2.

n.a.  Not available.

a.  Note that "manufacturing" is a subset of "industry." "Services and other" includes unallocated items.

b.  Italian data are for 1970, rather than 1965.

use, Brazil's partial transformation emerges clearly. In automotive production and usage, Brazil, Mexico, and Korea are in the same general bracket, only slightly behind Italy and Spain. In all these respects, however, one should note the contrast between Brazil's slowing rates of growth in the last twenty years and the sustained expansion in Korea.

Physical infrastructure provides another indicator of modernization. Table 4-4 shows two major aspects: electrification and telephone communications, together with two indicators of technological advance. It also shows (1) rapid rates of development in the entire group of countries, (2) a substantial continuing lead in Spain and Italy, and (3) Brazil in an intermediate position while Korea is closing rapidly on the leaders, already in their league in numbers of telephones. On technology, Brazil lags badly, little ahead of India in resources devoted to research and development, while Korea has made its way into the third industrial revolution. In computer density, Brazil stands at tenfold that of India but only one-tenth of the first world. In high-tech manufacturing, Brazil has found some successful niches in the information revolution but, unlike Korea, is still far from becoming a full participant. Data on scientific and technical personnel are discussed later.

## International Trade

In recent decades, international trade and financial flows have played an increasing part in the growth of first world economies, making them par-

Table 4-3. *Urbanization, Energy, and Transport in Selected Countries, 1960–98*

| Country | Urban population share (percent) | | Per capita use (kg. oil equivalent) | | Motor vehicle production (thousands) | | | Motor vehicle registration (persons/vehicle) | | |
|---|---|---|---|---|---|---|---|---|---|---|
| | 1960 | 1998 | 1965 | 1997 | 1965 | 1975 | 1998 | 1965 | 1975 | 1997 |
| Brazil | 45 | 80 | 286 | 896 | 185 | 930 | 1,573[a] | 41 | 16 | 14 |
| India | 18 | 28 | 100 | 352 | 71 | 74 | 513 | 659 | 421 | 440 |
| Mexico | 51 | 74 | 605 | 1,501 | n.a. | 361 | 1,453 | 34 | 18 | 20 |
| Korea | 28 | 80 | 238 | 3,834 | n.a. | n.a. | 1,954 | 1,047 | 180 | 5 |
| Spain | 57 | 77 | 901 | 2,729 | 225 | 814 | 2,826 | 26 | 6 | 3 |
| Italy | 59 | 67 | 1,568 | 2,839 | 1,175 | 1,459 | 1,693 | 8 | 3 | 2 |
| High-income | 64 | 77 | 3,707 | 5,369 | n.a. | n.a. | 2,173[b] | 4 | 3 | 2 |

Sources: Urban population data are from World Bank, *World Development Report, 1992* (Oxford University Press, 1992); World Bank, *World Development Indicators, 2000*, table 3-10. Energy use data are from World Bank, *World Development Report, 1984*, table 8; World Bank, *World Development Indicators, 2000*, table 3.7. Motor vehicle data are from American Motor Vehicle Manufacturers' Association (Detroit, Michigan), *Motor Vehicle Facts and Figures* (Detroit, 1967, 1977); *Ward's Motor Vehicle Facts and Figures, 1999* (Southfield, Mich.: Ward's Communications, 1999).

n.a. Not available.

a. In 1997 production was 2,052,004 vehicles. See *Conjuntura Econômica* (April, 2000), statistical section, p. xvi.

b. Figure is for Canada.

Table 4-4. *Infrastructure and Technology, Selected Countries, 1971–98*

| Item | Brazil | India | Mexico | Korea | Spain | Italy | High-income |
|---|---|---|---|---|---|---|---|
| *Electricity production (kWh billions)* | | | | | | | |
| 1971 | 51 | 66 | 31 | 10 | 62 | 124 | n.a. |
| 1980 | 139 | 119 | 67 | 37 | 109 | 184 | n.a. |
| 1990 | 222 | 289 | 123 | 108 | 151 | 213 | n.a. |
| 1997 | 307 | 463 | 175 | 244 | 186 | 246 | n.a. |
| *Electricity consumption (kWh/per capita)* | | | | | | | |
| 1971 | 431 | 92 | 496 | 282 | 1,382 | 1,984 | n.a. |
| 1980 | 974 | 130 | 846 | 859 | 2,401 | 2,831 | n.a. |
| 1990 | 1,425 | 254 | 1,204 | 2,202 | 3,239 | 3,784 | n.a. |
| 1997 | 1,743 | 363 | 1,459 | 4,847 | 3,899 | 4,315 | 8,238 |
| *Telephones (main lines/1,000 persons)* | | | | | | | |
| 1975 | 20 | 2.5 | 28 | 30 | 132 | 174 | n.a. |
| 1985 | 53 | 4 | 50 | 160 | 243 | 305 | n.a. |
| 1998 | 121 | 22 | 104 | 433 | 414 | 451 | 567 |
| *Technology, 1997* | | | | | | | |
| R&D expenditures[a] (percent of GDP) | 0.81 | 0.73 | 0.33 | 2.82 | 0.90 | 2.21 | 2.36 |
| Computers/ 1,000 persons | 30 | 3 | 47 | 157 | 145 | 173 | 311 |

Source: Calculated from data in World Bank, *World Development Indicators, 2000* (book and CD-ROM).
n.a. Not available.
a. Latest available data for the period 1987–97.

ticipants in the global economy. World trade has risen more rapidly than world production and most world trade is conducted by first world countries.[2] There is also a near-consensus among development specialists that, whatever the merits of past policies of import substitution or of protecting infant industry, economic growth in newly industrializing countries such as Brazil, Mexico, and Argentina can now best be accelerated by reducing obstacles to trade with and investment from the first world. Korea led the way along that path. The dramatic results there, as elsewhere in East and Southeast Asia, are a major factor in this new consensus.

2. Between 1965 and 1998, world production increased about 2.8 times, but world trade increased more than six times. In 1998, "industrial countries" (mostly OECD members) accounted for about two-thirds of both exports and imports. Calculated from data in World Bank, *World Development Indicators 2000* (Washington, 2000), table 1-4; and International Monetary Fund, *Direction of Trade Statistics Yearbook, 1999* (Washington, 1999).

On this score, as table 4-5 demonstrates, Brazil seems to lag well behind the first world and also the other industrializing nations. It should be recognized, however, that as a country of continental dimensions and variegated resources, Brazil should not be expected to show the high foreign trade ratios of the much smaller European or Southeast Asian nations. A better comparison would be with the European Union as a whole, where trade among its members accounts for almost 60 percent of the total.[3] For the United States, the ratios to GDP in 1998 were 8.6 percent for exports and 11.9 percent for imports, not much larger than Brazil's. These data confirm Brazil's intermediate position as a country moving toward participation in the global systems, but still with substantial ground to cover.

At the same time, there have been massive changes in the absolute volume, commodity composition, and geographical spread of Brazil's foreign trade. The practice and attitudes have altered dramatically from the decades-long era of the "law of similars," virtually prohibiting imports of anything produced at home in "sufficient quality and quantity." Under that policy, which yielded only gradually from the mid-1960s through the 1980s, exports other than the traditional agricultural specialties were often discouraged as robbing the nation of its God-given mineral heritage or inducing scarcities in domestic markets. Exports are now viewed with pride and have been helped by a variety of governmental incentives. On the import side, however, market opening to competition from abroad, although greatly expanded since 1990, remains controversial and subject to important exceptions, notably in automobiles and computers.

Table 4-6 shows changes in the volume and composition of trade between 1965 and 1998 for our international comparison group. Brazil's share of world exports has declined slightly since 1965 (from 0.955 to 0.934 percent), while the share of imports has risen significantly. Nevertheless, the expansion in volume of exports is impressive, even though less spectacular than the levels of Korea and Spain. The most striking change, affecting the entire group of countries, is in the structure of exports, with primary products giving way to a great variety of manufactured goods. In both categories, a more refined breakdown would show a great increase in sophistication: Brazil's primary exports now include high value added items such as frozen orange juice, soybean products, wood pulp, aluminum, steel sheets and shapes, and processed metal ores, while manufactured exports include petrochemicals, automobiles and automotive components, small aircraft, and mechanical instruments,

3. If the European Union were treated as a single country, the ratio of exports to GDP for 1998 from the "state of Spain" would fall to 5.6 percent and from Italy to 8.3 percent, with import ratios at 7.8 and 6.3 percent, respectively.

Table 4-5.  *Merchandise Trade as a Percentage of GDP, Selected Countries,* *1965–98*
Percent

| Country | Exports (fob)[a] | | | | Imports (cif)[a] | | | |
|---|---|---|---|---|---|---|---|---|
| | 1965 | 1975 | 1985 | 1998 | 1965 | 1975 | 1985 | 1998 |
| Brazil | 8.3 | 7.0 | 13.6 | 6.7 | 5.7 | 11.0 | 7.6 | 7.5 |
| India | 3.6 | 4.8 | 5.1 | 7.9 | 6.1 | 6.9 | 9.2 | 10.0 |
| Mexico | 5.5 | 4.2 | 3.7 | 31.9 | 7.7 | 7.0 | 31.9 | 35.5 |
| Korea | 5.8 | 24.0 | 35.1 | 33.2 | 15.3 | 34.5 | 33.2 | 23.4 |
| Spain | 4.0 | 7.3 | 14.8 | 19.7 | 13.0 | 15.6 | 19.7 | 24.0 |
| Italy | 11.5 | 18.1 | 22.0 | 20.9 | 11.8 | 21.7 | 20.9 | 18.7 |
| OECD | 9.2 | 14.8 | 14.7 | 16.2 | 9.6 | 13.6 | 16.2 | 16.5 |

Source: Calculated from data in International Monetary Fund, *Direction of Trade Statistics* (various years); and World Bank, *World Tables* (on diskette).
a. fob = free on board; cif = cost, insurance, freight.

along with the more traditional textile, leather, and wood products typical of low-wage developing countries in the early stages of industrialization. Consumer durable goods for the domestic market are produced almost entirely within Brazil.

## Technology

Technological capacity is a critical element in Brazil's economic modernization. On this front, the country made great progress during the twenty-five-year wave of industrial expansion, 1955–80, mainly by importing production methods along with direct foreign investments. During the subsequent period of macroeconomic stagnation, however, and in sharp contrast to the East Asian tigers, Brazil made little further progress. These were years when technology in the first world was opening spectacular new frontiers. In the words of a major Brazilian interuniversity study of competitiveness: "Compared with international standards, at the beginning of the 1990s a large part of Brazilian industry was working with obsolete facilities and equipment, was deficient in process technology, behindhand in product technology, and devoted a very small fraction of its income to research and development (R&D)." At the same time, however, the report noted a "significant number" of exceptional technological successes.[4]

4. Luciano Coutinho and João Carlos Ferraz (coordinators), *Estudo da Competitividade da Indústria Brasileira* (A Study of of Brazilian Industry's Competitiveness), 2d ed. (Campinas: Editora da

Table 4-6. *Volume and Composition of Trade, Selected Countries, 1965 and 1998*

| | Exports, 1998 prices (millions of U.S. dollars) | | Structure of exports (percent) | | | | Imports, 1998 prices (millions of U.S. dollars) | | Structure of imports (percent) | | | |
| | | | 1965 | | 1998 | | | | 1965 | | 1998 | |
| | 1965 | 1998 | Food and raw materials | Manufactures | Food and raw materials | Manufactures | 1965 | 1998 | Food and raw materials | Manufactures | Food and raw materials | Manufactures |
|---|---|---|---|---|---|---|---|---|---|---|---|---|
| Brazil | 7,669 | 51,136 | 91 | 9 | 45 | 55 | 5,266 | 57,739 | 50 | 50 | 24 | 76 |
| India | 8,108 | 34,076 | 51 | 49 | 25 | 75 | 13,638 | 44,828 | 41 | 59 | 43 | 57 |
| Mexico | 5,383 | 117,459 | 84 | 16 | 15 | 85 | 7,497 | 125,374 | 17 | 83 | 13 | 87 |
| Korea | 841 | 132,122 | 41 | 59 | 9 | 91 | 2,225 | 90,495 | 48 | 52 | 38 | 62 |
| Spain | 4,493 | 109,814 | 61 | 39 | 21 | 79 | 14,609 | 128,521 | 45 | 55 | 24 | 76 |
| Italy | 34,600 | 242,572 | 22 | 78 | 10 | 90 | 35,455 | 206,941 | 64 | 36 | 26 | 74 |
| High-income (billions of U.S. dollars) | 618.3 | 4,075.0 | 30 | 70 | 16 | 84 | 649.0 | 4,031.0 | 50 | 50 | 20 | 80 |

Sources: Export and import values for 1998 are from International Monetary Fund, *Direction of Trade Statistics Yearbook, 1999.* For 1965, values in current dollars from IMF, *International Financial Statistics, 1977 Supplement, Annual Data, 1952–76,* are adjusted to 1998 prices using U.S. GDP deflators (1992 = 100), as shown in *Economic Report of the President, 2000,* p. 310. Trade shares for 1965 are from World Bank, *World Development Report, 1990,* tables 15 and 16; for 1998, from World Bank, *World Development Indicators, 2000,* tables 4.5 and 4.6.

Many economic historians view the present age as a third great industrial revolution. The first was based on coal, steel, and railroads; the second on electricity, chemistry, and the automobile; while the third (sometimes called the knowledge or information revolution) includes microelectronics, computers, satellite communications, molecular biology, and synthetic materials. The most advanced countries devote substantial quantities of public and private resources to the training of scientists, engineers, and technicians and to both basic and applied R&D.

In this field, unfortunately, available data do not permit close international comparisons, since classifications of researchers are very imprecise. As rough orders of magnitude, table 4-7 presents data from the United Nations Educational, Scientific, and Cultural Organization (UNESCO) on numbers of scientists and engineers engaged in research and experimental development, along with World Intellectual Property Organization data on patents. Brazil's numbers are far surpassed by Korea's, with only 30 percent of Brazil's population.

Quality is at least as important as quantity in assessing technological modernization and is even harder to measure. Brazil's capacity for basic scientific research is very limited, so most innovations in generic new technology are imported rather than homegrown. Until the 1960s, the universities gave scant attention to engineering and the natural sciences, and they are still far behind their counterparts in North America, Europe, and East Asia. The weak structures in primary and secondary education (see chapter 6) entail large wastage of potential technological talent. A promising start during the 1970s in systematic governmental support for basic and industrially applied R&D was badly set back during the stagnant years of the 1980s, following severe reductions in both public R&D support and private capital investments.[5]

The Brazilian interuniversity project's special studies in the late 1980s on the automotive assembly and parts industries illustrate these weaknesses dramatically. Table 4-8 compares critical indicators on automotive assembly, based on an international comparison study at the Massachusetts Institute of

Unicamp, 1994), pp. 33–34 (my informal translation). The successes are noted at p. 127. The study is marked by its vigorous advocacy of national policies for technology promotion.

5. For a review and highly optimistic assessment of the promotional efforts, see Emanuel Adler, *The Power of Ideology: The Quest for Technological Autonomy in Argentina and Brazil* (University of California Press, 1987). For a more tempered assessment, but still favorable on balance, see Carl J. Dahlman and Claudio R. Frischtak, "National Systems Supporting Technical Advance in Industry: The Brazilian Experience," in Richard R. Nelson, ed., *National Innovations Systems: A Comparative Analysis* (Oxford University Press, 1993), pp. 415–50.

Table 4-7. *Research Scientists, Technicians, and Patents in Selected Countries, 1994–96*

| Country | Research scientists | Technicians | Patents Applications | Patents Granted | Patents In force |
|---------|--------------------|-------------|------------|---------|----------|
| Brazil | 26,754 | 9,327 | 32,106 | 1,487 | 15,429 |
| India | 336,589 | 136,503 | 8,292 | 1,020 | 9,448 |
| Mexico | 33,297 | 19,434 | 30,694 | 3,186 | 31,027 |
| Korea | 135,703 | 99,433 | 113,994 | 16,516 | 74,379 |
| Spain | 87,263 | 51,633 | 83,983 | 19,817 | 153,832 |
| Italy | 141,789 | 75,536 | 80,852 | 37,935 | n.a. |

Sources: Data on personnel are from *UNESCO Statistical Yearbook, 1999* (Paris), table III.2, pp. III-20 to III-28. Patent data are from the World Intellectual Property Organization, Geneva, as reported in *UN Statistical Yearbook, 1996* (New York), table 71, pp. 677–82.

n.a. Not available.

Technology. Some of Brazil's lags in introducing advanced technology may be due to low wage rates and high costs of capital, which make it uneconomic to apply certain labor-saving but capital-intensive modes of production. Lags might also result from decisions of the foreign-controlled automobile assemblers to build models already obsolete in their home markets, using the old dies and tools. That factor, however, would not apply to parts-makers, most of which are Brazilian-owned. Nor would it account for thickness defects in

Table 4-8. *Automotive Industry Technology, Selected Countries, 1988–89*

| Country | Hours worked per car produced | Assembly defects per 100 vehicles | Robotic applications per vehicle-hour | Percentage of automation |
|---------|------------------------------|-----------------------------------|--------------------------------------|-------------------------|
| Brazil | 48.1 | 92.5 | 0.2 | 3.9 |
| Mexico | 45.7 | 69.0 | 0.7 | 6.6 |
| Korea | 30.3 | 87.5 | 1.9 | 22.6 |
| Europe | 36.0 | 105.0 | 2.9 | 32.8 |
| North America | 25.1 | 82.0 | 2.0 | 30.6 |
| Japan | 16.0 | 60.0 | 3.9 | 38.0 |
| Japanese plants in the United States | 21.2 | 65.0 | 4.6 | 34.7 |

Source: José Roberto Ferro, "Para Sair da Estagnação e Diminuir o Atraso Tecnológico da Indústria Automobilística Brasileira" (To Emerge from Stagnation and Reduce the Technological Lag of the Brazilian Automotive Industry), unpublished paper, Technological Development Project, Instituto de Economia, Universidade Estadual de Campinas, 1990, section 4.

steel sheets or the limited R&D activities of all but a handful of companies in the industry.[6]

Notwithstanding the shortcomings summarized here, anecdotal and survey evidence points to a rapidly growing capacity in Brazil to absorb imported technology and to adapt it to local circumstances in both industry and agriculture. One example is the ISO-9000 quality certification system of the Geneva-based International Organization for Standards, inaugurated in 1987. It is not a measure of relative quality certified by a single objective international body, since each country makes its own arrangements for certification, industry by industry. But the system does indicate serious concern for "assuring the consistent conformity of products or services to a defined set of standards or expectations."[7] Table 4-9 shows how rapidly Brazilian industry has adopted this system, keeping pace with our standard comparison countries, except for Korea, and with the main industrialized regions of the world.

A five-country study in 1994 of labor productivity in Latin America by the McKinsey Global Institute showed Brazil at 44 percent of U.S. levels in steel, 29 percent in processed food, 31 percent in retail banking, and 89 per-

Table 4-9. *ISO-9000 Certifications, Selected Countries, 1993–98*

| Country or region | January 1993 | June 1994 | March 1995 | December 1998 |
|---|---|---|---|---|
| Brazil | 19 | 384 | 548 | 3,712 |
| India | 8 | 328 | 585 | 3,344 |
| Mexico | 16 | 85 | 145 | 978 |
| South Korea | 27 | 226 | 390 | 7,729 |
| Spain | 43 | 586 | 942 | 6,412 |
| Italy | 188 | 2,008 | 3,146 | 18,095 |
| Europe | 23,092 | 55,400 | 71,918 | 166,255 |
| Far East | 683 | 3,091 | 5,979 | 38,037 |
| North America | 1,201 | 4,915 | 7,389 | 33,550 |

Sources: For 1993–95, John Symonds, *The Mobil Survey of ISO-9000 Certificates Awarded Worldwide* (London: Mobil Europe Ltd., August 1995). For 1998, International Organization for Standardization, *The ISO Survey of ISO-9000 and ISO-14000 Certificates* (Geneva, 1999), annex A (accessed on the Internet). I am obliged to Mr. Symonds for a highly informative interview on this subject in London in October 1994.

6. See table 4-8, source note. See also, from the same Campinas project, Caren Addis, "O Setor de Autopeças no Brasil."

7. See U.S Department of Commerce, National Institute of Standards and Technology, *Questions and Answers on Quality, the ISO 9000 Standard Series, Quality System Registration, and Related Issues,* NISTIR 4721 and 5122 (April 1993).

cent in telecommunications.[8] A Georgia Institute of Technology study, "Indicators of Technology-Based Competitiveness," ranked Brazil at roughly the following ratios with respect to the United States:[9]

| Indicator | Percent |
|---|---|
| National orientation | 90 |
| Socioeconomic infrastructure | 65 |
| Technological infrastructure | 45 |
| Productive capacity | 50 |
| Technological standing | 20 |
| Technological emphasis | 20 |
| Rate of technical change | 70 |
| Overall high-tech production | |
| Present capacity | 55 |
| Expected in 15 years | 80 |

On most of these counts, the Brazilian ratings are well ahead of those for Argentina and Mexico. The World Competitiveness Report prepared for the annual World Economic Forum at Davos, Switzerland, placed Brazil as thirty-seventh out of forty-six countries in 1998 and thirty-sixth in scientific and technological capacity.[10]

These findings highlight the point that technology is by no means the sole determinant of international competitiveness. Other major factors include comparative wage costs and macroeconomic policies affecting price stability and exchange rates (see chapter 7). The structural category treated in this chapter also contains impediments known colloquially as "Custo Brasil" (Brazilian costs): gross inefficiencies in the seaports; decaying infrastructure, notably in road conditions and rail transportation; a precarious energy supply balance threatening serious shortages, especially in times of drought; inadequate and costly communications (now being rapidly improved); and a residue of bureaucratic constraints remaining from the "cartorial" tradition.

8. McKinsey Global Institute, Latin American Productivity (Washington: June 1994).

9. Technology Policy and Assessment Center, Georgia Institute of Technology, Implementation and Further Analysis of Indicators of Technology-Based Competitiveness (Atlanta, March 1995). The study covers thirteen OECD member countries, two from Eastern Europe, the four Asian tigers, six so-called Asian cubs, and three from Latin America. Since these indicators are only very rough orders of magnitude, I have rounded them off to the nearest 5 percent.

10. The World Competitiveness Report is published each year by IMD International (Lausanne, Switzerland). Brazil's overall ranking between 1995 and 1998 has hovered between thirty-eighth and thirty-third.

## Informatics

There is a controversy about whether Brazil's technological lags were exacerbated during the 1980s by questionable public policies, notably the effort known as *informática* (informatics). Its goal was to create in a few years an integrated domestic information-processing industry free from reliance on foreign technology or foreign investment. The chosen policy instrument, called market reserve, went beyond the prohibition of imports to include prohibitive restrictions on direct foreign investment in selected segments of the industry, starting with microcomputers and peripherals and progressively extended to larger units and additional fields of information processing.[11]

Informatics was launched in the mid-1970s by a curious combination of (a) young technologists and economists (colorfully described by one scholar as "pragmatic anti-dependency guerrillas") rebelling against excessive dependency on first world multinational corporations and (b) naval officers and other military groups who believed that an "independent" information industry was essential to Brazil's national security. They formed a kind of companionate marriage between left- and right-wing nationalisms. Both viewpoints were strongly represented in the relevant administrative agency, known as the Special Secretariat for Informatics (SEI). In 1984 market reservation was embodied in formal legislation, with a term of eight years. In 1985 it was challenged by the U.S. government as an unfair trade practice. During the following three years, it became a major issue in dispute between Washington and Brasília.[12]

In 1988 the barriers to multinational participation were somewhat relaxed. By 1990 many industrial users of information processing had

---

11. From the mid-1970s through the 1980s and beyond, informatics became a subject of intense study and controversy, both within Brazil and internationally. From 1985 to 1990, it was a prime issue of contention between the Brazilian and American governments. It attracted the attention of social scientists in Europe, North America, and Latin America. Outside assessments ranged from favorable on balance (Sussex, England, Institute of Development Studies) to mainly negative (William S. Cline, Claudio Frischtak). The Sussex studies are summarized in Hubert Schmitz and José Cassiolato, eds., *Hi-tech for Industrial Development: Lessons from the Brazilian Experience in Electronics and Automation* (Routledge, 1992). More critical analyses are in William S. Cline, *Informatics and Development: Trade and Industrial Policy in Argentina, Brazil, and Mexico* (Washington: Economics International, 1987); and Claudio Frischtak, "Brazil," in Francis W. Rushing and Carole Ganz Brown, eds., *National Policies for Developing High-Technology Industries: International Comparisons* (Boulder, Colo.: Westview Press, 1986), chap. 3.

12. For a detailed account of this dispute and the evolution of negotiating positions on both sides, see Ellene A. Felder and Andrew Hurrell, *The U.S.-Brazilian Informatics Dispute*, Pew Case Studies in International Affairs, Case 122 (Washington: Pew Case Studies Center, 1988).

become strenuous opponents of the policy on the ground that it condemned them to technological backwardness and excessive costs, a concern only partly offset by the widespread smuggling of computers and components from North America, Europe, and East Asia. By then, the Collor administration's more open attitudes toward international trade and investment foreshadowed the termination of the policy when the legislation expired in 1992, but residues still remain in the year 2000.

At its inception, informatics was complemented by a strong governmental push to expand both research and technological training at the university level. These efforts, however, floundered during the administrative and fiscal disarray of the 1980s. Nor could they compensate for the basic weaknesses of Brazil's elementary and secondary educational systems, which contrast so sharply with those of East Asia.

Viewed in retrospect, the informatics experience appears negative on balance, although not wholly so. Compared with a complete "hands-off" policy, it probably accelerated the development of a substantial cadre of qualified engineering and technical personnel and helped some Brazilian-owned enterprises to locate niches in which they could become genuinely competitive. Examples include banking automation and mass production of certain computer peripherals whose basic technology came from abroad. But the results never remotely approached the goal of an autonomous Brazilian industry, even one excluding the largest machines and ultra-high-technology subsectors such as microelectronic chips. It was impossibly ambitious to aim at catching up in a few years with a set of technologies in which "generational" advances often take place every year or two. The effort imposed a considerable cost on the user industries, retarding Brazil's participation in the third industrial revolution. A far more rewarding alternative would have been to promote alliances between promising Brazilian firms and first world leaders in information technology, taking advantage of the intense competitiveness of the industry and the inherent attractiveness of Brazil's large potential market. That course has now become open again.

## The Financial Sector

Chapter 3 pointed to the remarkable structural changes in the financial sector during the military era, including the creation of a genuine central bank and the move toward modern-style capital markets. During the two decades of increasing inflation, commercial banks became highly sophisticated in providing middle- and upper-class Brazilians with means to protect against erosion of their assets and to profit from the high interest rates that accompanied the central bank's efforts to avoid outright hyperinflation. "Overnight" deposits in interest-bearing accounts became a household term, but they were only one of many inflation-hedging instruments. The financial sector expanded rapidly, and during the late 1980s accounted for almost one-fifth of GDP, a proportion about double the norm in low-inflation first world countries.

A bloated private banking industry thus took its place alongside the heavily politicized national Banco do Brasil and state-owned banks, attracting an undue share of talent into parasitical activities that contributed little or nothing to long-term capital formation. Profits came easily as long as mega-inflation persisted, but this hypertrophy would evidently demand a difficult and costly restructuring when the time came for genuine stabilization, as it did in the mid-1990s.

## Conclusion

By the early 1980s Brazil's economic structures seemed well along the road toward the first world, although with lags imposed by educational backwardness and nationalistic statism. The economy then entered a twelve-year phase (1982–94) of galloping inflation and stop-and-go production, analyzed in chapter 7. During that lost decade, the first world continued its movement into new technologies and new patterns of trade and investment, in which Brazil participated only minimally and far less successfully than Korea and the other East Asian tigers. After 1994—with financial stabilization, opening to the global economy, and revival of large-scale investment from both domestic and foreign sources—there was a good prospect that growth rates could be restored to the high levels of earlier decades. Much would depend, however, on the nation's capacity to overcome its lags in modernizing social and political structures, the topics of chapters 5 and 6.

# 5

## *The Social Dimension*

In contrast to its economic structures, Brazil's social conditions present a darker picture of progress to date, with much larger shortfalls from first world norms. The economic and social dimensions overlap. Income inequalities and poverty are social concerns, but measurable in economic terms. Unemployment insurance and other safety-net measures are classified as both social and economic in character. Education enhances human beings in all respects, but it can also be considered more narrowly as an economic good, a capital investment in human skills, productivity, and earning capacity. In many circumstances, as Korea and its neighbors have shown, education can be the most productive kind of capital. It is also a social good, enabling individuals and communities to broaden their horizons and raise the quality of life. Health care likewise combines social and economic aspects. Public health measures, including sanitation and potable water supply, are a major factor in decreasing morbidity, increasing life expectancy, and helping to raise productivity. Preventive health care may therefore be considered a kind of capital investment, but that is much less the case for remedial or curative care. Quality of housing and community facilities also combine social and economic elements. Such matters as race relations, religious observance, crime and violence, abandonment of children, and family instability, on the other hand, are essentially social, or sociopolitical concerns, even though they all have economic consequences.

## Income Distribution

Brazil has achieved an unenviable notoriety for inequality in income distribution. Table 5-1 (illustrated by figure 5-1) shows, for the set of countries being compared here, the ratio between the incomes or consumption levels of the highest and lowest quintiles (fifths) of the population, together with the fraction secured by the highest decile (tenth).[1] Severe inequalities are common to most of Latin America, but even within the region, Brazil stands out, as seen in table 5-2, comparing Gini coefficients from household surveys.[2]

In this particular, unlike per capita output or incomes, Brazil is in an extreme position, not intermediate between the poorest and richest countries (contrast figures 4-1 and 5-1). Nor has the overall income distribution substantially improved during the four decades of intensive industrialization and urbanization. As noted in chapter 3, the degree of inequality stabilized during the high growth period of the 1970s but again worsened during the lost decade beginning in 1982. In contrast, as shown in figure 5-2, the times of relative price stability—1986 under the Cruzado Plan and 1995–99 with the Real Plan—have substantially improved the relative standing of the lowest quintile and slightly reduced the position of the top decile, while also securing increases in average incomes for all households. Yet the inequalities remain huge by general world standards.

There is a large literature on income distribution in various countries and much debate among economic historians concerning its relationship to structural change and economic growth.[3] The economic failures of the communist regimes, along with their record of political repression, have downgraded the attractiveness of equality as an end in itself, so that, in Brazil as elsewhere, most centrist and center-left ideologues and political leaders claim to seek equality of opportunity rather than equality of results. There is certainly no consensus, either in world public opinion or among philosophers, concerning the tolerable—or perhaps essential—degree of inequality

1. Also included here are two first world countries, Japan and the United States, both with very high average incomes but contrasting patterns of income distribution.
2. The Gini scale runs from 0 to 1: zero representing total equality and 1 a complete concentration of income in a single recipient. For OECD countries, the values range from 0.3 to 0.5.
3. For a summary treatment, with extensive references, see Jeffrey G. Williamson, *Inequality, Poverty, and History* (Cambridge, Mass.: Basil Blackwell, 1991). See also Inter-American Development Bank, *Facing Up to Inequality in Latin America*, Economic and Social Progress in Latin America, 1998–1999 Report (Washington, 1998); Andrés Solimano, ed., *Social Inequality: Values, Growth, and the State* (University of Michigan Press, 1998).

Table 5-1. *Income Inequality in Selected Countries*

| Country and year | Ratio of highest to lowest fifth | Top tenth share of total (percent) |
|---|---|---|
| Brazil, 1996 | 25.5 | 47.6 |
| India, 1997 | 5.7 | 33.5 |
| Mexico, 1995 | 16.2 | 42.8 |
| Korea, 1993 | 5.2 | 24.3 |
| Spain, 1990 | 5.4 | 25.2 |
| Italy, 1995 | 4.2 | 21.8 |
| Japan, 1993 | 3.4 | 21.7 |
| United States, 1997 | 8.9 | 30.5 |

Source: Calculated from data in World Bank, *World Development Indicators, 2000* (Washington, 2000), table 2.8.

in an ideal society. In Brazil, inequality of incomes is so severe as to rule out equality of opportunity. Substantial segments of society are at best only marginal participants in economic modernization. First world status not only tolerates, but even requires, some degree of inequality to provide inducements and rewards for vigorous entrepreneurship and high productivity. But inequality evidently need not exceed the magnitudes shown for the four OECD nations charted at the right side of figure 5-1. They illustrate a goal still far from attainment by Brazil.

Figure 5-1. *Income Inequalities in Selected Countries, 1996–97*

Ratio and percentage

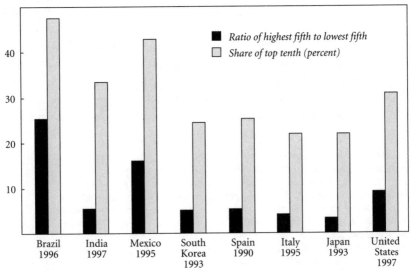

Source: Table 5-1.

Table 5-2.  *Income Inequality in Latin America*

| Country and year | Gini coefficient | Country and year | Gini coefficient |
|---|---|---|---|
| Argentina, 1989[a] | 0.48 | Mexico, 1989 | 0.54 |
| Bolivia, 1990 | 0.42 | Panama, 1997 | 0.48 |
| Brazil, 1996 | 0.60 | Paraguay, 1995 | 0.59 |
| Chile, 1994 | 0.56 | Peru, 1996 | 0.46 |
| Colombia, 1996 | 0.57 | Uruguay, 1989[b] | 0.42 |
| Costa Rica, 1996 | 0.47 | Venezuela, 1996 | 0.49 |
| Guatemala, 1989 | 0.60 | | |

Source: For Argentina, Guatemala, and Uruguay, Samuel A. Morley, *Poverty and Inequality in Latin America* (Johns Hopkins University Press, 1995), pp. 30–31, where the original sources are cited in detail. For all other countries, World Bank, *World Development Indicators, 2000*, table 2.8, pp. 66–69.

a. Buenos Aires.

b. Urban.

The main reasons for this lamentable condition can be found in Brazil's early social and economic history, but its continuance through the twentieth century results in part from defects in development strategy. Until 1888, Brazil was still predominantly a semifeudal agrarian society, based mainly on Afro-Brazilian slave labor producing subsistence crops and livestock and

Figure 5-2.  *Income Inequalities in Brazil, 1985–96*

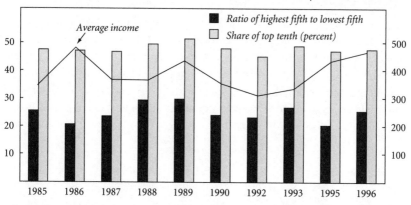

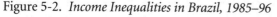

Sources: For 1985–95, calculated from IBGE, National Sample Household Survey (PNAD), 1995, tables 7.2.3 and 7.2.7. Monthly average income figures are for employed workers and are converted to reais of constant value (September 1995). Data exclude Amazonia. For 1996, shares of quintiles and deciles from World Bank, *World Development Indicators 2000*, table 2-8. Monthly earnings in 1996 from *Conjuntura Econômica*, April 2000, Statistical Section, p. 18.

exporting sugar, cotton, coffee, and some minerals.[4] That heritage concentrated wealth in the landowning classes and entailed a grossly uneven income distribution following the abolition of slavery. In Charles Wagley's words, "Traditionally there were only two social classes in Brazil: an upper class consisting of landowners, merchants, professionals, government officials, and bureaucrats, and a lower class of manual laborers and artisans."[5]

In the twentieth century, and especially after World War II, immigration, urbanization, and industrialization greatly altered this social structure, as shown in chapter 1, but did not completely destroy it. A large and still growing middle class has come into being. Social mobility, both upward and downward, has become the order of the day. But unlike Japan, Korea, Taiwan, and the antebellum American South, where landed elites were eliminated by war or decolonization, Brazil retained substantial residues of the old two-class social structure, especially in the rural Northeast and North. There is continuing de facto racial discrimination against the large black minority, limiting both schooling and employment opportunities.[6] Income inequalities have also been sustained by differential birth rates, with large families predominant in the poorer regions and the lower classes.

As to development strategies, it is noteworthy that during the Vargas and Kubitschek eras the distribution of income was not a central topic of political discussion and reduction in inequality was not a declared objective of policy. Chapter 3 summarized the inconclusive debate on this issue during the 1970s, a period of very rapid overall economic growth in which income distribution was stable or slightly improving and poverty was being greatly reduced. Even within the political constraints of the military era, however, one can imagine alternative strategies that would have promoted greater equality. In rural Brazil, implementation of the 1964 Land Statute would have encouraged family farming and the use or sale of idle land. On the industrial side, inequality could have been eased through more substantial encouragement of small enterprises and an earlier start at integration into the world economy. More attention to water supply, sanitation, and nutri-

---

4. The polarized social structure was reflected in the titles chosen by Brazil's great social historian Gilberto Freyre: *Casa Grande e Senzala* (Rio de Janeiro: Schmidt, 1936), translated as *The Masters and the Slaves* (Knopf, 1946; literally "The great house and the slave quarters"); and *Sobrados e Mucambos* (Rio de Janeiro: Olympio, 1961), translated *The Mansions and the Shanties* (Knopf, 1963).

5. Charles Wagley, *An Introduction to Brazil*, rev. ed. (Columbia University Press, 1971), p. 93.

6. In Brazil, unlike the United States, the words "negro" and "mulatto" are in common use, without pejorative connotations, and a term such as "Afro-Brasileiro" has not entered into use.

tion, especially in the poor rural Northeast, could have reduced ill health as a force perpetuating poverty.

The critical failure shared by civilian and military regimes alike, however, was inadequate investment in human capital through basic education. This failure was in flagrant disregard of the 1946 Constitution's injunction for universal, free, and compulsory primary education.[7] Since education is the principal means for expanding equality of opportunity, this shortfall has been a cardinal deficiency in developmental strategy. The scope of the shortfall is discussed later in this chapter.

## Land Reform

Although reliable data are not available, wealth distribution in Brazil is certainly more unequal than income distribution. That is clearly the case with ownership of land, the most traditional form of wealth although no longer the dominant one.[8] Poverty is twice as prevalent in the countryside as in the cities, and landless peasants are the largest group among the rural poor. Their settlement through occupation of empty land (called "colonization") or redistribution of unproductive land has been a perennial issue in Brazilian politics for generations.

In polar contrast to the family farming patterns of British settlement in New England and the Middle Atlantic colonies, the Portuguese monarchy and its "captaincy" agents in Brazil parceled out land in huge estates for sugar cultivation near the coast and for cattle raising inland. By the late seventeenth century that practice had already become a cause for regret. A modern English-language historian writes of this issue in terms still applicable three centuries later:

> Realizing that the gigantic estates created a type of semifeudalism in practice if not in name and that they kept much of the best land fallow and hence unproductive, the king belatedly tried to reverse the course. Repeatedly promulgated decrees [starting in 1695] ... sought vainly to limit the size of the estates. One of the viceroys late in the eighteenth century ... pointed to the unused fields held by their owners as symbols of prestige, while at the same time he noted that farmers petitioned him for land to till.[9]

---

7. Article 168, Constitution of 1946.

8. Gini coefficients for land distribution were in the 0.83–0.85 range, compared with 0.63 for income distribution in 1989. See W. C. Thiesenhusen and J. Melmud-Sanjak, "Brazil's Agrarian Structure: Changes from 1970 through 1980," World Development, vol. 18 (March 1990), p. 396.

9. E. Bradford Burns, A History of Brazil, 2d ed. (Columbia University Press, 1980), p. 31.

Over the century since the abolition of slavery, vast changes have taken place in patterns of land ownership and use. Enormous new areas have been opened to cultivation by pushing back the frontier in the Northwest and West and by soil treatment in the central *cerrado* plateau. (Amazônia is a tangled and much less successful story.) In the South, large regions have been devoted to family farming by immigrant streams from Japan and Europe, especially Italy, Spain, and Germany. More recently, there has developed a major segment of highly capitalized agro-industry on first world patterns. Urbanization and industrialization have reduced the rural population and rural birth rates have greatly declined.

Nevertheless, the failures of social modernization—poverty, illiteracy, child labor, and ill health—are still disproportionately concentrated in the countryside.[10] Intense political pressure continues, including violent direct action, for access to ownership by landless peasants, whether contract employees of large estates, sharecroppers, or the migratory seasonal rural workers known as *boias frias* (literally "cold lunches").

During the post–World War II decades examined in this study, there have been three waves of active political pressure for land reform. Rural workers had been excluded from the corporativist employer and labor organization implanted during the Vargas dictatorship. During the 1950s, substantial numbers, mainly in the Northeast, were organized in "peasant leagues" (*ligas camponeses*) under the leadership of the charismatic socialist lawyer, Francisco Julião. Expropriation and redistribution of idle land in large estates, however, was ruled out by the 1946 Constitution's requirement for immediate and full monetary compensation. President Kubitschek's push for accelerated development focused mainly on infrastructure and industry, with the land hunger in the Northeast to be satisfied mainly by new settlements in the unoccupied semihumid regions of Maranhão. Under President Goulart, the labor federation system was extended to rural workers. Land reform became a topic of heated political oratory but little substantive action before the military coup of 1964 and dissolution of the peasant leagues.

The second wave was initiated by the military regime from the top down, reflecting the personal interest of President Castello Branco, a Northeast-

10. Morley's data for 1980 and 1989 (in *Poverty and Inequality in Latin America* [Johns Hopkins University Press, 1995], pp. 38 and 42) show a decrease in the rural share of total population from 34 to 24 percent, but an increase in the incidence of rural poverty from 55 to 63 percent, leaving the total rural numbers in poverty constant at 22 million, about 15 percent of the total national population.

erner by heritage. In November 1964, Congress agreed to his initiative for a constitutional amendment permitting compensation for expropriated land in long-term bonds (twenty-year terms, with full protection against inflation). There followed the Estatuto da Terra (Land Statute), on its face the most comprehensive land law in Brazilian history, which is still on the books. It was adopted only after intense controversy within the political coalition that had supported the military takeover.[11]

The Land Statute called for an updated cadastral survey of all rural land-holdings, with regionally differentiated definitions of family-size farms and classification of large holdings as either *latifundia,* if idle or used unproductively (and also when used productively but of immense size), or *rural enterprises,* if used efficiently. The former were to be taxed heavily, as an inducement to get the land on the market, and the latter to be taxed lightly. The latifundia could also be expropriated for resettlement in family farm units, with the price based on the owner's declaration of value to the taxing authorities. At the same time, uneconomically small *minifundia* were to be consolidated into viable units. Land redistribution via sale or expropriation was to be accompanied by technical assistance and agricultural research to improve farm productivity, along with continuing settlement of public lands. The proponents hoped that this statute would not only help satisfy the legitimate land hunger of tenant farmers and rural migrant workers but also limit the rural exodus into city slums beyond the absorptive capacity of urban industry and modern services.

Although a serious start was made on the cadastral survey, the Land Statute proved almost a dead letter during the remainder of the military regime. The later presidents did not share Castello Branco's personal interest in land reform, and the expansion of industry during the economic miracle years seemed to be absorbing the surplus rural migrants. In the recession of the 1980s, however, that was clearly no longer the case. Violent clashes in the countryside again became widespread. The politics of land reform became radicalized between a new peasant Movement of Landless Rural Workers (Movimento de Trabalhadores Rurais Sem Terra, or MST) and a new Democratic Ruralist Union (UDR) organized by conservative landowners. One wing of the Catholic Church also became a proponent of

11. A vivid account can be found in the memoirs of Roberto Campos, planning minister under Castello Branco and the principal author of the legislation. See Roberto Campos, *A Lanterna na Popa: Memórias* (The Lantern on the Stern—Memoirs) (Rio de Janeiro: Topbooks, 1994), pp. 680–96.

communitarian land reform, which was endorsed by the influential National Conference of Brazilian Bishops.[12]

The third wave of active interest coincided with the return to civilian government in the mid-1980s. Land reform had figured in statements of Tancredo Neves in 1984 as candidate for president and in his program as president-elect (elected by a special Electoral College). Starting as a project for implementation of the 1964 Land Statute, this initiative proved beyond the political and administrative capacity of the transitional regime led by President José Sarney after the death of Neves. It had little net effect on the agrarian structure.[13] The radicalized political environment ruled out rational modernization of rural tenure and technology along the lines advocated by international institutions and Brazilian agronomists.[14] In the framing of the 1988 Constitution, the UDR secured protection against expropriation of all productive land holdings, thus eliminating the 1964 concept of "latifundium by size," huge estates more than 600 times the family farm "module" for each region. Another constitutional clause required immediate payments in cash for any improvements on the land.[15] Then the third reform wave receded as Brazilian politics became preoccupied with inflation control, corruption, and new electoral alignments.

In the mid-1990s, land reform was not a high priority in the early plans of the Cardoso administration, whose central concern was with macroeconomic stabilization. The issue was forced onto public attention by another wave of rural violence, precipitated by MST-organized "invasions" or "occupations" of large estates in many regions of the country, along with sit-ins at regional offices of INCRA and other government agencies and blocking of highways and railroads. Popular news magazines, not unsympathetic to land reform in principle, expressed concern about the ideological radi-

12. See Antônio M. Galvão, *Terra: Dom de Deus* (Land: Gift of God) (São Paulo: Paulinas, 1994), and Fernando Castro da Cruz, *Reforma Agrária e Sua Evolução* (Land Reform and Its Evolution) (São Paulo: Livraria e Editora Universitária de Direito, 1987).

13. A colorful firsthand account by the state director for São Paulo of INCRA (the National Institute of Colonization and Land Reform) during this period is presented in José Eli da Veiga, *A Reforma que Virou Suco* (The Reform That Turned into Sap) (Petropolis: Vozes, 1990). An account in English appears in Anthony W. Pereira, *The End of the Peasantry* (University of Pittsburgh Press, 1997), pp. 139–43.

14. See, for example, the collection of studies published by IPEA, the government-supported Institute for Economic and Social Planning. Antônio Salazar P. Brandão, ed., *Os Principais Problemas da Agricultura Brasileira: Análise e Sugestões* (The Main Problems of Brazilian Agriculture: Analysis and Suggestions) (Rio de Janeiro: IPEA/INPES, 1988).

15. Articles 184 and 185, Constitution of 1988.

calism of the MST leadership.[16] There were frequent clashes with military police and private armed guards, with widely publicized loss of life.

In April 1996, state military police fired on an MST demonstration blocking a highway in southern Pará, killing nineteen peasants, wounding forty-one, and creating a cause célèbre in the domestic and foreign press. In response, INCRA was placed under new leadership and the pace of settlement on public and previously expropriated land was accelerated. The government achieved the annual target of settling 100,000 families by 1998, making for a total of 400,000 by early 2000 on about 40 million acres. In addition, Congress enacted a substantial tax on unproductive land and a summary procedure to avoid endless delays in expropriation cases.[17] In 2000, the government launched a new program for registering land titles. Meanwhile, however, the MST has increasingly assumed the role of a left-wing populist political movement, appealing to urban unemployed as well as would-be farmers.

In Brazil's overall economic structure and numbers of people involved, the ongoing processes of urbanization, industrialization, and declining birth rates have made land reform in the new millennium less important than it seemed in the 1960s and less salient a national issue than elsewhere in Latin America. If renewed economic growth brings urban unemployment down to normal levels, land reform will again recede as a national issue. Nevertheless, family farming will remain an important sector in a fully modernized Brazil. In the first world, family farming on medium-sized holdings has been a successful use of land for most crops other than capital-intensive monoculture items.[18] At this stage, not only poverty, but also illiteracy and ill health are disproportionately concentrated among Brazil's landless rural workers and the holders of minifundia. As noted by two North American specialists: "While 33 million agricultural hectares are idle, there may be as

16. See, for example, "Vontade radical," VEJA, August 28, 1996, pp. 68–74, and "Luta sem trégua," ISTO E, February 5, 1997.

17. Quantitative data from Ministério do Desenvolvimento Agrário by Internet, May 2000. A recent World Bank analysis shows that market-based land redistribution could be greatly advanced through institutional reforms going beyond more effective taxation of underused holdings. They include a modernized system for securing and registering clear titles, together with access to mortgage financing and rapid-acting procedures for debt collection and adjudication of land disputes. See Coralie Bryant, "Brazil: Land Ownership, Land Reform and Property Rights," unpublished World Bank paper, 1997.

18. See Hans P. Binswanger, Klaus Deininger, and Gershon Feder, Power, Distortions, Revolt and Reform in Agricultural Land Relations (Washington: World Bank, 1995), pp. 44–45; also William C. Thiesenhusen, Broken Promises: Agrarian Reform and the Latin American Campesino (Boulder, Colo.: Westview Press, 1995), p. 10.

many as 9 million landless or partially landless farmers who are desirous of a production unit in Brazil."[19] To become participants at first world standards, they clearly require easier access to land ownership. The efforts currently under way, combining some formal land reform with market transfers induced by effective taxation, modernized land registration, and further settlement of public lands, are steps in the right direction.

## Poverty

For any given level of per capita incomes, extreme inequality in their distribution implies a greater extent of absolute poverty. That is clearly the case in Brazil, where, in the World Bank's words, "the level of poverty ... is well above the norm for a middle-income country." Using the Bank's severe poverty line of $1.00 consumption per person per day (in U.S. 1985 prices), about 23 percent of Latin America's population was in poverty in the early 1990s, compared with 28 percent in East Asia, 43 percent in South Asia, and 39 percent in sub-Saharan Africa.[20] Within Latin America, however, Brazil accounts for a disproportionately large share of the impoverished population.

Using the less stringent, but still austere, poverty line of $2.00 per person per day, table 5-3 shows the situation in 1989 for Latin America as a whole and for all the larger individual countries, with updating to the mid-1990s. The Brazilian numbers are dismaying: they accounted in 1989 for 35 percent of Latin America's population but 45 percent of those in poverty. The poverty rate was outmatched only by Haiti, Central America, Bolivia, and Peru—all far behind Brazil in progress toward First World status. The reduction to 17 percent in 1997 was a dramatic improvement, but those gains were later somewhat eroded by increasing unemployment.

The incidence of poverty is very sensitive to fluctuations in overall economic growth and in rates of inflation. During the 1980s, one study shows, the fraction of Brazil's population in poverty was as low as 16 percent in 1986 but 27 percent in 1988. For metropolitan areas alone, another study

19. William C. Thiesenhusen and Jolyne Melmed-Sanjak, "Brazil's Agrarian Structure: Changes from 1970 through 1980," *World Development*, vol. 18, no. 3 (1990), p. 400.

20. The quotation is from World Bank, *Poverty Reduction and the World Bank: Progress and Challenges in the 1990s* (Washington, 1996), p. 79; the percentages are from p. 4. International comparisons are hampered by differences in national definitions of the "poverty line," difficulties in measuring nonmarket consumption, and questions concerning the applicability to the poor of purchasing power parity exchange rates calculated for entire national populations.

Table 5-3. *Poverty in Latin America, 1989–96*

Percent

| Country | Proportion of population in poverty | | | | Share of total population in region, 1989 | Share of total population in poverty in region, 1989 |
|---|---|---|---|---|---|---|
| | Urban, 1989 | Rural, 1989 | Total, 1989 | Updated total (year) | | |
| Argentina | 6.4 | 23.4 | 8.8 | n.a. | 7.6 | 2.1 |
| Bolivia | 54.0 | 76.3 | 65.0 | 38.6 (1991) | 1.7 | 3.5 |
| Brazil | 33.2 | 63.1 | 40.3 | 17.4 (1997) | 34.9 | 45.3 |
| Chile | 9.9 | 10.4 | 10.0 | 20.3 (1994) | 3.1 | 1.0 |
| Colombia | 8.0 | 40.6 | 17.9 | 28.7 (1996) | 7.7 | 4.4 |
| Costa Rica | 3.5 | 3.2 | 3.3 | 26.3 (1996) | 0.6 | 0.7 |
| Ecuador | 24.2 | 47.4 | 34.4 | 52.3 (1995) | 2.5 | 2.7 |
| Guatemala | 54.8 | 79.4 | 71.4 | 64.3 (1989) | 2.1 | 4.9 |
| Haiti | 79.7 | 98.5 | 92.9 | n.a. | 1.5 | 4.6 |
| Honduras | 54.4 | 82.6 | 70.5 | 68.8 (1996) | 1.2 | 2.7 |
| Mexico | 9.1 | 31.6 | 15.4 | 42.5 (1995) | 20.3 | 10.1 |
| Peru | 49.5 | 73.4 | 56.7 | 41.4 (1996) | 5.0 | 9.2 |
| Venezuela | 10.8 | 23.5 | 12.9 | 36.4 (1996) | 4.6 | 1.9 |
| Latin America and Caribbean | 22.0 | 53.4 | 31.0 | n.a. | 100 | 100 |

Source: Based on Morley, *Poverty and Inequality in Latin America,* table 2-3, pp. 38–39. Updating column is from World Bank, *World Development Indicators 2000,* table 2.7.

n.a. Not available.

shows, the fraction varied between 23 and 29 percent.[21] More recently, Brazil's household surveys show a drastic reduction in numbers of workers receiving less than one-half the minimum wage, from 9.4 million in 1992 and 8.0 million in 1993 to 4.4 million in 1995. An income level of half the minimum wage is close to the Morley poverty line, and the 50 percent reduction in poverty results mainly from price stabilization under the Real Plan (see chapter 7).[22] On the negative side, the 1995 survey showed 3.8 million children under age fifteen in the work force (2.4 million in agriculture), including more than half a million under age ten. These are indicators of both poverty and inadequate schooling, as well as a violation of domestic constitutional provisions and of international commitments prohibiting child labor.

In the longer run, the goals of poverty reduction and lessened income inequalities overlap, with investment in human capital, especially through education, being the key instrument along with effective macroeconomic growth policies. In South and Southeast Asia, overall economic growth has greatly reduced poverty, but in Latin America, including Brazil, the correlation between growth rates and poverty reduction has been weaker or nonexistent. Overall growth provides more ample resources for poverty alleviation ("welfare" in the U.S. terminology, or *assistencialismo* in Brazil), but welfare measures alone do not remedy the underlying structural causes. This dilemma has led national governments and international institutions concerned with development—such as the World Bank, the Inter-American Development Bank, and the United Nations Development Programme—to search for policy measures focused on structural poverty reduction.[23] Experimental measures include provision of capital for microenterprises, special support for education in poverty areas, subsidies for families to replace child labor by schooling, school nutrition programs, targeted income support for workers displaced by economic modernization, and remedial education and vocational training for the generations deprived of adequate schooling in childhood.

21. See Morley, *Poverty and Inequality in Latin America*, table 6-1, p. 153; and Ricardo Paes de Barros, Rosane Mendonça, and Sonia Rocha, "Brazil: Welfare, Inequality, Poverty, Social Indicators, and Social Programs in the 1980s," in Nora Lustig, ed., *Coping with Austerity: Poverty and Inequality in Latin America*, chap. 7 (Brookings, 1995), p. 255.

22. IBGE, *Pesquisa Nacional por Amostra de Domicílios* (National Household Sample Study), 1992, 1993, and 1995, table 4.1.

23. For a general discussion of these issues, see Nancy Birdsall, Carol Graham, and Richard H. Sabot, eds., *Beyond Tradeoffs: Market Reforms and Equitable Growth in Latin America* (Washington: Inter-American Development Bank and Brookings, 1998).

Most measures of this sort in Brazil are at the state or municipal level rather than the federal, and almost every type is being tried somewhere in the country. They are all limited, however, by the budgetary constraints and high interest rates discussed in chapter 7. Meanwhile, the heavy continuing incidence of poverty entails social costs as well as individual and family deprivation. They include urban and rural violence, abandoned children, petty thievery, stealing of automobiles, kidnappings for ransom, retreat of the wealthy to isolated fortress communities with private guards, peasant land seizures, spreading of the drug culture, drug gang warfare in urban slums, and emigration of talented professionals to more congenial environments. Urban violence is strongly correlated with increased unemployment. By the late 1990s, these phenomena were posing serious challenges to the Brazilian national traditions of optimism and resilience.

## Basic Education

As noted in chapter 1, adult literacy in Brazil has improved vastly since World War II, rising from 49 percent in 1950 to 86 percent in 1998. That progress reflects the substantial national effort in primary education, which has been maintained without regard to changes in political regime or in general economic conditions. Nevertheless, in both qualitative and quantitative terms, the educational structure still lags well behind first world standards and also falls short compared with other large countries of Latin America. Table 5-4 reports the basic data for the latter group, along with the standard set of countries used in this book for international comparisons.

Three Brazilian items stand out in those comparisons: the improved participation in primary education, the continuing shortfall in access to secondary education, and the small numbers of university students. In the words of a leading expert on the educational system, "The real Brazilian miracle is to have progressed so far in our development with such poor education."[24]

Brazil's public expenditure on education (table 5-5) makes a respectable showing by international standards. The overall levels have been maintained despite the macroeconomic difficulties of the 1980s and early 1990s. The distribution of these funds, however, is widely criticized as providing too little

---

24. Claudio de Moura Castro, *Educação Brasileira: Consertos e Remendos* (Brazilian Education: Repairing and Patching) (Rio de Janeiro: Rocco, 1994), p. 15. See also Nancy Birdsall and Richard H. Sabot, eds., *Opportunity Foregone: Education in Brazil* (Washington: Inter-American Development Bank, 1996).

Table 5-4. *Literacy and Schooling, Selected Countries*

| | Adult literacy, 1999 (percent) | Net enrollment ratios[a] (percent) | | | | University students per 100,000 of population[b] |
| | | Primary | | Secondary | | |
| | | 1980 | 1997 | 1980 | 1997 | |
|---|---|---|---|---|---|---|
| Brazil | 85.3 | 80 | 97 | 46 | 66 | 1,141 |
| India | 55.8 | 65 | 77 | 41 | 60 | 630 |
| Mexico | 91.0 | 98 | 100 | 67 | 66 | 1,710 |
| Korea | 97.8 | 100 | 100 | 76 | 100 | 3,385 |
| Spain | 97.7 | 100 | 100 | 79 | 92 | 4,286 |
| Italy | 98.5 | 98 | 96 | 71 | 70 | 3,291 |
| Argentina | 96.9 | 97 | 100 | 59 | 77 | 2,074 |
| Chile | 95.7 | 93 | 90 | 70 | 85 | 2,230 |
| Colombia | 91.8 | 73 | 89 | 60 | 76 | 1,407 |
| Peru | 89.9 | 87 | 94 | 80 | 84 | 1,446 |
| Uruguay | 97.8 | 87 | 94 | 70 | 84 | 2,045 |
| Venezuela | 93.0 | 83 | 83 | 24 | 49 | n.a. |

Source: Data on adult literacy from UNESCO, *Statistical Yearbook* (Paris, 1999), table II.2; on university enrollments from table II.7 (then divided by population data from World Bank, *World Development Indicators 1999*, table II.1). Net enrollment ratios are UNESCO enrollment estimates and projections as assessed in 1999 and reported in World Bank, *World Development Indicators 2000*.

n.a. Not available.

a. Enrollment ratios are the share of the relevant age groups actually enrolled in school.

b. Data are for 1996 or 1997 except for Argentina, 1994, and Venezuela, 1992.

for free and high-quality public secondary education, and too much for universities charging no tuition regardless of capacity to pay. Periodic initiatives to introduce tuition charges, even for a modest fraction of university costs, have been frustrated by the political opposition of student organizations and middle-class parents.

Constitutional guarantees of free primary education for all Brazilian citizens go back as far as Article 179 of the Imperial Constitution of 1824, which included this item in a long list of "political and civil rights of citizens," not including slaves. In all constitutions since 1934, primary education (eight years in the Brazilian system) is described as both free and compulsory. Until World War II, reality fell woefully short of these aspirations.

Since 1960, however, the actual coverage has greatly expanded. Scarcity of school buildings is no longer a substantial problem, although teaching and library materials are still woefully deficient in the rural Northeast. As late as 1996, the official household sample study showed 9 percent of chil-

Table 5-5.  *Public Expenditure on Education, Selected Countries*
Percent

| Country | Share of GDP | Distribution by level | | | |
|---------|--------------|----------------------|---|---|---|
| | | Preprimary and primary | Secondary | Tertiary | Other and nondistributed |
| Brazil, 1995 | 5.1 | 54 | 20 | 26 | n.a. |
| India, 1996 | 3.2 | 40 | 26 | 14 | 20 |
| Mexico, 1995 | 4.9 | 50 | 33 | 17 | n.a. |
| Korea, 1995 | 3.7 | 45 | 37 | 8 | 10 |
| Spain, 1996 | 5.0 | 33 | 48 | 17 | 2 |
| Italy, 1996 | 4.9 | 32 | 49 | 15 | 4 |
| Argentina, 1996 | 3.5 | 46 | 35 | 19 | n.a. |
| Chile, 1997 | 3.6 | 58 | 19 | 16 | 7 |
| Colombia, 1996 | 4.4 | 40 | 32 | 19 | 9 |
| Peru, 1996 | 2.9 | 35 | 21 | 16 | 28 |
| Uruguay, 1996 | 3.3 | 33 | 29 | 20 | 18 |
| Venezuela, 1994 | 5.2 | n.a. | 30[a] | 35 | 35 |

Source: UNESCO, *Statistical Yearbook 1999*, table II.18, for share of GDP and table II.19 for distribution by level.

n.a. Not available.

a. Primary plus secondary.

dren aged seven to fourteen with no schooling.[25] In addition, the repetition of grade levels has been a notorious feature of Brazilian primary education, along with dropping out entirely in the early grades. Truncated schooling is highly correlated with low earnings.[26]

On the encouraging side, public opinion in recent years has shown increasing interest in educational reform, especially at the primary level, and remedial measures have been a high priority for the Cardoso administration. With encouragement from the federal ministry, Minas Gerais, Paraná, the Federal District, and the city of São Paulo have led the way in reducing dropouts and grade repetition, improving teacher qualifications, and measuring results by systematic testing.[27] Since competitiveness in the modern

25. IBGE, *Indicadores Sociais Mínimos* (Key Social Indicators), table 3, by Internet (May, 2000).

26. See Divonzir Arthur Gusso, "Educação básica no Brasil: um desafio à democratização e à competitividade" (Basic Education in Brazil: A Challenge to Democratization and to Competitiveness), in *A Questão Social no Brasil* (The Social Question in Brazil), Fórum Nacional (João Paulo dos Reis Velloso, organizer) (São Paulo: Livraria Nobel, 1991), pp. 208–10.

27. In Minas Gerais, grade repetition in the first four years was reduced from 41 percent in 1991 to 18 percent in 1996. See reportage in "O desafio da educação" (The Challenge of Education),

industrial and service sectors requires most of the work force to be educated at least through high school, a goal still reached by only one-third of the Brazilian age cohort, the leading states are also upgrading and expanding public secondary education. They are attracting patronage from middle-class families previously relying on private schools at that level. Night schools are also expanding to cater to former school dropouts. There are promising experiments in vocational training in cooperation with local business federations and prospective employers. Although parts of the Northeast and North remain far behind, and teacher unions are often resistant to change (as in the United States), these are substantial steps toward overcoming the shortfall from first world standards. That is far less true at the university level, where the weaknesses in relation to technological modernization have already been noted.

## Health

Major indicators of health conditions and availability of health care are shown in table 5-6 for the standard country set. They fall into a now familiar pattern: an intermediate position for Brazil between very poor countries and OECD members; radical improvements in life expectancy and child mortality since 1960; yet also a striking contrast with Korea, which has approached first world results with a much smaller number of doctors and nurses. As with education, Korea achieves these results with lower relative expenditure levels, a result that implies greater efficiency in the application of public resources. Brazil's record also compares unfavorably with Mexico's, showing lesser life expectancy and higher infant mortality despite the greater numbers of doctors and nurses.

Health care, like education, is a form of investment in human capital but is less clearly linked with the social objectives of reducing poverty and increasing equality of opportunity. On the one hand, poverty leads to ill health by way of malnutrition. Impoverished communities, whether rural or urban, are the most vulnerable to epidemic diseases. The great improvements in life expectancy and child mortality shown in table 5-6 result mainly from public health measures, such as vaccinations, potable water supplies, and sanitary waste disposal. On the other hand, a large share of health care expenditures goes to the treatment of illnesses and accidents unrelated to

*ISTOE*, November 27, 1996; also oral presentation by Claudio de Moura Castro at Woodrow Wilson Center symposium, Washington, D.C., February 25, 1997.

Table 5-6. Health and Health Care, Selected Countries

| Country | Life expectancy (years) | | Infant mortality rate/1,000 live births | | | Doctors/100,000 population, 1993 | Nurses/100,000 population, 1993 | Public expenditure on health, 1995 (percent of GDP) |
|---|---|---|---|---|---|---|---|---|
| | 1960 | 1997 | 1960 | 1975 | 1993 | | | |
| Brazil | 52 | 63 | 179 | 110 | 37 | 134 | 41 | 1.9 |
| India | 47 | 67 | 235 | 195 | 71 | 48 | n.a. | 0.7 |
| Mexico | 56 | 72 | 148 | 95 | 29 | 107 | 40 | 2.8 |
| Korea | 53 | 72 | 133 | 29 | 6 | 127 | 232 | 1.9 |
| Spain | 68 | 78 | 56 | 22 | 5 | 122 | 400 | 5.8 |
| Italy | 68 | 78 | 56 | 25 | 5 | n.a. | n.a. | 5.4 |
| United States | 70 | 77 | 31 | 19 | 7 | 245 | 878 | 6.5 |

Sources: UNDP, *Human Development Report, 1999*, table 8, pp. 168–71 (for life expectancy and infant mortality), table 9, pp. 172–75 (doctors and nurses), and table 13, pp. 188–91 (public expenditures).

n.a. Not available.

income levels and constituting an open-ended potential claim on resources, as rich countries the world over have discovered.

Before the twentieth-century era of industrialization and urbanization, health care in Brazil was a private matter for those who could afford it. For the poor, it was nonexistent or provided by religious or municipal charities. In 1934 the Vargas regime included health care insurance among the social security benefits extended to organized urban workers, laying the foundation for Brazil's unusual array of mixed public-private arrangements.[28]

Under the military regime, publicly financed health care benefits were extended to much larger segments of the population, accompanied by a boom in hospital construction and medical training. Coverage increased from about 25 percent of the population in 1962 to over 80 percent in 1985.

For higher-income groups, there developed a parallel private insurance system much like the American, with payments mainly on a fee-for-service basis but with the most costly procedures still financed through the public system. Administrative supervision was provided mainly at the state level (in large urban centers at the municipal level), but with most of the funding flowing through the social security system and with some coordination by the federal Ministry of Health. The economic recession of the 1980s reduced the financial resources for health care just when popular desires for more comprehensive service were soaring. The 1946 Constitution had made only the briefest reference to providing for "medical assistance, including hospitalization and preventive medicine for workers and expectant mothers" (Article 156-XIV). In 1988, however, the constitution for the New Republic devoted five articles to an entire section labeled Health, beginning with a ringing declaration: "Article 196. Health is a right of all and a duty of the State and shall be guaranteed by means of economic and social policies aimed at reducing the risk of illness and other hazards and at the universal and equal access to actions and services for its promotion, protection and recovery." It also called for reorganization of the publicly financed health services into a "single system," but one that was to be decentralized and fully open to private and nonprofit entities, excluding foreign ownership.

In the late 1990s, however, the practice was still far short of these aspirations and the term "single health system" (Sistema Único de Saúde, or SUS)

---

28. For a concise summary of the historical evolution of Brazil's health care system until the early 1980s, see Milton I. Roemer, *National Health Systems of the World* (Oxford University Press, 1991), vol. 1, pp. 316–35. For more recent developments, see World Bank, *Brazil: The Organization, Delivery and Financing of Health Care in Brazil: Agenda for the '90s*, Report 12655BR (Washington, June 1994), chap. 3.

was a misnomer. Several of the states and most of the *municípios* were unable to manage their nominally decentralized responsibilities. The system was riddled with fraudulent claims for the reimbursement of private providers from public funds. There was inadequate regulation of sanitary procedures in hospitals. Public financing fluctuated from year to year, forcing ministers of health to concentrate on fund-raising rather than administrative reform. For the poor, there was widespread rationing via the queue, while physicians shifted their attention to higher-paid private practice.[29]

At the same time, some states and metropolitan centers used decentralization to good advantage in weeding out abuses and improving the quality and timeliness of care. But Brazil cannot escape the worldwide dilemma of all health care systems: the combination of expensive technological advances in medical procedures with increasing life expectancies, a dilemma that makes some kind of rationing inescapable, even though rarely acknowledged. In Brazil, this dilemma is intensified by the overambitious constitutional promise and the perverse incentive of income tax deductibility for all private medical expenditures. At the margins, Brazil has secured some financial and technical assistance from the World Bank and Inter-American Development Bank in confronting these challenges. The task ahead of continuing administrative, fiscal, and even conceptual reform remains a thorny one.[30]

## Reflections on the Social Sector—Patience and Persistence

This cursory review of Brazil's social issues leaves me with one major reflection. The shortfalls from first world standards are being reduced, but they are still large and deeply embedded in Brazilian history and social structures. In the democratic political framework that seems increasingly secure, there is very little space for simple fiscal policies to transfer income from rich to poor. The basic remedies are structural, focused on incorporation of excluded groups into the modern sectors of the economy. Measures should

29. Many of these problems are documented in André Cezar Médici, *Economia e Financiamento do Setor Saúde no Brasil* (The Economics and Financing of the Health Sector in Brazil) (São Paulo: Universidade de São Paulo, Faculdade de Saúde Publica, 1994). See also World Bank, *Brazil: The Organization, Delivery and Financing of Health Care*, fn. 27.

30. In late March 1997, President Cardoso announced budgetary goals in the health sector for 1998, as part of an announced Year of Health. The Health Ministry budget was to be raised from R\$14.5 billion in 1996 and R\$20.3 billion in 1997 to R\$31.1 billion in 1998. The successive macroeconomic crises of 1998 and 1999 (see chapter 7) made it impossible to meet these goals, but in 2000 Congress has earmarked substantial supplementary resources for health care.

combine economic and social policies and actions in both the public and private sectors, looking toward a healthy and well-educated work force with productive employment opportunities, along with special care for the very young, the very old, and the disabled. Bitter experience elsewhere has shown that a social revolution with those aims would end up doing more harm than good. In any event, the Brazilian public is in no mood for revolution.

Genuine social progress, therefore, can only come from the participation of successive segments of society in the dynamic processes of economic modernization. The consciousness of "social debt" is widespread in Brazilian public opinion, but the remedies will require prolonged application over a long period. A good deal can be done through measures focused directly on poverty reduction, such as capital for microenterprises, infrastructure in urban or rural areas of concentrated poverty, and technical assistance to family farming. The key to large-scale transformations, however, is job-creating overall economic growth and price stability, combined with radical improvements in education at all levels, suited to a modern economy. The watchwords must be persistence and patience.

# 6

## The Political Structure

I n the opening pages of this study I described the political criterion of first world membership as "a condition of stable pluralist democracy, with representative government based on free elections, competition among political parties, constitutional protection of individual and minority rights, and unconditional acceptance of electoral results." Toward the end of the 1950s, Brazil's Second Republic appeared to be close to meeting this definition, only to have the regime suspended in 1964 by a coup d'état and a twenty-one year interval of authoritarian government under military direction. As previously noted, the restoration of civilian control in 1985 was immensely popular, and the Constitution of 1988 was intended to consolidate political democracy and civil liberties in the República Nova (New Republic).

On its face, the political criterion now appears to be met in all respects but one. At the start of the new millennium, the armed forces show no disposition to reassume political power. There are free and frequent elections based on universal franchise, honest counting of the ballots, vigorous competition among political parties, constitutional clauses protecting individual and minority rights, and unconditional acceptance of electoral results. The exception concerns the *stability* of the political system: how far democracy can be judged as *consolidated*. The doubts as to stability arise from structural weaknesses: weaknesses in the federal-state division of powers and the separation of powers at the federal level, systemic weaknesses in the political parties, operational weaknesses conducive to corruption, and impunity for abuses of civil liberties. All combine to undermine popular respect for governmental institutions and politicians. I review those weaknesses in detail in this chapter, but only after posing a more ephemeral question: whether today's Brazilian society possesses a genuine democratic ethos, a readiness to subject critical decisions of policy and leadership to the ultimate test of rule by popular majority.

## A Democratic Ethos?

Although an elected legislature figured prominently in the imperial Constitution of 1824, Brazil can scarcely be credited with a democratic ethos during its first century of national existence. Under the Empire (1822–89) and the Old Republic (1889–1930), political power was concentrated in the owners of large inherited estates: sugar growers in the Northeast, cattle raisers in the Center, and later the coffee growers of the Center-South. Most of the population were illiterate peasants and (until 1888) slaves. In those two historical eras, Brazil clearly merited the sobriquet "patrimonial society." Yet the landowners did not have a total monopoly of power. Under the Empire, it was qualified by the monarch's "moderating power" and partly shared with the coastal merchant class, court circles in Rio de Janeiro (including a nascent bureaucracy), professionals (mainly in law and medicine), and military officers. These modernizing elements were the forces behind the late-nineteenth-century abolitionist movement (strengthened after the American Civil War), the philosophical and partly political movement called Positivism, and the republican movement that overthrew the monarchy in 1889.

The Old Republic was in some ways even more dominated by the landowning class than the Empire, since there was no longer an imperial court as a rival source of power and the 1891 constitution greatly strengthened the states at the expense of the Union. On the other hand, the coffee barons of the Center-South were not as backward-looking as the northeastern sugar *coroneis* ("colonels"). Their labor force was composed mainly of new immigrants from Europe and Japan, and the population was becoming progressively urbanized and industrialized. Especially in the southern region, new wealth was rivaling inherited wealth, making the term "patrimonial" increasingly inappropriate as a description of the social structure.[1]

---

1. In his widely read study of Brazilian politics, Riordan Roett has preserved the term "patrimonial society" even in the fourth edition published in 1992. He also uses the terms "patrimonial state" and "patrimonial order" (see *Brazil: Politics in a Patrimonial Society*, 4th ed. [Westport, Conn.: Praeger, 1992], p. 23). The terminology follows Max Weber's usage (see H. H. Gerth and C. Wright

The revolution of 1930, led by Getúlio Vargas, perhaps constituted the sharpest discontinuity in Brazil's entire political history, putting an end to landowner hegemony. In the words of historian Bradford Burns:

> The coffee interests lost their absolute control of the nation and the urban middle class and proletariat strengthened their positions. The landed class, while still powerful, had to learn to compromise and to share some of its power with those two newly potent elements. Vargas enlisted both to support his government and skillfully identified his program with the increasingly powerful force of nationalism. Waves of nationalism, the drive for modernization, and the effects of urbanization and industrialization combined to alter much of the social structure.[2]

In subsequent decades, as noted in chapter 1, urbanization and industrialization continued apace, further strengthening the political weight of the nonagricultural sectors. But the political structure imposed by Vargas in his Estado Novo constitution, decreed by fiat in 1937, was essentially antidemocratic, connecting state with society through a fascist system of corporative representation rather than the electoral competition of political parties. A formally democratic structure was restored only after the military overthrow of Vargas in 1945, popular elections of a new president and Congress, and the adoption in 1946 of a constitution for the Second Republic. While substantially more democratic than any earlier regime, the Second Republic still denied the vote to illiterates. With further urbanization and industrialization, however, especially during the Kubitschek presidency, literacy was spreading rapidly. As shown in figure 6-1, electoral participation after World War II was a full order of magnitude greater than in the Old Republic.[3]

---

Mills, *From Max Weber: Essays in Sociology* [reprint, Oxford University Press, 1958], pp. 296–97) but may be confusing to the modern reader, since the words "patrimony" and "patrimonial" connote inherited wealth. Such wealth remains significant in Brazil but has not been dominant since the Vargas revolution of 1930. Roett also uses the term "ruling class" to refer to the old landed aristocracy, but notes that it "has been in a process of decline and decadence since 1930" (*Brazil*, p. 30). Thus it is clearly no longer "ruling," having been displaced by what Roett calls the "political elite," a much larger grouping that is not homogeneous in either its composition or its political attitudes. In his explicit discussion of the term "Patrimonial State" (*Brazil*, pp. 33–37), Roett describes attributes such as widely encompassing state authority, Brazilian methods of exerting political influence (several of which are reviewed later in this chapter), and a philosophy of the state derived from Brazilian historical processes. Since none of these attributes relates to inherited property, the term "patrimonial" does not describe them accurately.

2. E. Bradford Burns, *A History of Brazil* (Columbia University Press, 1970), p. 272.

3. The sharp fall in percentage between 1872 and the next entry, which is for 1886, resulted from a major change in voting eligibility in 1881. Until then, elections for the Chamber of Deputies were

Figure 6-1.  *Electorate as Percentage of Voting-Age Population, 1872–1994*[a]

Percent

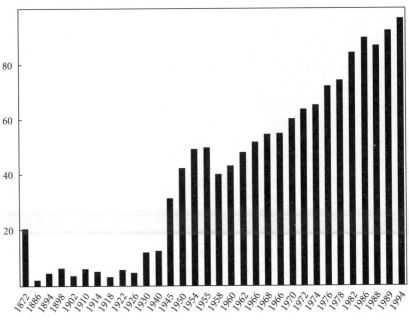

Empire    Old Republic    Vargas    Second Republic    Military Regime    New Republic

Sources: Voting age population calculated from periodic national censuses as published in *Anuário Estatístico 1991*, p. 177, with arithmetical interpolations for intercensal years. Electorate figures for 1872 to 1930 from text references in Ronald M. Schneider, *"Order and Progress": A Political History of Brazil* (Boulder, Colo.: Westview, 1991); for 1940 to 1950, from IBGE, *Estatísticas Históricas do Brasil*, (1987), pp. 590–91; for 1954 to 1989 from *Anuário Estatístico*, 1991, p. 446; for 1994 from *Anuário Estatístico*, 1995, p. 2–247.

a.  The minimum voting age from 1822 to 1934 was twenty-one years; from 1934 to 1988 it was eighteen years; and since 1988 it has been sixteen years.

In interpreting those data, it should be kept in mind that there were no presidential elections during the military regime of 1964–85, so the participation for that period refers only to legislative and municipal elections. The first postmilitary civilian president-elect (Tancredo Neves) was indirectly chosen in 1985 by a special electoral college. Direct popular elections for president took place in 1989 for the first time since 1960, the electorate now

---

indirect, the voting citizens first electing parochial assemblies, which then elected national and provincial assemblies (in that era, today's states were called provinces). Although the basic electorate was limited by a property qualification, which became progressively more severe for membership in the assemblies, there was no literacy requirement until 1881, when deputies came to be elected directly by a much more restricted basic electorate.

being further enlarged by abolition of the literacy requirement and lowering of the voting age to sixteen.

In the nine years following the end of military government, Brazil's newly restored and amplified democratic institutions were severely strained. The first civilian president-elect, Tancredo Neves, died before being able to take office. The first president chosen by popular vote, Fernando Collor de Melo, was impeached after two years by the Chamber of Deputies on charges of far-reaching financial corruption and convicted by the Senate in December 1992. The respective successors, José Sarney and Itamar Franco, had not been considered of presidential stature when they were put on the ballots as running mates in 1984 and 1989.

In 1986 Sarney enjoyed several months of great popularity because of the initial success of the Cruzado Plan for price stabilization (see chapter 7), followed by disillusion when that plan collapsed in early 1987. The failure of four subsequent anti-inflation efforts, combined with the slowdown in economic growth and a series of financial scandals involving prominent political figures at both state and federal levels, compounded popular cynicism at the seeming incompetence of elected governments. Opinion polling showed a low regard for the political class as a whole. In this lost decade, moreover, there was evidence of significant "reverse migration" of Brazilians to Portugal. Books by prominent intellectuals, who had rejoiced at the ending of the military regime, came to be marked by a tone of despair.[4]

On the favorable side, there were waves of popular enthusiasm when the new constitution was promulgated in 1988, when President Collor was elected in 1989, and—somewhat paradoxically—when Collor was removed in 1992 by constitutional means with no threat of military intervention. A seemingly more durable period of renewed confidence in democracy began with the apparent success of the Real Plan for inflation control. It led to the election of President Fernando Henrique Cardoso on the first ballot in October 1994 and his first-ballot reelection in 1998.

In all this period, the armed forces have shown no significant signs of ambitions for political power. The prevalence of democracy among the world's leading nations except China also makes it a natural aspect of Brazilian ambitions to be counted among the leading nations. On balance, then, Brazilians appear to prefer democracy to any visible alternative. They take pleasure in electoral competition even if regarded only as a game. A national

4. As examples, see Hélio Jaguaribe and others, *Reforma ou Caos* (Reform or Chaos) (Rio de Janeiro: Paz e Terra, 1989); Cándido Mendes, *A Democracia Desperdiçada* (The Wasted Democracy) (Rio de Janeiro: Editora Nova Fronteira, 1992).

democratic ethos exists, but it may be precarious until there is a resumption of sustained economic growth without inflation and sufficient political reform to channel the interest groupings and political aspirations of the electorate into workable public policies.

Political reform might involve the formal structure of government, federalism, the electoral system, the character of political parties, the judicial system, and the relations between state and society. The next sections present the main reform issues arising since the restoration of civilian government in 1985.

## Presidentialism versus Parliamentarism

For many decades, Brazilian political and intellectual circles have debated exhaustively the relative merits of presidential and parliamentary systems of government. During the Constitutional Congress of 1987–88, a shift to parliamentarism (or mixed "premier-presidentialism," as in France) was strongly supported and seemed likely to prevail, only to be defeated by a vote of 344 to 212 because of intense opposition by then President Sarney and on condition that the question be submitted in 1993 to a popular plebiscite.[5] In the run-up to that vote, prominent political scientists, backed by widespread agreement among international scholars of the subject, argued strenuously for the change, pointing to the German Federal Republic as their preferred model.[6] Public opinion polls seemed to foreshadow its adoption in the wake of corruption scandals and the ouster of President Collor. Nevertheless, when the plebiscite took place in late April, parliamentarism was routed by a majority of 55 to 25 percent (with 20 percent of the ballots blank or spoiled).[7]

The arguments favoring parliamentarism are so widely known as to require here only a brief recapitulation:[8]

5. See Bolívar Lamounier, organizer, *A Opção Parlamentarista* (The Choice for Parliamentarism) (São Paulo: Editora Sumaré, 1991), p. 50. See also Bolívar Lamounier and Dieter Nohlen, organizers, *Presidencialismo ou Parlamentarismo: Perspectivas sobre a Reorganização Institucional Brasileira* (Presidentialism or Parliamentarism: Perspectives on Brazil's Institutional Reorganization) (São Paulo: Edicões Loyola, 1993).

6. The arguments are set forth systematically in Juan J. Linz and Arturo Valenzuela, eds., *The Failure of Presidential Democracy: The Case of Latin America* (Johns Hopkins University Press, 1994). A striking exception to the consensus is Matthew Soberg Shugart and Scott Mainwaring, eds., *Presidentialism and Democracy in Latin America* (Cambridge University Press, 1997), especially chap. 1 by the joint editors.

7. Xinhua General Overseas News Service bulletin, April 26, 1993.

8. For a comprehensive review, see Linz and Valenzuela, *The Failure of Presidential Democracy*.

—Among well-established democratic regimes, parliamentary systems outnumber presidential ones by a very wide margin.

—Parliamentarism ensures affinity between the executive and legislative branches of government, since the legislature can remove the cabinet through a vote of nonconfidence, while the executive can appeal to the electorate by dissolving parliament and calling for new elections. Facility in changing cabinets reduces the danger of crises of regime. (In this regard, there are many variations of detail, most of them designed to avoid excessive instability and "revolving-door cabinets" such as those in Germany between the two World Wars and in France both before and after World War II, until de Gaulle's constitution of 1958.)

—Parliamentarism promotes the formation of durable coalitions in countries with a multiplicity of political parties.

—Parliamentarism permits flexibility in the timing of general elections.

—In parliamentary regimes, the path to the office of prime minister normally goes through a succession of lesser cabinet posts, thereby ensuring a degree of competence in the head of government and avoiding charismatic demagogues with aspirations of *caudillismo.*

—Parliamentarism can be protected against excessive governmental instability by devices such as the German "constructive vote of nonconfidence" (requiring majority endorsement of a replacement prime minister before the current one can be ousted), and by a minimum threshold requirement for a party to win seats in the legislature.

The main counterargument, based on British practice, is that for the life of an elected parliament, party discipline is so strong that the prime minister has almost dictatorial powers, a danger avoided in classic American presidentialism by the checks and balances provided in the Constitution of 1787. In Brazil, however, there is a further compelling counterargument in the popular desire to participate directly in the selection of the head of state. Since the essence of parliamentary regimes is to permit parliaments to overthrow cabinets, a monarch-equivalent is needed to give the system formal stability and often a real voice in identifying potential prime ministers where no single party has a parliamentary majority. But a popularly elected head of state is likely to become a rival to the prime minister elected by parliament; hence the frequent provision for some kind of electoral college for the head of state "above the fray" of partisan politics. Another arrangement is sometimes called premier-presidentialism, an uneasy hybrid dividing fields of responsibility between president and prime minister; the classic example is the French constitution designed by Charles de Gaulle. That system runs the risk of re-creating the kinds of stalemate that parliamentary systems are supposed to avoid.

In my opinion, the desire for direct connection between electorate and chief executive is an insuperable obstacle to parliamentarism in Brazil. After a century of restricted suffrage and a recent long period of military government, Brazil's entire adult population is at last participating in the selection of the president. In the absence of well-established national parties with recognized leaders, voters could not predict with assurance who might emerge as prime minister from political jockeying among members of Congress in Brasília. For reasons summarized later in this chapter, members of Congress are generally held in low esteem. It is therefore not credible that the public at large would entrust them with selection of the nation's chief executive. Viewed in this light, the overwhelming rejection of parliamentarism in 1993 was not a surprise.[9]

Short of a basic change of structure, there is ample room for improvement in executive-legislative relationships. On paper, the 1988 Constitution gives the president a large role in legislation, in striking contrast to presidential authority in the United States. He has exclusive initiative on major issues of administrative organization and the size of the armed forces and can secure priority consideration of bills in these fields (Articles 61 and 64). He can veto parts of bills as well as whole bills, subject to overriding by an absolute majority of the membership of both houses in joint session (Article 66).

Most important in practice, he can issue decree-laws (*medidas provisórias,* "provisional measures") on "important and urgent matters," which have the force of law for thirty days (Article 62). In principle, such measures lapse, retroactively, unless confirmed by Congress within the thirty-day deadline, but in practice they have been kept in force through repeated reissuance. Both the constitutional wording and the 1988 legislative history indicate that this power was intended for use only in genuine emergencies, but the practice under four presidents has made it a customary mode of legislation.[10] It cannot be used, however, for constitutional amendments, which must be voted in two separate sessions by three-fifths majorities of the full membership of each house (Senate and Chamber of Deputies). Since the 1988 Constitution is very long and replete with provisions treated in most countries

9. An additional obstacle was posed by objections from state governors, who generally prefer direct election by the voters.

10. Scott Mainwaring reports that up until May 1995, the four presidents had issued 1,004 "provisional measures," 640 of which were renewals. See Mainwaring and Shugart, *Presidentialism and Democracy in Latin America,* p. 63.

by ordinary legislation, and since the common practice of absenteeism amounts to a de facto negative vote, this limitation on provisional measures is more consequential than might be supposed from a mere reading of the constitutional text. In addition, congressional discontent with the arrangement leads to repeated proposals for further limitations on its use, a live topic on the political agenda for the new millennium.

Another arena of potential conflict is the management of public finances, extensively and confusingly dealt with in the 1988 Constitution. In practice, monetary policy is reserved to the Finance Ministry and the central bank, while multiyear and annual revenues and expenditures are initiated by the executive but then subjected to detailed legislative revision. The constitution (Title VI) divides types of taxation among federal, state, and municipal authorities, and then transfers substantial portions of federal revenues to the state and municipal levels, reserving a sizable share of each level's revenue for expenditure on education (Article 212).

During the era of high inflation, the actual revenue and expenditures fluctuated with economic activity, rates of inflation, and efficiency in tax collection. Rather than engage in bureaucratic battles with various spending ministries and then with the Congress, the Finance Ministry accepted nominal appropriations far beyond prospective real resources, depending on the "inflation tax"—the rapid erosion of real values—to keep expenditures within bounds. With inflation reduced under the Real Plan to annual single-digit percentages, that solution became untenable. In the late 1990s, the practice was to take the actual federal revenues ten days at a time, allocate the constitutional shares to states and *municípios,* cover current interest on the public debt, meet the payroll for federal employees, and then apportion the residue to investment and other current expenditures in proportion to congressional appropriations, but at much lower levels. Individual ministries then have wide discretion on which specific projects or programs to finance, providing a broad arena for bargaining between the national administration and politicians at the state and local levels.[11] This bargaining becomes a major element in securing congressional support for legislation, catering to what Brazilians term the "physiological" interest of members, known in American jargon as "pork and patronage."

The weakness and fragmentation of Brazil's political parties, sustained by the electoral mechanics described later in this chapter, rule out the possibil-

---

11. The procedures were described to me in August 1997 by Murilo Portugal, Brazilian executive director of the World Bank and former secretary of the national treasury within the Finance Ministry.

ity of coherent congressional initiatives on broad issues of economic or social policy. Such initiatives can come only from the executive branch. But the party weakness and fragmentation also rule out coherent confrontation with the executive on policy grounds. Instead, the capacity of Congress to delay and obstruct is used as bargaining leverage in seeking federal projects, patronage, and financial assistance to states and *municípios*, making the path of reform steep and rocky, even for a popular president.[12] Although there is no prospect for parliamentarism as a remedy for these difficulties, they could certainly be reduced through less ambitious measures for party restructuring of the kinds discussed below.

## The Federal Structure

Brazilian culture has been marked by regional differences since the earliest European settlements, reflecting the diversity of economic activities and the differing social origins and interests of the various streams of immigration. The formal political structure, however, was basically centralized prior to independence. Today's coastal states are descendants of the "captaincies" (*capitanias*) established by the Portuguese crown in the 1530s, but in 1548 they were subordinated to a colony-wide governor-general, first residing in Salvador da Bahia and after 1763 in Rio de Janeiro.[13]

The move of the Portuguese court to Rio in 1808, to escape from Napoleon's invasion of Portugal, strengthened the power of the capital in relation to the captaincies. When Pedro I declared independence in 1822, therefore, sovereignty was concentrated in his hands as emperor. The presidents (now governors) of the provinces (now states) were selected by him. Imperial Brazil was a unitary state, transformed into a federation only after the republican revolution of 1889. The federal status was formalized by the

12. Thus President Fernando Henrique Cardoso, despite an unprecedented first-round electoral victory in 1994 and a nominal congressional majority for the parties represented in his cabinet, suffered numerous postponements and several serious defeats on proposed constitutional amendments during his first three years in office. For a detailed review of these difficulties during the first two years, see Peter Flynn, "Brazil: The Politics of the 'Plano Real,'" *Third World Quarterly*, September 1996.

13. The practice, however, did not necessarily match the theoretical lines of authority. In the words of historian E. Bradford Burns: "Distance, intrigues, the varying effectiveness of personalities, the vagueness of the law, often meant that the governor-general and later the viceroy exercised little authority over the various governors of the captaincies." On the other hand, central authority was strengthened in the eighteenth century, especially during the tenure of the powerful Portuguese prime minister, the Marqués de Pombal. Burns, *A History of Brazil*, pp. 81–82.

Constitution of 1891 in the nation's new name: the United States of Brazil, now the Federal Republic of Brazil.

This history contrasts with federations, such as the United States and Switzerland, formed by the voluntary association of previously sovereign component states.[14] Over the subsequent century, power alternated between the states and the center. The Old Republic (1891–1930) carried devolution to the extreme, with power concentrated at the state level in São Paulo and Minas Gerais.[15] That tendency was sharply reversed by Getúlio Vargas after 1930; he named "interventors" in place of elected governors and assumed total power in the Estado Novo of 1937–45. The Second Republic (1945–64) returned to a less extreme decentralization, which was again reversed by the military regime of 1964–85. In the New Republic's constitution of 1988, decentralization is promoted through a new device: earmarking of large proportions of specified federal tax revenues for reallocation to states and *municípios* (counties or towns), but without a corresponding reallocation of functions.

Since 1946 there have been three senators per state. In the lower House, moreover, the American model of proportionality to population has been modified to favor the small states, usually through ceilings on numbers of deputies for the larger states and floors for the smaller.[16] In the latter stages of the military regime, when opposition was concentrated in the more developed southern states, the government intensified the overrepresentation of the less populous states of the Northeast and North. This bias was continued in the 1988 Constitution (Article 45), which provides a maximum of seventy deputies per state and a minimum of eight. Inequality of representation was further augmented by the admission to statehood of thinly populated Amazonian territories and the carving out of new states from Mato Grosso and Goiás. In consequence, a deputy from São Paulo now represents 450,000 inhabitants on the average, while the population bases for deputies from Roraíma, Acre, and Amapá are only 27,000, 36,000, and 52,000, respectively. Coming on top of equal representation in the Senate, this over-

14. For a comparative legal perspective on federalism in North America and four South American countries, including Brazil, see Keith S. Rosenn, "Federalism in the Americas in Comparative Perspective," *Inter-American Law Review,* vol. 26 (Miami, Fall 1994), pp. 1–50.

15. Since these states dominated the production of coffee and cattle, respectively, it was termed the republic of *café com leite* (coffee and milk).

16. The extreme example was Article 48 of Getúlio Vargas's Estado Novo Constitution of 1937, which had a maximum of ten and a minimum of three, but that had little practical effect since most legislation in that period was by executive decree.

weighting of the least developed regions is a significant impediment to modernizing reforms. It also reinforces the parochialism of Congress and the institutional obstacles to the development of nationwide political parties, as noted later in this chapter.

All the states are financially dependent on the central government, both for budgetary appropriations and for a variety of loans and "bailouts." Yet the political influence of the states is pervasive.[17] In contrast to the situation in the United States, governors are generally more powerful than senators. Their control over state patronage and funds for municipal projects gives them enormous political influence, without having to share power with other statewide elected officials. The absence of strong political parties makes them undisputed leaders in state legislation, while local governments, except in large cities, are financially dependent on state largesse.[18]

Members of Congress give up seats for mayoralties, even of moderate-sized *municípios*. New *municípios* are frequently created to provide additional patronage jobs, paid for out of state or federal funds, even when local resources are not able to sustain them.[19] The electoral mechanics for the Chamber of Deputies and for state assemblies, both based on "open lists" instead of party lists, give governors a pivotal influence over the selection of candidates and electoral prospects for members of Congress and of state assemblies (*deputados*). Coupled with the extreme weakness of national parties, this system makes the voting behavior of state *bancadas* (delegations in Congress) highly responsive to the governors, even when the congressmen

17. During the era of extreme inflation, 1980–94, public borrowing at both state and federal levels was unconstrained because repayment obligations were rapidly eroded and real interest rates were negative. Public payrolls became grossly expanded. With financial stabilization under the Real Plan after 1995, such "easy money" was no longer available. Most state-owned banks and other enterprises were threatened with failure, with the result that state governments and related institutions sought financial relief from the Ministry of Finance (Fazenda) and the central bank. The federal authorities have made bailouts conditional on state agreements for repayment over long terms, together with promises of fiscal and institutional reform akin to IMF conditions for international financial assistance, but political constraints limit the enforcement of such conditions.

18. A recent analysis of Brazilian federalism, based on intensive study of fifteen states, describes its functioning at the state level as "ultrapresidentialism," totally lacking in the legislative and judicial checks and balances common to the states in North America. That is decidedly not the case at the federal level in Brazil. See Fernando Luiz Abrucio, *Os Barões da Federação: Os Governadores e a Redemocratização Brasileira* (The Barons of the Federation: Governors and Brazilian Redemocratization) (São Paulo: Editora Hucitec, 1998), chap. 3.

19. The *Estado de S. Paulo* of August 17, 1997, reported data from IBGE showing that the number of *municípios* increased from 3,990 in 1980 to 4,979 in 1995 and 6,040 in mid-1997, 533 of which had been created during the previous six months. A constitutional amendment was passed by Congress in September 1996 to restrain this process, but it had not yet been "regulated" by the needed complementary statute.

are not nominally members of the governor's party. The resulting influence of governors over national legislation can be bargained by them for federal projects, patronage, and financial assistance. It constitutes a kind of state-dominated federalism, which is a serious hindrance to coherent national policymaking.[20]

## Political Parties and Electoral Mechanics

The fundamental weakness in Brazil's political structure lies in the nearly total absence of broadly based political parties mediating between the electorate and the government, despite a multiplicity of nominal parties created for electoral purposes. That weakness derives in part from the relatively short experience with a broadly based electorate, which began only with the Second Republic in 1945 and then suffered a long interruption from 1964 to 1985. It is greatly exacerbated by Brazil's peculiar electoral mechanics for both federal and state legislators.[21]

During the Second Republic, the political scene was dominated by three parties of national scope. Two—the PSD (Social Democratic Party) and PTB (Brazilian Labor Party)—had been organized by Vargas before the termination of the Estado Novo in 1945. The UDN (National Democratic Union) brought together elements that had opposed Vargas during most of the 1930s and 1940s. By the early 1960s, it seemed possible that they would gradually take on the aspect of national parties in much of Western Europe: the UDN right of center; the PTB left of center, with an extreme wing including significant Communist elements; and the PSD as a centrist balancing group. These parties were dissolved by the military regime in 1965 and replaced by a two-party system decreed from on high. When a multiparty system again became possible in 1979, as part of the guided transition away from military

20. See Abrucio, *Os Barões da Federação,* chap. 4. These practices show a strong historical linkage with the Old Republic, when federal deputies could be seated only with the approval of state governors. See Kurt von Mettenheim, *The Brazilian Voter: Mass Politics in Democratic Transition* (University of Pittsburgh Press, 1995), pp. 65–66. See also Mainwaring and Shugart, *Presidentialism and Democracy in Latin America,* pp. 83–84; and Antônio Carlos de Medeiros, "The Politics of Decentralization in Brazil," *European Review of Latin American and Caribbean Studies,* vol. 57 (December 1994), pp. 7–27.

21. The weaknesses of Brazilian political parties and their connection with electoral mechanics have been extensively documented in recent years by Brazilian political scientists and foreign scholars. This discussion draws from Bolívar Lamounier, Amaury de Souza, José Alvaro Moisés, Hélio Jaguaribe, Kurt von Mettenheim, Scott Mainwaring, Alfred Stepan, Juan Linz, David Fleischer, and Barry Ames. For a detailed account of the kaleidoscopic formation of new parties and party groupings between 1982 and 1994, see Jairo Marconi Nicolau, *Multipartidarismo e Democracia* (Rio de Janeiro: Fundação Getúlio Vargas, 1996).

control, the parties of the Second Republic were not revived, showing that they had not sunk broad roots in Brazilian society, as had the major political parties of Chile, Argentina, or Germany.

In reaction against the two-party straitjacket imposed by the military regime, a constitutional amendment in 1985 opened the political market to a proliferation of nominal parties with little or no programmatic content. The parties of the late 1990s were all (except the small communist groupings) creations of the last two decades, lacking historical roots or traditions. Some of them are personalistic groupings tied to charismatic individuals. In the Chamber of Deputies early in 2000, with 513 seats in total, seventeen parties were represented, eight of which had more than 30 members and the largest only 128. The 81-member Senate had nine parties.[22] Party cohesion and party loyalty are weak; there is no penalty for changing party affiliations and over 250 changes were recorded in the Congress elected in 1991.

Except for the Workers' Party (PT) and the communists, party discipline is very loose, with congressmen frequently voting against positions favored by their parties' majorities. Of the three parties holding the largest numbers of seats in the chambers elected in 1994 and 1998, it is difficult to make more than broad characterizations. Thus the Party of the Liberal Front (PFL) is right of center. The Social Democratic Party of Brazil (PSDB), whose founders included President Fernando Henrique Cardoso, began in 1988 as a left-of-center breakaway from the Party of the Brazilian Democratic Movement (PMDB) but shifted toward the center or even center-right as macroeconomic stabilization became the main preoccupation of the Cardoso administration. The PMDB was founded in the 1970s by opponents of the military regime during the transition back to democracy and was greatly expanded by the enormous popularity of the short-lived Cruzado Plan for price stabilization in 1987. Yet it has no consistent ideological position beyond being vaguely in the center; its voting patterns are often sharply divided. Together with many smaller groupings, it falls into the category of nonprogrammatic "catchall parties" providing little discipline in congressional voting, accepting candidates with a wide variety of ideological histories, and subject to frequent party switching.[23]

---

22. Data from official Internet websites of the Senado and Cámara dos Deputados.

23. See Scott Mainwaring, "Brazil: Weak Parties, Feckless Democracy," in Scott Mainwaring and Timothy Scully, eds., *Building Democratic Institutions: Party Systems in Latin America* (Stanford University Press, 1995), pp. 354–98, esp. 376–87. At that writing, Mainwaring placed the PSDB in his middle category of "moderately disciplined parties with moderate programmatic commitments," but its evolution since 1995 has made it more heterogeneous.

In contrast, the PT has a genuine grass-roots base in the electorate. It started with the São Paulo metallurgical unions, although today its greatest strength is among public employees. It requires party discipline from its candidates, uses intraparty primary elections for their selection, and demonstrates remarkable cohesion in congressional voting. In organizational aspects, therefore, it resembles parties in more mature European democracies. Like many other social-democratic or socialist parties, however, in both third world and first, it is sharply divided on such basic issues as how to adjust to the end of the cold war, the discrediting of state-run economic enterprises, the proper place for Brazil in a rapidly changing world economy, and the need for fiscal discipline as an essential ingredient of macroeconomic price stabilization.

As already noted, geographical representation of the electorate is skewed, even in the lower federal chamber, by the severe overweighting of small and thinly populated states that are also the least developed economically and educationally. The electoral districts are all statewide. The individual voter casts a ballot either (a) for a specific party or an electoral coalition of parties formed to contest a particular election in that state or (b) for a single candidate who is affiliated with a party. From state to state, electoral coalitions (sometimes called "alliances") need not be made up of the same group of parties.[24] In practice, almost all voters cast their ballots for a specific candidate. Ballots are sorted by parties (or by party alliances) and the state's total of seats is then assigned to parties in proportion to the votes cast, as near as can be done using the "D'Hondt method" for proportional representation. The quota for each party (or alliance) is then assigned to the individual candidates receiving the most votes within that party or alliance grouping; they become the elected members of Congress.

This system, known as open-list proportional representation with statewide districts, contrasts sharply with voting procedures for federal and state legislatures in the United States, Europe, and most other democratic

---

24. Amaury de Souza notes that in the 1986 elections, interparty alliances accounted for 57.3 percent of the votes for the Chamber of Deputies. He continues (informal translation): "Ideological differences apparently were not an insuperable obstacle. Of the 91 electoral alliances which included at least one center-left party (PDT, PT, PCB, PC do B, or PSB), 71.4 percent also included parties of the center (PMDB) or the center-right (PDT, PFL, PDS, PL, PDC, and PDM). Three parties of the center-left (PDT, PCB, and PC do B) were represented in almost all the alliances with parties of the center-right." See "O Sistema Político-Partidário (The Political Party System)," in Hélio Jaguaribe, organizer, Sociedade, Estado e Partidos na Atualidade Brasileira (Society, State, and Party in Contemporary Brazil), chap. 3 (São Paulo: Paz e Terra, 1992), p. 190, fn. 30. These data may help the reader appreciate the confusion facing the ordinary Brazilian voter.

electoral systems.[25] The very large districts make it easier for small parties to elect one or a few *deputados,* thus encouraging the multiplicity of parties. Fringe parties can be formed mainly to secure a morsel of free television time for sale to other parties in a coalition. The large districts also impede direct contact between constituents and representatives, undermining the basic concept of responsibility to the electorate. The open-list system in effect merges the intraparty selection of candidates (the primary in the United States) with the interparty general election. For an individual candidate, therefore, a battle against other candidates from the same party is likely to be more rewarding than fighting competing parties. A single well-known big name in a party may drag in several unknown and unqualified fellow members. The voter is faced with a baffling array of numbers, names, and party labels. It is difficult to imagine electoral mechanics more adverse to the classic function of democratic political parties.

The absence of effective accountability permits legislators to regard their offices more as personal prizes than as public trusts. At both federal and state levels, there are lavish legal perquisites in office expenditures, housing and travel allowances, and extra pay for special sessions, along with frequent examples of extra-legal nepotism and outright vote-selling. They are often reported in Brazil's totally free and very energetic press, but only rarely followed by punishment at the polls or through the courts.[26] Beyond direct personal advantage, congressional attention is heavily concentrated on what Brazilians call "physiological" politics, that is, job creation and appointments and local public works projects, rather than on broader interest groupings or public policy issues of national concern.

Although the word *fisiologismo* is a typically light-hearted Brazilian coinage, its substance is a universal component of democratic politics. In the United States, as mentioned earlier, it is called pork and patronage, provided by legislators in return for votes. At the turn of the twentieth century, this was the basis of "machine politics" in the large cities, in the mold of New York's Tammany Hall. In democracies with only a few large parties, however, a greater share of political attention goes to special interest groups, which seek favorable legislation in return for their financial and organizational support to a party's candidates. And a large share of political atten-

25. See Rein Taagepera and Matthew Soberg Shugart, *Seats and Votes* (Yale University Press, 1989); Bernard Grofman and Arend Lijphart, eds., *Electoral Laws and Their Political Consequences* (New York: Agathon Press, 1986); and Matthew Soberg Shugart and John M. Carey, *Presidents and Assemblies: Constitutional Design and Electoral Dynamics* (Cambridge University Press, 1992).

26. A striking exception was the expulsion of members of Congress known as the "seven dwarfs" in the budgetary scandals of 1994.

tion and discourse goes to a third level: public interest politics, in which votes are sought in order to promote the adoption of broadly defined policies in the national interest, such as macroeconomic growth, price stability, improved education and health care, environmental protection, safety from crime and accident, administrative efficiency, or national security. All these kinds of issues play some part in Brazilian politics, but compared with more mature democracies, Brazil has an overwhelming proportion of *fisiologismo*. That fact results in part from the multiplicity of small, essentially nonprogrammatic parties generated by the electoral system. That is undoubtedly why politicians, especially legislators, are held in low esteem, even though democratic institutions are generally favored.[27]

The near unanimity of academic criticism of Brazil's political party structure is frequently supported in media editorials and statements by prominent political leaders. Unlike a total shift to parliamentarism, reform in party legislation and electoral mechanics seems difficult but not impossible. Although it would change the rules under which the congressmen voting the reforms were elected, many could hope to be reelected under a changed system and a large turnover in membership is not uncommon in any case. In the run-up to the Constitutional Congress of 1987–88, a preliminary drafting commission appointed by President Sarney and chaired by the widely respected academic jurist Afonso Arinos de Melo Franco, had recommended an electoral system similar to that of the German Federal Republic, in which half the *deputados* would be elected from single-member districts of roughly equal population (as in the United States) and the other half would be drawn from party lists in numbers sufficient to provide proportional representation of parties on a national basis in the chamber as a whole. Fringe parties would be eliminated by requiring a minimum of 3 percent of the total national vote to be represented at all (in Germany, the threshold is 5 percent).[28] Party switching would be discouraged by depriving a *deputado* of his seat if he switched parties during a congressional session.

---

27. José Alvaro Moisés reports a late 1989 political culture survey in which the performance of politicians was evaluated with the following total results: "Take care of friends and relatives," 30.1%; "Get rich off public money," 44.8%; "Defend constituents' interests," 9.1%; "Other and don't know," 16.1%. See "Elections, Political Parties and Political Culture in Brazil: Changes and Continuities," *Journal of Latin American Studies*, vol. 25 (1993), p. 602.

28. Nicolau, *Multipartidarismo e Democracia*, p. 14, fn. 8, notes that a new party law (No. 9096, dated September 1995) strengthens the requirements for the registration of a new party and also provides that a party must have 5 percent of the total vote to secure representation in Congress. The new law, however, would only become operative for the elections of 2002, and it remains to be seen whether it will be kept in force when the time comes.

Responsibility for preparing national party lists to fill out the proportional representation quotas would strengthen party organizations at the national level and concentrate their attention on national issues. Parties would be free to determine how to prepare these lists, whether by the leadership, party conventions, primary elections within the party membership at large, or some combination. Advocates of this reform make a plausible argument that party lists on a national basis would provide more highly qualified candidates than the state-level open lists now in use.[29]

These kinds of party and electoral reform were endorsed by most Brazilian political scientists in the mid-1980s. They appeared likely to prevail in the constitutional convention until they were caught up in President Sarney's battle to retain the presidential system in general and a five-year term for himself. They remain lively issues on the Brazilian national agenda, potentially as decisive as the macroeconomic reforms on which political attention has been focused since 1994. In 1997 many observers supposed that political reform might be enacted in President Cardoso's second "honeymoon" period, assuming that he would be reelected in 1998. The reelection took place, but it was followed by financial crisis instead of honeymoon (see chapter 7). In early 2000, there is still some possibility of reform to discourage meaningless tiny parties and to limit party switching, but more far-reaching changes seem unlikely before the presidential and congressional elections of 2002.

## Corruption and Violence

Corruption and violence are the dark side of political underdevelopment, reflecting failures in the rule of law. In most countries they appear together, although there are exceptions such as modern Japan, where tight gun control minimizes violence, notwithstanding large-scale financial corruption. Holding them within bounds requires substantial institutional development, without which they can badly impede economic development and undermine confidence in the political order.[30]

29. See Jaguaribe, *Sociedade, Estado e Partidos na Atualidade Brasileira*, pp. 55–60.

30. For an elaborate cross-country statistical analysis concluding that corruption impedes growth by reducing investment, see Paolo Mauro, "Corruption and Growth," *Quarterly Journal of Economics*, vol. 110 (August 1995), pp. 681–712. Unfortunately, the basic data relate to the period 1980–83, the beginning of Latin America's lost decade.

Both in folklore and in practice, Brazilians have traditionally regarded a degree of corruption as normal, especially if it caters to family or patriarchal relationships.[31] That view is implicit in the term *jeito*, a way of getting around inconvenient regulations. Another saying distinguishes mere laws from "laws that really matter" (*leis para valer*) or "laws that take hold" (*leis que pegam*). Favoritism for relatives and friends and kickbacks on public contracts have long been taken for granted, along with tax-avoiding double bookkeeping by corporations (known as *caixa dois,* the second treasury). A twice-elected governor of São Paulo in the 1960s was not embarrassed by the motto *Rouba mas Faz!* ("Steals but Achieves!"). It is not surprising that a business survey of 54 countries ranks Brazil as the fifteenth most corrupt.[32]

A parallel tradition tolerates a degree of political violence, especially in the smaller and less developed states of the Northeast and Amazônia, where land-grabbing has been common with the help of hired thugs (*jagunços*), and family and clan feuds are sometimes maintained over decades.[33] Chapter 5 noted the frequency of violence in connection with land reform. In recent years, a new source of violence has developed around drug trafficking in the larger cities, especially Rio de Janeiro and São Paulo.

All these examples have counterparts in American history. They bring to mind nineteenth-century land-grabbing in Oklahoma and blood feuds in Kentucky and West Virginia, along with the Prohibition Era and present-day urban gang violence. It is plausible to expect that economic and social modernization will in time reduce the levels of Brazilian political violence, following patterns already established there in the Southeast and South. Corruption is likely to be more tenacious, since it is linked to

31. See Marcos Otávio Bezerra, *Corrupção: Um Estudo sobre Poder Público e Relações Pessoais no Brasil* (Corruption: A Study of Public Power and Personal Relations in Brazil) (Rio de Janeiro: Relume-Dumará, ANPOCS, 1995). A historical review of Brazilian corruption going back to antecedents in Portugal appears in Pedro Rodrigues de Albuquerque Cavalcanti, *A Corrupção no Brasil* (Corruption in Brazil) (São Paulo: Edições Siciliano, 1991). An analytical discussion of various common types of corruption is in Ricardo Nahat, *Anatomia da Corrupção* (Anatomy of Corruption) (São Paulo: Câmara Brasileiro do Livro, 1991).

32. The survey by Transparency International, an NGO based in Berlin, is noted in *Brazil 1997 Country Report* (Washington: Orbis Publications, 1997), p. 116. A 1996 World Bank survey of more than 3,600 firms, both domestic and foreign-owned, in sixty-nine countries rated corruption in Latin America as a major obstacle to economic activity, although less severe than in Sub-Saharan Africa or the former Soviet Union. See *World Development Report 1997: The State in a Changing World* (Oxford University Press, 1997), pp. 35, 42.

33. For a colorful description of these practices in the small state of Alagoas, as part of a detailed journalistic account of the corruption scandals leading to the impeachment of President Collor de Mello in 1992, see José Neumanne Pinto, *A República na Lama,* 3d ed. (The Republic in the Mud) (São Paulo: Geração Editorial, 1992).

underpaid civil servants and police forces largely appointed through patronage, poorly enforced systems of business and public accounting, inadequate controls of both public and private financial institutions, and lavish political campaign expenditures, notwithstanding the availability of free television time.

On the brighter side, the Brazilian public since the restoration of civilian government has become more conscious and less tolerant of both violence and corruption. There are illuminating historical models and encouraging signs of parallel changes in Brazilian public opinion.[34] In 1992 a combination of a vigorous free press, family and personal rivalries, and diligent congressional inquiry brought to light the massive scale of corruption engineered by President Collor's campaign manager, P. C. Farias, and led to the first impeachment of a sitting president in Brazil's history. Opinion surveys showed deep civic pride in securing this dramatic punishment through constitutional procedures. Subsequent parliamentary committees of inquiry (CPIs) unearthed major congressional corruption involving budgetary manipulations (1993–94) and a large-scale fraudulent misuse of state and municipal bond issues intended to finance judicial settlements (1997). Farias was jailed for a time, a number of congressmen were expelled, and a state governor was nearly impeached. Major scandals in the banking sector, involving both government and privately owned banks, have encountered severe criticism in the media and in some cases led to fines for violation of laws against white-collar crime.

Privatization reduces opportunities for corruption in public contracting and hiring. Tentative steps toward professionalization of the civil service were taken by Vargas before World War II and greatly expanded under the Second Republic and the military regime. There are islands of high technical competence in several government ministries and the central bank. On the other hand, payrolls at all levels of government continue to be padded with thousands of patronage appointments and numerous cases of "no-shows," payment without any work. Civil service reform, especially in state and municipal bureaucracies, remains a critical necessity if corruption is to be brought within tolerable limits.

---

34. In early nineteenth-century Britain, political corruption and urban and rural violence were endemic; a century later, they had been brought under control through political reform and professionalization of civil service and police forces. In the late nineteenth century, in a much shorter period of time, the notorious patterns of corruption by political "machines" in large American cities were largely corrected by the movement for urban political reform.

## Judicial Reform

The judicial structure established in the 1988 constitution also creates impediments to Brazil's economic and social modernization. As part of its broader reaction against the military regime, the constituent assembly adopted sweeping provisions designed to ensure judicial independence, competence, and accessibility. Twelve years later, a close American scholar of judicial reform in Latin America writes:

> Apparently sensible judicial reform inputs failed to produce the desired outputs. The backlog of cases clogging the court system increased by a factor of ten in just over a decade, and trial delays increased so dramatically—more than doubling—that access for everyone resulted, paradoxically, in access for no one. The goal of promoting individual and structural judicial independence clearly was successful . . . and the courts frequently ruled against other branches of government on sensitive political and economic questions. . . . The post-reform judiciary was rife with nepotism and corruption, indifferent to public and congressional calls for transparency, and capable of resisting any measure that would improve its efficiency or scale back the generous and unjustifiable perquisites the courts had granted themselves. It was, in the words of one legislator, "a power above the law."[35]

The scope and complexity of the 1988 Constitution, including its economic provisions, make almost any governmental initiative subject to challenge on constitutional grounds. The Supreme Court's docket rose from 14,000 cases in 1987 to 35,000 in 1996. An especially bizarre aspect of the system is the absence of binding precedents; as a result, lower courts need not apply principles laid down by higher courts in similar cases. An effort to introduce binding precedents has been resisted by the judiciary on the curious ground that having to follow the rulings of another court would interfere with the individual independence of judges.[36] On this point, however, there are indications that Congress may overrule the courts, if necessary through constitutional amendment.

Judicial review has delayed or disrupted a number of measures important to the macroeconomic reforms of the 1990s. Every substantial privatization

---

35. William C. Prillaman, *The Judiciary and Democratic Decay in Latin America* (Westport, Conn.: Praeger, 2000), pp. 75–76. Chapter 4, "Brazil: A Shotgun Approach to Judicial Reform," contains an extensive bibliography.

36. Prillaman, *The Judiciary and Democratic Decay in Latin America,* p. 97.

has required the clearance of dozens or hundreds of temporary injunctions. More serious, the taxation of better-off pensioners to help restore solvency to social security was still under injunction at the beginning of the year 2000, with no certainty as to the ultimate outcome. The equalization (*isonomia*) principle has led the courts to ratchet up payrolls for other classes of civil servants whenever a particular class secures a pay increase. Some court decisions are reminiscent of the U.S. Supreme Court's actions at the start of Franklin Roosevelt's New Deal, with the 1937 strategic adaptation to economic and political realities still for the future.

## The Political Structure in Perspective

To sum up, the modernization of Brazil's political structure can be assessed as intermediate, less advanced than the economic but more advanced than the social. The basic concepts of consolidated democracy are all in place: the rule of law, respect for civil liberties, an independent judiciary, freedom of political organization (now including a wealth of NGOs), vigorously critical and competitive media, and ultimate responsibility to an all-inclusive electorate. The weaknesses lie in an absurdly overdetailed constitution, educational deficiencies and the absence of modern-sector employment for a large fraction of the population, the antiquated structure of public employment, and the absence of political parties capable of crystallizing the large issues of national direction into workable form for guidance by the electorate and legislative resolution.

These weaknesses are widely recognized, and some remedial action has been directed against each of them in recent years. Those efforts, however, have not sufficiently recognized the strategic priority of political party reform, linked to electoral mechanics and fairer geographical representation. Reform on those fronts would facilitate progress on all the others; it may even prove indispensable to the achievement of first world status.

# 7

## From Debt and Drift to Real—and Stability?

arlier chapters have traced changes in Brazil's economic structures during the past half century, along with changes in the social and political
arenas. Here we turn to the macroeconomic conditions and policies since
the 1980s: inflation, balance of payments, trade and capital flows, domestic
and foreign indebtedness, and the results in economic growth or stagnation,
employment levels, and standards of living.

### The Lost Decades

Table 7-1 provides a global overview of the domestic economy since the
"economic miracle" of 1968–74. The dramatic shifts in two key magnitudes,
growth and inflation (table 7-1, columns 3 and 7), are charted in figure 7-1.
The miracle was followed by six more years (1975–80) of quite substantial
growth, only to be abruptly reversed by the debt crisis of the 1980s. The late
1970s were also marked by an ominous rise in inflation, which reached triple
digits in 1980. In 1981 growth and investment shrank, never to recover the
levels of the miracle era. The woeful lost decade that followed, prolonged far
into the 1990s, witnessed the worst macroeconomic performance in Brazilian history. Output per capita stagnated through two decades, with almost
no improvement from 1980 to 1999 (table 7-1, column 4).

The proximate causes of this reversal, as summarized in chapter 3, were
external shocks, starting with the quadrupling of world oil prices in 1973–74
and their further doubling in 1979. In the early 1980s, oil prices collapsed,
but the balance of payments came under even greater stress from the huge

Table 7-1. The Lurching Domestic Economy, 1968–99

| Phase and year | 1. Population (millions) | 2. GDP (billions of current dollars) | 3. GDP, real increase (percent) | 4. GNP per capita (constant 1995 dollars) | 5. Gross domestic investment (percent of GDP) | 6. Domestic savings[a] (percent of GDP) | 7. Annual inflation[b] (percent, year end) | 8. Rate of open unemployment (percent) |
|---|---|---|---|---|---|---|---|---|
| "Economic Miracle" | | | | | | | | |
| 1968 | 91.3 | 34.1 | 11.4 | 2,219 | 18.6 | 17.4 | 25 | n.a. |
| 1969 | 93.7 | 37.4 | 9.7 | 2,373 | 19.0 | 21.1 | 19 | n.a. |
| 1970 | 96.0 | 42.6 | 8.8 | 2,548 | 18.7 | 19.0 | 19 | n.a. |
| 1971 | 98.4 | 49.2 | 11.3 | 2,768 | 19.9 | 18.6 | 19 | n.a. |
| 1972 | 100.8 | 58.8 | 12.1 | 3,028 | 20.3 | 18.7 | 16 | n.a. |
| 1973 | 103.2 | 84.1 | 14.0 | 3,372 | 20.4 | 20.0 | 16 | n.a. |
| Adjustment to external shocks | | | | | | | | |
| 1974 | 105.6 | 110.4 | 9.0 | 3,593 | 21.8 | 17.9 | 35 | n.a. |
| 1975 | 108.2 | 129.9 | 5.2 | 3,671 | 23.3 | 20.5 | 29 | n.a. |
| 1976 | 110.8 | 154.0 | 9.8 | 3,932 | 22.4 | 19.1 | 46 | n.a. |
| 1977 | 113.4 | 177.2 | 4.6 | 4,012 | 21.3 | 19.8 | 39 | n.a. |
| 1978 | 116.2 | 201.2 | 3.2 | 4,014 | 22.3 | 19.6 | 41 | n.a. |
| 1979 | 118.9 | 223.5 | 6.8 | 4,170 | 23.4 | 18.3 | 77 | n.a. |
| 1980 | 121.7 | 237.8 | 9.1 | 4,423 | 22.9 | 17.9 | 110 | 6.5 |
| Debt crisis and redemocratization | | | | | | | | |
| 1981 | 124.4 | 258.6 | -4.4 | 4,101 | 24.3 | 19.9 | 95 | 7.9 |
| 1982 | 127.2 | 271.3 | 0.6 | 3,995 | 23.0 | 16.6 | 100 | 6.3 |
| 1983 | 129.9 | 189.5 | -3.4 | 3,751 | 19.9 | 14.8 | 211 | 6.7 |
| 1984 | 132.6 | 189.7 | 5.3 | 3,873 | 18.9 | 17.7 | 224 | 7.1 |
| 1985 | 135.2 | 211.1 | 7.9 | 4,116 | 18.0 | 20.3 | 235 | 5.3 |

*Stagnation and inflation*

| | | | | | | | | |
|---|---|---|---|---|---|---|---|---|
| 1986 | 137.9 | 257.8 | 8.0 | 4,396 | 20.0 | 18.0 | 65 | 3.6 |
| 1987 | 140.4 | 282.4 | 3.6 | 4,505 | 23.2 | 22.7 | 416 | 3.7 |
| 1988 | 143.0 | 305.7 | -0.1 | 4,410 | 24.3 | 25.7 | 1,038 | 3.8 |
| 1989 | 145.5 | 415.9 | 3.3 | 4,524 | 26.9 | 27.1 | 1,783 | 3.3 |
| 1990 | 147.9 | 469.3 | -4.3 | 4,026 | 20.2 | 18.0 | 1,477 | 4.3 |
| 1991 | 150.3 | 405.7 | 1.3 | 4,003 | 18.1 | 11.4 | 480 | 4.8 |
| 1992 | 152.7 | 387.3 | -0.5 | 4,046 | 18.4 | 12.9 | 1,158 | 5.8 |
| 1993 | 155.0 | 429.7 | 4.9 | 4,040 | 19.3 | 14.6 | 2,708 | 5.3 |
| *Stabilization* | | | | | | | | |
| 1994 | 157.2 | 543.1 | 5.9 | 4,221 | 20.8 | 16.6 | 1,094 | 5.1 |
| 1995 | 159.4 | 705.4 | 4.2 | 4,349 | 20.5 | 20.3 | 14.8 | 4.6 |
| 1996 | 161.5 | 775.5 | 2.8 | 4,428 | 19.3 | 19.3 | 9.3 | 5.4 |
| *Renewed uncertainty* | | | | | | | | |
| 1997 | 163.7 | 801.7 | 3.2 | 4,514 | 19.9 | 20.8 | 7.5 | 5.7 |
| 1998 | 165.8 | 775.5 | -0.1 | 4,453 | 19.9 | 17.4 | 1.7 | 7.6 |
| 1999 | 167.8 | 556.8 | 0.9 | 4,427 | n.a. | n.a. | 20.0 | 7.6 |

Sources: Population data from Instituto Brasileiro de Geografia e Estatística (IBGE). Economic data from IBGE and Banco Central, except GDP real increase and per capita GNP from World Bank, *World Development Indicators, 2000*, on CD-ROM.

n.a. Not available.

a. Brazil's national income accounting procedures calculate domestic savings as a residual, so that apparent fluctuations in periods of high inflation may not reflect the underlying savings behavior in the real economy.

b. Annual inflation is IGP-DI (General Price Index—Domestic Availabilities), a weighted average of wholesale, retail, and construction price indexes.

Figure 7-1. *Growth and Inflation, 1968–99*

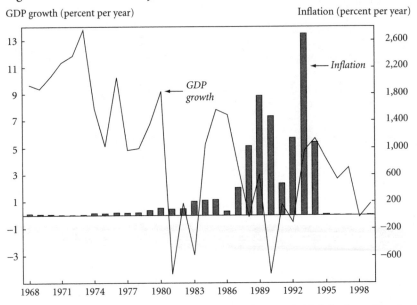

GDP growth (percent per year)                                    Inflation (percent per year)

Sources: GDP data are from IBGE (Instituto Brasileiro de Geografia e Estatística). Inflation data are December to December increases in IGP-DI (General Price Index, Domestic Availabilities), a weighted average of wholesale, retail, and construction price indexes compiled monthly by the Fundação Getúlio Vargas. Both series are republished monthly in *Conjuntura Econômica*.

rise in world interest rates, mainly due to counterinflationary policies in the United States. At the same time, Brazil's export earnings were depressed by a slowdown in worldwide rates of growth and the consequent decline in primary product prices. The culminating event in this gloomy record came in August 1982 with Mexico's default on payments to foreign commercial creditors, inducing a sharp reduction in foreign bank lending to the rest of Latin America, including Brazil.

The external shocks were compounded by Brazilian policies that amplified their effects, notably the huge borrowings abroad at variable interest rates and the weakness of domestic fiscal and monetary discipline. Chapter 3 described the overall economic responses under Presidents Geisel and Figueiredo (1974–85) as an alternation of stop-and-go policies. At first, in the 1970s, they sought to maintain high rates of growth, financing the needed imports by borrowing petro-dollars from American, European, and Japanese banks, by promoting a major new phase of import substitution in capital goods, and in 1979 by a maxi-devaluation of the exchange rate. From 1981 on, however, the mode shifted perforce to crisis management, accepting a major growth recession and vigorously promoting exports in order to sustain a minimum essential level of imports while warding off outright hyperinflation.[1] This was also the period of major political transition—the final but extended phase of return to democratic control and civilian leadership, in which executive attention was distracted by popular demonstrations, labor disputes, and rearguard actions by hard-line military officers. Especially under President Figueiredo, macroeconomic policy was subordinated to efforts—ultimately defeated—to secure a civilian succession on the political right of center.[2]

## The Balance of Payments and the Debt Crisis

During the early 1980s, economic policy attention was focused on foreign debt and the balance of payments. The goal was to maintain an indispensable volume of imports while promoting major shifts in trade patterns and reducing the burden of foreign interest payments. Table 7-2 presents the year-by-year evolution of all the main variables. (see also figures 7-2, 7-3, and 7-4).

The shifts in trade patterns stand out in figure 7-2 (table 7-2, columns 1, 2, and 3). The near balance of imports and exports in the miracle years was destroyed by the oil price shocks, which generated trade deficits for six years out of seven in 1974–80. Then, starting in 1981, export promotion was combined with intensified import substitution and compression to produce large annual trade surpluses—in the range of $10 billion to $20 billion—for more than a decade, spanning the return to civilian government in 1985.[3]

1. Many writers apply the term "hyperinflation" to Brazil's record in the late 1980s and early 1990s, when in four years the annual rate ranged from 1,300 to 2,600 percent. I prefer to reserve that term for cases where the currency becomes completely worthless, an experience that Brazil managed to avoid. The most thorough and professional analysis of these events and policies is in Donald V. Coes, *Macroeconomic Crises, Policies, and Growth in Brazil, 1964–1990* (Washington: World Bank, 1995).

2. The intensity of these preoccupations emerges vividly from a detailed account by a younger close associate of Tancredo Neves, based on extensive interviewing along with documentary sources. See Ronaldo Costa Couto, *História Indiscreta da Ditadura e da Abertura; Brasil, 1964–1985* (Indiscreet History of the Dictatorship and the Opening: Brazil, 1964–1985) (Rio de Janeiro: Editora Record, 1999). See also Gláucio Ary Dillon Soares and others, *21 Anos de Regime Militar—Balanços e Perspectivas* (Twenty-One Years of Military Rule—Assessments and Perspectives) (Rio de Janeiro: Editora da Fundação Getúlio Vargas, 1994).

3. The trade data are in current U.S. dollars, uncorrected for inflation in the United States. They show exports in 1988 as 2.8 times the value of 1977. When corrected by the U.S. wholesale price index, that ratio falls to 1.7 times, still a remarkable achievement. A similar correction would also apply to the import side.

Table 7-2. Balance of International Payments, 1968–99[a]
Millions of dollars, except as indicated

| Year | 1. Exports | 2. Imports | 3. Trade balance | 4. Terms of trade (1968–96 = 100) | 5. Services balance | 6. Interest and profits | 7. Current account balance | 8. Capital account balance | 9. Overall balance | International reserves | | 12. Gross foreign debt |
|---|---|---|---|---|---|---|---|---|---|---|---|---|
| | | | | | | | | | | 10. Quantity | 11. Months of imports | |
| 1968 | 1,881 | 1,855 | +26 | 112 | −556 | −228 | −508 | +541 | +32 | 266 | 1.7 | 3,780 |
| 1969 | 2,311 | 1,993 | +318 | 118 | −630 | −263 | −281 | +871 | +549 | 657 | 4.0 | 4,403 |
| 1970 | 2,739 | 2,507 | +232 | 130 | −815 | −353 | −562 | +1,015 | +545 | 1,190 | 5.7 | 5,295 |
| 1971 | 2,905 | 3,245 | −341 | 121 | −980 | −420 | −1,307 | +1,846 | +530 | 1,754 | 6.5 | 6,622 |
| 1972 | 3,991 | 4,235 | −244 | 139 | −1,250 | −520 | −1,489 | +3,492 | +2,439 | 4,219 | 12.0 | 9,521 |
| 1973 | 6,199 | 6,192 | +7 | 140 | −1,722 | −712 | −1,688 | +3,512 | +2,179 | 6,509 | 12.6 | 12,572 |
| 1974 | 7,951 | 12,641 | −4,690 | 121 | −2,433 | −900 | −7,123 | +6,254 | −936 | 5,463 | 5.2 | 17,166 |
| 1975 | 8,670 | 12,210 | −3,540 | 112 | −3,162 | −1,732 | −6,702 | +6,189 | −950 | 4,166 | 4.1 | 21,171 |
| 1976 | 10,128 | 12,383 | −2,255 | 125 | −3,763 | −2,189 | −6,017 | +6,594 | +1,192 | 6,667 | 6.5 | 25,985 |
| 1977 | 12,120 | 12,023 | +97 | 147 | −4,134 | −2,559 | −4,037 | +5,278 | +630 | 7,442 | 7.4 | 32,037 |
| 1978 | 12,659 | 13,683 | −1,024 | 126 | −6,037 | −4,232 | −6,990 | +11,891 | +4,262 | 12,190 | 10.7 | 43,511 |
| 1979 | 15,244 | 18,084 | −2,840 | 116 | −7,920 | −5,542 | −10,742 | +7,657 | −3,215 | 9,839 | 6.4 | 49,904 |
| 1980 | 20,132 | 22,955 | −2,823 | 96 | −10,152 | −6,621 | −12,807 | +9,679 | −3,472 | 6,913 | 3.1 | 53,848 |
| 1981 | 23,293 | 22,091 | +1,202 | 81 | −13,135 | −9,531 | −11,734 | +12,773 | +625 | 7,507 | 3.6 | 61,411 |
| 1982 | 20,175 | 19,395 | +780 | 79 | −17,082 | −11,935 | −16,310 | +7,851 | −8,828 | 3,994 | 2.5 | 69,654 |
| 1983 | 21,899 | 15,429 | +6,470 | 79 | −14,415 | −10,313 | −6,837 | +2,103 | −5,405 | 4,563 | 3.1 | 81,319 |
| 1984 | 27,005 | 13,916 | +13,089 | 85 | −13,215 | −10,999 | +45 | +253 | +700 | 11,995 | 10.3 | 91,091 |
| 1985 | 25,639 | 13,153 | +12,486 | 85 | −12,877 | −10,716 | −242 | −2,554 | −3,200 | 11,608 | 10.6 | 95,857 |

| 1986 | 22,349 | 14,044 | +8,305 | 92 | −13,695 | −10,677 | −5,304 | −7,108 | −12,356 | 6,760 | 5.8 | 101,759 |
| 1987 | 26,224 | 15,051 | +11,173 | 98 | −12,678 | −9,702 | −1,436 | −746 | −2,987 | 7,458 | 5.9 | 107,514 |
| 1988 | 33,789 | 14,605 | +19,184 | 101 | −15,103 | −11,371 | +4,175 | +3,365 | +6,977 | 9,140 | 7.5 | 102,555 |
| 1989 | 34,383 | 18,263 | +16,120 | 79 | −15,331 | −12,016 | +1,033 | −3,648 | −3,391 | 9,679 | 6.4 | 99,285 |
| 1990 | 31,414 | 20,661 | +10,753 | 67 | −15,369 | −11,340 | −3,782 | −4,715 | −8,825 | 9,973 | 5.8 | 96,546 |
| 1991 | 31,620 | 21,041 | +10,579 | 74 | −13,542 | −9,286 | −1,407 | −4,148 | −4,679 | 9,406 | 5.4 | 92,996 |
| 1992 | 35,793 | 20,554 | +15,239 | 90 | −11,339 | −7,827 | +6,143 | +25,271 | +30,028 | 23,754 | 13.9 | 110,835 |
| 1993 | 38,563 | 25,256 | +13,307 | 84 | −15,585 | −10,111 | −592 | +10,115 | +8,404 | 32,211 | 15.3 | 114,270 |
| 1994 | 43,545 | 33,079 | +10,466 | 71 | −14,743 | −8,821 | −1,689 | +14,294 | +12,939 | 38,806 | 14.1 | 119,668 |
| 1995 | 46,506 | 49,858 | −3,352 | 61 | −18,594 | −10,748 | −17,972 | +29,359 | +13,480 | 51,840 | 12.5 | 129,313 |
| 1996 | 47,747 | 53,286 | −5,539 | 71 | −21,707 | −12,214 | −24,347 | +32,148 | +8,774 | 60,110 | 13.5 | 142,148 |
| 1997 | 52,990 | 61,347 | −8,357 | 51 | −26,897 | −15,988 | −33,054 | +25,864 | −7,865 | 52,173 | 10.2 | 163,283 |
| 1998 | 51,120 | 57,594 | −6,484 | 51 | −30,351 | −19,129 | −34,981 | +15,924 | −17,265 | 44,556 | 9.3 | 210,458 |
| 1999 | 48,006 | 49,212 | −1,206 | n.a. | −25,212 | −19,228 | −24,375 | +16,552 | −7,822 | 36,342 | 8.9 | 213,585 |

Sources: Banco Central, data reported monthly and republished in *Conjuntura Econômica*.

a. Column 7 differs from the sum of columns 3 and 5 because of unilateral transfers. Column 9 differs from the sum of columns 7 and 8 because of "errors and omissions." The data in column 6 are included in column 5.

Figure 7-2. *Balance of Trade, 1968–99*

Billions of U.S. dollars                                    Terms (1968–96 = 100) of trade

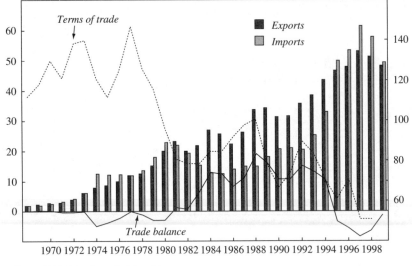

Source: Table 7-2, columns 1, 2, 3, and 4.

That record was all the more remarkable since in those years Brazil's terms of trade (the ratio of export prices to import prices) were suffering a long-term deterioration that far outlasted the era of high oil prices (see figure 7-2 and table 7-2, column 4).

Until 1984, however, the gains on the trade account were offset by increased deficits in services, which consisted mainly of interest payments and profit remittances to foreign investors (table 7-2, columns 4 and 5 and figure 7-3). Overall equilibrium, therefore, required a continuous inflow of foreign capital (table 7-2, column 8 and figure 7-4), mainly in the form of bank loans to both governmental entities and private business, but they were in large part cut off after the Mexican moratorium.[4] Brazil's international reserves then fell to only three months' imports during four years on end (1980–83, table 7-2, column 11), well below levels considered essential for national safety. The capital account (table 7-2, column 8 and figure 7-4) shifted dramatically, from a five-year surplus of almost $50 billion in 1978–82 to a

4. Table 7-2, column 12, shows a continuing increase in gross foreign debt in the years 1983–87, but, in the words of Donald Coes: "Part, if not all, of the increase ... was simply forced lending to finance interest payments. It did not have a real counterpart in the form of additional resources entering the country through the capital account." Coes, *Macroeconomic Crises, Policies, and Growth in Brazil*, p. 117.

Figure 7-3.  *Balance on Current Account, 1968–99*

Billions of U.S. dollars

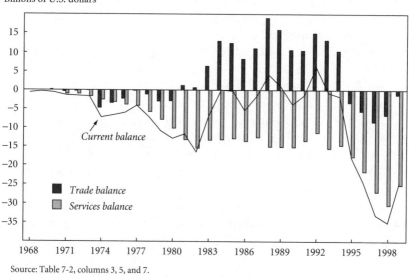

Source: Table 7-2, columns 3, 5, and 7.

Figure 7-4.  *Overall Payments Balance and Reserves, 1968–99*

Billions of U.S. dollars

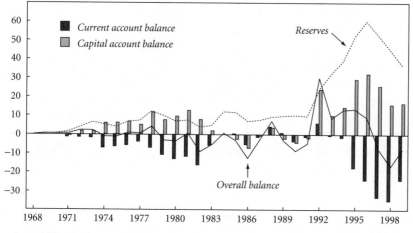

Source: Table 7-2, columns 7, 8, 9, and 10.

deficit of $8 billion in 1983–87, a net unfavorable shift of 4 percent a year of GDP. That movement ran counter to the normal expectation that capital should flow from richer to poorer countries. It sharply reduced gross investment rates and helped inaugurate Brazil's long era of "stagflation." From 1980 to 1983, per capita output fell by 12 percent, while the inflation rate doubled from 100 to 200 percent a year (table 7-1, columns 4 and 7).

The Mexican default had stunned the world of international finance. The main lending banks suspended the almost automatic rollover of expiring credits to developing country debtors. In some of the large banks, especially in New York, there were spreading doubts about the adequacy of loan loss reserves. Defaults in Latin America might even threaten their solvency, raising in some minds the specter of a second 1929–31, a global financial crisis bringing on another Great Depression.

Diagnosing the problem as a shortage of short-term liquidity, the International Monetary Fund joined with the U.S. Federal Reserve system in organizing emergency rescue packages to permit uninterrupted interest payments by Mexico, Brazil, and the other debtor countries, while encouraging reschedulings of principal payments through negotiations by the governments with a representative committee of the main lending banks. Brazil's policymakers perforce gave top priority to maintaining international lines of credit at least for short-term trade financing. Although their negotiating position would have been strengthened by formal IMF approval of macroeconomic policies, the IMF had become a whipping boy of populist politics. The decaying military regime therefore deferred the submittal of a letter of intent to the IMF until after the congressional elections of late 1982. The next two years witnessed no less than seven such letters. Although there were repeated suspensions and revisions as inflation rates regularly exceeded the targets,[5] IMF support sufficed to avoid a rupture in trade financing and to underpin negotiations for rescheduling repayments of principal, but not interest, with both governmental and banking creditors. In 1984 and 1985, the successful export drive and improved terms of trade, especially with falling oil prices, relieved Brazil's balance of payments enough to secure substantial increases in international reserves. Inflation rates, however, were running at more than 200 percent a year as the military regime came to an end.

---

5. For a detailed account, see Maria Silvia Bastos Marques, "FMI: A Experiência Brasileira Recente" (IMF: Brazil's Recent Experience), in Paulo Nogueira Batista Jr., organizer, *Novos Ensaios sobre o Setor Externo da Economia Brasileira* (New Essays on the External Sector of the Brazilian Economy) (Rio de Janeiro: Editora da Fundação Getúlio Vargas, 1988), pp. 261–91.

In North-South political relations more broadly, already soured by two decades of endless and fruitless debate on a "New International Economic Order," the debt crisis fueled new recriminations on moral responsibilities, but with little practical effect on availability of foreign funds.[6] With historical perspective, it is clear that both lenders and borrowers had taken undue risks during the 1970s and had a common interest in avoiding outright ruptures, but all felt sufficiently endangered to make them bargain hard and long. The bitter experience also laid the foundation for constructively revolutionary changes in macroeconomic policies in all the larger economies of Latin America. In Brazil, however, those changes were delayed by the institutional transition and a series of political misadventures, so the lead in working out new relationships with creditors fell to Mexico.

For Brazil, the years 1985 to 1992 showed elements of Greek tragedy in both politics and economics—an alternation of euphoria and despair. On the political side, euphoria at the restoration of civilian government and full political liberties was followed by despair at the tragic death of president-elect Tancredo Neves from botched surgery on the eve of his scheduled inauguration. On assuming the presidency, Vice President José Sarney appointed the cabinet ministers already designated by Neves, but at first the new president seemed a weak leader. In 1986 the apparent success of the Cruzado Plan generated a new wave of euphoria, sufficient to win him a commanding congressional majority in the October elections. By year's end, however, disillusion set in again as the Cruzado Plan collapsed. Then political attention shifted to constitution-drafting by the full Congress, with a wave of euphoria in 1988 at its guarantees of political liberties and democratic participation. Unfortunately, however, the new constitution also entrenched privileges for a vast array of special interest groups, including government employees, and rigid fiscal privileges for states and municipalities. By 1989, when annual inflation reached four digits, the government's popularity had fallen to new lows. Attention then shifted to the first direct presidential election since 1960.

6. The Latin American debt crisis generated a large literature in English, Spanish, and Portuguese over the decade 1983–93, most of which was ephemeral. Of more lasting interest is Pedro-Pablo Kuczynski, *Latin American Debt* (Johns Hopkins University Press, 1988). Kuczynski was raised in Peru and had been a cabinet minister there before migrating to the United States and taking up a prominent career in international banking. The book combines a highly competent technical analysis of the subject with a sympathetic understanding of the motivations of all the actors involved and the impact on the real economies of Latin America.

On the economic side, by 1985 accelerating inflation was replacing the foreign debt problem as the major concern.[7] Some of the foreign creditor banks had become more accommodating after improving their loan loss reserve positions. In 1986, however, as the Cruzado Plan was giving way to a major new surge of inflation, Brazil's capital balance turned sharply negative and reserves were again approaching dangerous levels. In February 1987, Finance Minister Dilson Funaro surprised the financial world by declaring a moratorium on interest payments to the foreign banks, apparently hoping, but vainly, that the shock might precipitate a negotiated reduction. Later that year, Brazil resumed interest payments, and Sarney's last finance minister, Maílson da Nóbrega, forswore further shock treatments, domestic or external.

By 1989 first world governments and bankers were wearying of endless rescheduling negotiations and anxious to reopen Latin American markets for both loans and equity investments. The 1985 initiative of U.S. Treasury Secretary James Baker, intended to increase commercial bank lending in Latin America, was not yielding the hoped-for results. The way out was finally pointed by the new treasury secretary, Nicholas Brady. His plan combined substantial debt write-down with expanded support from the international financial institutions (IMF, World Bank, and Inter-American Development Bank) and U.S. government guarantees of commercial bank loans at longer terms and lower interest rates, all on condition of market-oriented macroeconomic reforms by the borrowing country governments.[8] Mexico responded immediately to the Brady Plan, followed by the Philippines, Costa Rica, Venezuela, and Uruguay. By then, however, the Sarney administration in Brasília was a "lame duck," demoralized by the collapse of the Cruzado Plan and the subsequent "Bresser" and "Summer" plans. It was focused on warding off runaway hyperinflation, pending the installation of

7. There was also a significant competing school of thought that downplayed the problem of inflation, arguing that the prime necessity was maintenance of growth through accelerated changes in economic structures on the lines pursued in the mid-1970s, rather than orthodox fiscal and monetary measures to achieve price stability. See Antônio Barros de Castro and Francisco Eduardo Pires de Souza, *A Economia Brasileira em Marcha Forçada* (The Brazilian Economy in Forced March) (Rio de Janeiro: Paz e Terra, 1985). Brazilian economists and policy analysts continued throughout the 1990s to debate the merits of priority for inflation control versus priority for renewed growth. My own opinion is that this debate is misplaced, since inflation control is a necessary, but decidedly not sufficient, condition for renewed and sustained growth. The debate should be shifted to the domain beyond inflation control: inflation control plus what?

8. A full description of the elaborate steps involved in a Brady Plan renegotiation is in World Bank, *World Debt Tables 1994–95*, vol. 1, p. 69. For a critical review of these developments, see Benjamin J. Cohen, "U.S. Debt Policy in Latin America: The Melody Lingers on," in *In the Shadow of the Debt: Emerging Issues in Latin America* (New York: Twentieth Century Fund Press, 1992), chap. 8.

newly elected President Fernando Collor de Mello, and in no condition to initiate a major new negotiation with foreign creditors.

On his inauguration in March 1990, Collor announced three macroeconomic policy goals: (1) to end inflation "with a single bullet"; (2) to open the economy to foreign trade and investment; and (3) to privatize state-owned firms in potentially competitive sectors, starting with the steel industry. The first goal proved illusory, but the other two initiated far-reaching changes in Brazilian policies. Since regularizing the foreign debt was an essential requirement of all three goals, the government entered Brady-style negotiations with the bankers' advisory committee late in 1990. The arrears in interest payments were settled in May 1991 and the longer-term debt in July 1992.[9]

Even under the shadow of impeachment proceedings against Collor, 1992 turned out to be a banner year for Brazil's balance of payments. It included a $15 billion trade surplus, an overall positive balance of $30 billion, and a jump in international reserves to the record level of $24 billion, worth almost fourteen months of imports. The gross volume of foreign debt, which had fallen steadily since 1987 (see table 7-2, column 12), took another steep upward turn. By then, however, macroeconomic policy attention was focused on the control of inflation, which had reached four-digit annual rates in 1988.

## The Inflationary Tiger: Fiscal and Monetary Policies

Brazil has experienced chronic inflation since the earliest years of independence from Portugal. One historical researcher found a tenfold increase from the 1830s to the 1930s, compared with only 33 percent in the United States.[10] A tenfold increase in a century averages only 7 percent a year, but from World War II through 1994, much higher rates took over, with a dominant trend toward accelerating inflation. There were only four brief reversals of this trend (see figure 7-5): (1) the immediate postwar disinflation (1946–52); (2) the first decade of military rule (1964–73); (3) the short-lived

9. For the details, see Marcos Caramuru de Paiva, "A Dívida Externa e as Questões Financeiras Internacionais" (The Foreign Debt and International Financial Issues), in José Augusto Guilhon Albuquerque, Sessenta Anos de Política Externa Brasileira (1930–1990) (Sixty Years of Brazilian Foreign Policy) (São Paulo: Cultura Editores Associados, 1996), vol. 2, pp. 65–78.

10. Oliver Ónody, A Inflação Brasileira (Brazilian Inflation) (Rio de Janeiro, published by the author, 1960), p. 25. Note, however, the methodological criticisms in IBGE, Estatísticas Históricas, pp. 134–35. For the U.S. figure, see U.S. Department of Commerce, Historical Statistics of the United States, vol. 1, p. 211.

Figure 7-5. *The Inflationary Heritage, 1935–99*

Annual inflation (percent)                                    Monthly inflation (percent)

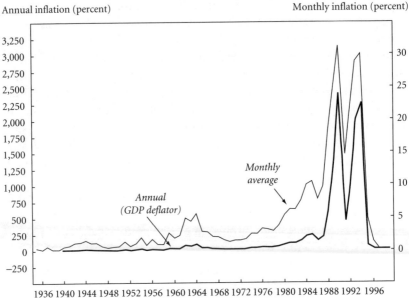

Source: Until 1947, IBGE, *Estatísticas Historicas*, table 5-2; after 1947, IBGE, National Accounts.

Cruzado Plan (1986); and (4) the Collor shock (1990). The annual rate moved up from two digits (1953–81) to three digits (1982–87) and four digits (1988–94), on the verge of unrestrained hyperinflation.

The underlying causes of accelerating inflation were hotly debated in the 1950s and 1960s between two schools of thought: "monetary" and "structural." The debate was somewhat contrived, since structuralists were concerned with underlying causes while monetarists focused on the institutional mechanisms generating price increases.[11] Whatever the ultimate causes, the proximate cause was monetization of fiscal deficits by the central bank. In Brazil, fiscal deficits were not limited to revenue shortfalls in the central government budgets. State governments and even municipalities borrowed heavily from state-owned banks, which never went bankrupt and whose accumulating bad loans were periodically taken over by the federal government's Bank of Brazil. Chronic inflation encouraged unrealistic budgeting, with seemingly generous promises eroding in real value and numerous projects left unfinished because funding became insufficient. Publicly owned enterprises, sometimes called *autarquias,* likewise operated with soft bud-

11. See Daniel Heymann and Axel Leijonhufvud, *High Inflation* (Oxford: Clarendon Press, 1995), chap. 2.

geting and no risk of bankruptcy. When the refinancing requirements of the Bank of Brazil came to exceed the public's willingness to lend at tolerable interest rates, the difference was monetized.[12]

In 1964 seemingly unrestrained inflation, with prices rising at annual rates above 100 percent (or 6 percent a month), had been one of the factors leading to the military assumption of power. The new regime, guided by Finance Minister Octávio Bulhões and Planning Minister Roberto Campos, gave top priority to combating inflation, essentially by the orthodox remedies of fiscal and monetary discipline and limitations on wage increases, backed by reforms in the tax structure and creation of the Central Bank.[13] The annual inflation rate was reduced progressively to a minimum of 12.5 percent in 1969. In 1968 the new finance minister, Antônio Delfim Netto, adopted a more permissive credit policy, coupled with massive foreign borrowing, to lay the foundation of the economic miracle. Recognizing that inflation rates would remain well over 10 percent for the indefinite future, and that such rates made it impossible to negotiate long-term contracts (including rents) at fixed prices, the government instituted a legal requirement for annual readjustments of wages and contracts in line with the consumer price index, thus introducing the policy known as indexation.

During the economic miracle period, this policy seemed to be eminently successful. In later years, however, as inflation rates increased and retail prices were raised every week, the interval between readjustments had to be made shorter and shorter: half-years, quarters, and then months. Indexation then came to be seen as a major factor in at least maintaining, and more likely accelerating, the rate of inflation, giving rise to the term "inflationary inertia" or "momentum"—a force propelling price increases in addition to fiscal and monetary imbalances.[14] With indexation adjustments occurring on different dates for various groups of wage earners and tenants, any freeze would be overly generous to workers and landlords who had just received their adjustments while severely penalizing those whose adjustment dates lay in the near future.

12. For a detailed quantitative analysis, see Coes, *Macroeconomic Crises, Policies, and Growth in Brazil,* chap. 5.

13. For a critical view of structural weaknesses built into the central bank from its inception, see Roberto Campos, *A Lanterna na Popa—Memórias* (The Lantern on the Stern—Memoirs) (Rio de Janeiro: Topbooks, 1994), pp. 661–74.

14. See, for example, Rudiger Dornbusch and Mário Henrique Simonsen, *Inflation, Debt, and Indexation* (MIT Press, 1983). See also Eliana Cardoso, "From Inertia to Megainflation: Brazil in the 1980s," in Michael Bruno and others, eds., *Lessons of Economic Stabilization and Its Aftermath,* (MIT Press, 1991), chap. 5, pp. 143–89. For a comprehensive bibliography, see Heymann and Leijonhufvud, *High Inflation,* pp. 208–26.

In the last two years of the military regime (1983–1985), annual inflation rates were running at more than 200 percent. Avoiding their explosion into total hyperinflation became the central preoccupation of the thirteen finance ministers who held office in the following ten years.[15] Policies fluctuated between "heterodox" shock treatments, mostly based on legislative price freezes, and more "orthodox" fiscal and monetary measures, but until 1994 the latter were aimed more at buying time than at genuine inflation control. As vividly portrayed in figure 7-6, they achieved neither price stability nor sustained economic growth.

The first and seemingly most successful of these efforts was the Cruzado Plan, launched in February 1986, by President Sarney's second finance minister, Dilson Funaro. In the previous four months, annual inflation rates had risen from 200 to more than 450 percent. The Cruzado Plan's central thrust was to attack inflationary momentum by a government-imposed price freeze, including ingenious provisions to avoid glaring inequities, along with promises of budgetary and monetary restraint. It generated immense popular enthusiasm, including volunteer "enforcers" of the price freeze at the retail level. Annual inflation rates fell to single digits for three months and low-range double digits for another four. By July, however, spreading black markets and unsustainable import surpluses pointed clearly to a basic demand-supply imbalance and an urgent need for corrective action.

With the first postmilitary congressional elections scheduled for November, Sarney rebuffed his economic advisers and postponed any macroeconomic contraction. His party won the elections, but the battle against inflation was lost, the rate returning to three digits in 1987 and four in 1988.[16] The experience cast a dark shadow on all subsequent proposals for radical anti-inflationary "shock" treatments. A short-lived price freeze, backed by more orthodox fiscal and monetary restraints, was initiated by Finance Minister Bresser Pereira in July 1987 but was abandoned after a few months. In early 1989, the Summer Plan, including another partial price freeze, also collapsed in short order. Then Sarney's last finance minister, Maílson da Nóbrega, settled for an orthodox policy, dubbed "beans and rice," designed to get through the remainder of the presidential term without outright hyperinflation. He barely succeeded, since the annual inflation rate surpassed 1,000 percent in December 1989.

15. For names and dates, see Coes, *Macroeconomic Crises, Policies, and Growth*, p. 183.

16. The Cruzado Plan generated a substantial analytical literature in both Portuguese and English. See Eliana Cardoso, "From Inertia to Megainflation," pp. 143–77, with references at pp. 176–77. See also André Lara Resende and others, *Por Que Não Deu Certo* (Why It Failed) (Porto Alegre: L&PM Editores, 1987).

Figure 7-6.  *From Roller Coaster to Stability, 1986–95*

Monthly price increases (percent)

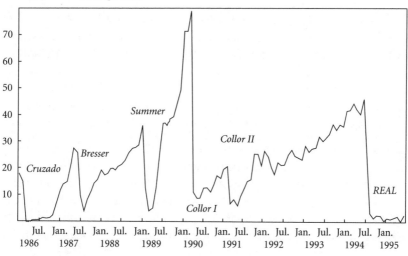

Source: General Price Index, Domestic Availabilities (IGP-DI), calculated by the Fundação Getúlio Vargas, published in *Conjuntura Econômica.*

Popularly elected President Fernando Collor de Mello took office in March 1990. He promptly launched another heterodox shock treatment, soon known as the Collor Plan. It sought not only to control prices by decree but also to reduce demand through an eighteen-month freeze of two-thirds of the economy's liquid assets, including personal savings accounts. The plan failed even at the start to reduce inflation below 9 percent monthly (an annual rate of 180 percent) and by year's end was in full retreat. Early in 1991, a second effort at price-fixing by decree (Collor II) collapsed even more rapidly.

That experience closed the era of shock treatments to fight inflation. As figure 7-6 demonstrates, the duration of stability had been shorter from shock to shock, and the subsequent inflation peaks became increasingly high, except for Collor I with its traumatic freezing of liquid assets. Thus inflation was not being overcome or even stabilized; it was accelerating, intensifying the fear of an utterly worthless currency.[17]

In mid-1991, Marcílio Marques Moreira was named Finance Minister to stave off disaster as the Collor presidency entered its terminal phase of cor-

17. For a detailed analysis of the monetary system mechanisms involved in this era of shock treatments and accelerating inflation, see World Bank, *Brazil: An Agenda for Stabilization,* Report 13168-BR (Washington 1994), chap. 3.

ruption investigations and impeachment. Looking back on the two failed plans a few years later, he wrote:

> Collor I ... embodied such great violence against the principles of an established legal order and the working rules of a market economy—unilateral breaking of contractual obligations, freezing of financial assets, disregard of vested rights—that it not only failed to achieve stabilization ... but also corroded the very idea of monetary restraint central to the Plan's logic; it also assaulted the holders of domestic private savings, alienating a large part of the new middle class which had brought Collor to victory at the polls.[18]

Experienced in both banking and diplomacy, Moreira applied more conventional fiscal and monetary instruments, ending price control, repaying the frozen assets with interest, and reversing a dangerous deficit in the balance of payments. The rate of inflation was stabilized, although still in the stratospheric range of 20–25 percent a month. A surge of capital imports relieved the balance of payments, although it also put additional pressure on prices.

With Collor's impeachment, the presidency fell to Vice President Itamar Franco, a provincial politician with populist leanings, unskilled in foreign affairs or issues of macroeconomic policy. In his first five months in office, three finance ministers were appointed and replaced. The new president refused to support more strenuous fiscal discipline, and monthly inflation rates moved into the 30–35 percent range (more than 3,000 percent a year). Then in May 1993, Itamar was persuaded to shift Foreign Minister Fernando Henrique Cardoso into the Finance Ministry.[19] That appointment laid the basis for the Real Plan, a fundamental sea change in Brazil's stormy macroeconomic history.

## The Real Plan

Cardoso had been a professor of sociology at the University of São Paulo and went into exile in Chile and France during the most repressive phase of the military regime. As political "decompression" took hold, he returned to

---

18. Marcílio Marques Moreira, "O Brasil e o Novo Contexto Econômico Internacional" (Brazil and the New International Economic Context), in José Augusto Guilhon Albuquerque, organizer, *Diplomacia Para o Desenvolvimento* (Diplomacy for Development), vol. 2 of *Sessenta Anos de Política Externa Brasileira* (Sixty Years of Brazilian Foreign Policy) (São Paulo: Cultora Editores Associados, 1996) p. 28. My informal translation.

19. Itamar Franco, elected governor of the state of Minas Gerais in 1998, is generally known by his distinctive first name rather than the common surname Franco.

Brazil and was soon elected senator from São Paulo, affiliated with the PMDB in opposition to the military. He was a principal founder of the breakaway PSDB (Social Democratic Party of Brazil), shedding the doctrinaire socialism of his youth in favor of progressive social democracy combined with market economics akin to "new Labour" in Britain. While not himself an economist or expert in macroeconomics, he was well acquainted with the highly qualified economists of the University of São Paulo and the Catholic University of Rio de Janeiro, who had been working intensively on policies to break the inflationary cycle. During Cardoso's first few months as finance minister, they developed a novel strategy for overcoming inflation without shock treatment, soon christened the Real Plan (Plano Real).[20]

In contrast to the five failed shock treatments, the Real Plan was introduced over a half-year period with each step announced in advance and without any general freezing of prices or confiscation of assets.[21] The most ingenious innovation was a transition period of four months, March through June 1994, in which wages, prices, and other contracts were calculated not only in cruzeiros, with monthly adjustments to the escalating cost of living, but also in Unidades Real de Valor (URVs, or real units of value). The wages in URVs were de facto dollar equivalents of the average wages received over the previous four-month period (November 1993 through February 1994), which became the base for adjusting the minimum wage during the transition. Although not required by law, wages above the minimum generally followed the same pattern. This device overcame the inflationary momentum generated by differences in timing of wage adjustments. In addition to wages, many rental agreements and other contracts were written in terms of URVs, and retailers began to post prices in both cruzeiros and URVs, even though the cruzeiro was still the formal unit of payment.

On July 1, 1994, all cruzeiro prices were converted to reais at the ratio 2,750:1, the then dollar exchange value of the cruzeiro, and the real became Brazil's unit of currency and means of payment. The transitional operation had been so smoothly conducted that it induced a huge inflow of capital. By

20. The name *real* for the new currency was a clever pun, since the word means royal but also real in the sense of actual or factual. In the former sense, it had been the name of a coin in Portugal and imperial Brazil, similar to the word "crown" in several European countries. In the latter sense, it implied a kind of solidity or stability that had been irretrievably lost by the cruzeiro and the cruzado. Between 1967 and 1993, there had been four 1:1000 currency replacements (making in combination a trillionfold depreciation) along with two changes of name without revaluation.

21. For a summary of the principal provisions, see Coes, *Macroeconomic Crises, Policies, and Growth in Brazil*, Epilogue, pp. 167–71. See also World Bank, *Brazil: An Agenda for Stabilization*, pp. 14–16.

December 1994, the "parallel market" exchange rate had strengthened to 87 centavos per dollar, or $1.17 per real. It then fell gradually, reaching par only in June 1996. After the conversion, price stability was to be pursued mainly through orthodox fiscal and monetary policies, including budgetary discipline at the state and local levels, along with major additional programs for privatizing state-owned enterprises and further opening of the economy to import competition.

As figure 7-7 demonstrates, the Real Plan was astoundingly successful in moving to price stability from mid-1994 through late 1998. Monthly inflation rates charted there include seasonal fluctuations, but the strong downward trend is unmistakable. Here are the year-by-year annual rates:[22]

| Full year | Percent |
|---|---|
| 1994 | 1,093.8 |
| Annual rate in second half | 91.3 |
| 1995 | 67.5 |
| 1996 | 11.1 |
| 1997 | 7.5 |
| 1998 | 1.7 |

The government's official four-year review, published in mid-1998 in English as well as Portuguese, was a paean of self-praise.[23] The achievement was the major factor in President Cardoso's first ballot reelection to a second term in October 1998. Although the downward trend was brusquely interrupted in early 1999 by the crisis discussed later in the chapter, the Real Plan, unlike its heterodox predecessors, did not collapse.

On fronts other than price stability, however, the early record of the plan was not an unambiguous success. One weak area concerned the balance of payments, as illustrated in figures 7-8 and 7-9. The black line and black bars in figure 7-8 show the sharp deterioration in the current account balance, coinciding with the introduction of the real. The surge in imports engendered by reduced trade barriers was in itself a healthy phenomenon, but it was not matched by increased exports. Growing trade deficits were financed by external investment and borrowing, leading to higher payments of interest and dividends, the main component of the services account. Foreign

22. These data are for the IGP-DI (General Price Index, Domestic Availabilities), a weighted average of wholesale, retail, and construction price indexes compiled monthly by the Fundação Getúlio Vargas and published in *Conjuntura Econômica*.

23. See Presidency of the Republic, *Real: 4 Anos que Mudaram o Brasil* (Real: Four Years That Changed Brazil) (Brasília, 1998).

Figure 7-7. *The Real Plan, 1994–99; Stabilization Progress and Setback*

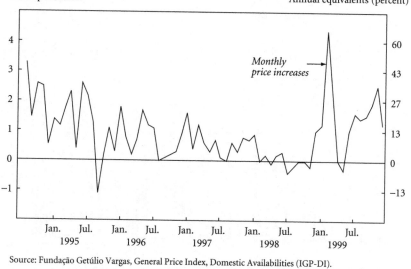

Percent per month

Annual equivalents (percent)

Source: Fundação Getúlio Vargas, General Price Index, Domestic Availabilities (IGP-DI).

Figure 7-8. *The Real and the Balance of Payments, 1992–99*

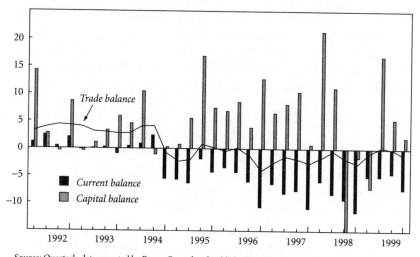

Billions of U.S. dollars

Source: Quarterly data reported by Banco Central and published in *Conjuntura Econômica*.

Figure 7-9. *External Debt and Reserves, 1992–99*

Billions of U.S. dollars

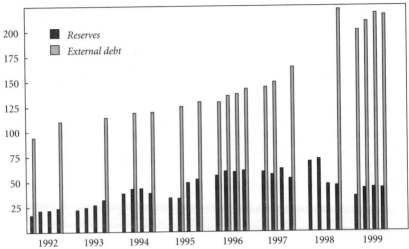

*Source:* Quarterly data reported by Banco Central and published in *Conjuntura Econômica.*

direct investments (FDI) would provide long-term benefits to the economy, but in the later 1990s a substantial share of FDI was going for privatization of existing government-owned enterprises rather than adding to the stock of fixed capital. The total current account deficit (shown as black bars in figure 7-8) was growing dangerously. Until the Asian and Russian crises of 1997–99, reserves remained at very healthy levels (figure 7-9), but at the cost of high interest rates needed to attract foreign capital and secure the domestic financing of rising public budget deficits.

Unlike Argentina's stabilization plan, which tied the peso to the dollar by statute, the exchange value of Brazil's real was not made a formal anchor for the stabilization effort. Until 1999, however, it served as a slowly moving de facto anchor, allowed to fluctuate within a narrow band that the central bank depreciated each month by about one-half percentage point. Exchange rate policy became increasingly disputed among economists and market analysts, with the São Paulo business community arguing that overvaluation was directly hampering exports and also discouraging domestic investment through its upward pressure on interest rates.[24] Those disputes were overtaken by the crises of 1997–99, discussed below.

24. For a well-informed analysis of the complex interactions among exchange rates, domestic and international interest rates and capital movements, public finance, and economic growth, see Affonso Celso Pastore, "Politica Econômica, Vulnerabilidade Externa e Crescimento" (Economic

A second area of weakness—even more critical than exchange rate policy and much more difficult to remedy—lay in fiscal performance, including state and local governments and government-owned enterprises. Here the policy goals were clear enough, but their achievement was hampered by constitutional obstacles and the deficiencies in political structure discussed in chapter 6. The Real Plan's designers were fully aware of the need for budget surpluses—or at least balance—to consolidate price stability and reduce interest rates to levels promoting sustained economic growth. As table 7-3 and figure 7-10 make painfully evident, however, the early years of the real were marked instead by a sharp worsening of the fiscal balance. (The "primary" balance excludes interest payments on public debt, while the "operational balance" includes interest payments but not the nominal marking up of the stock of debt during the era of high inflation.)

The privatization program has greatly reduced deficit financing by public enterprises and state governments can no longer turn to captive banks for unsecured loans or treat state-owned enterprises as "cash cows" by borrowing from them and not repaying. On the other hand, restrictions and entitlements in the 1988 Constitution, as well as political party competition, make it very hard to overcome the long-standing habits of dubious construction projects and wasteful public overemployment, with very generous retirement benefits.[25]

In the last few years, especially since 1997, deficits in the social security systems (Previdência) have become a major threat to budgetary discipline, a threat not foreseen when the real was introduced.[26] The contributory system for registered workers in the private sector, known as the National Institute for Social Security (INSS), moved from surpluses in the late 1980s to

Policy, External Vulnerability, and Growth), in João Paulo dos Reis Velloso, coordinator, *O Brasil e o Mundo, no limiar do novo século* (Brazil and the World at the Threshold of the New Century) (Rio de Janeiro: José Olympio, 1998), vol. 2, pp. 81–100.

25. Extreme examples are Transitory Article 19, giving life tenure to all civil servants who were on the public payrolls for five years or more when the constitution was adopted, whether or not they had been recruited by competitive examination; Article 37-XV, forbidding salary reductions; Article 40, providing retirement at full pay for men after thirty-five years and women after thirty years (thirty and twenty-five, respectively, for teachers) and increasing pensions to match any pay increases in the active service; and Article 41, giving tenure after two years to civil servants recruited by examination. In 1998 a constitutional amendment raised the ages for retirement at full pay to sixty for men and fifty-five for women, while civil service tenure under Article 41 required three years of service instead of two.

26. For an analysis by an outstanding authority on Brazilian public finance, see Raul Velloso, "A Situação das Contas Públicas Após o Real" (The Condition of the Public Accounts Following the Real), in João Paulo does Reis Velloso, coordinator, *O Brasil e o Mundo, no limiar do novo século* (Rio de Janeiro: José Olympio, 1998), vol. 2, pp. 101-35.

Table 7-3. *Primary and Operational Surpluses and Deficits, 1989–99*
Percent of GDP

| Year | Primary balance | Operational balance |
|------|-----------------|---------------------|
| 1989 | −1.00 | −6.90 |
| 1990 | +4.60 | +1.30 |
| 1991 | +2.85 | +1.35 |
| 1992 | +2.26 | −2.16 |
| 1993 | +2.67 | +0.25 |
| 1994 | +5.09 | +1.32 |
| 1995 | +0.36 | −4.88 |
| 1996 | −0.09 | −3.75 |
| 1997 | −0.92 | −4.33 |
| 1998 | +0.01 | −7.50 |
| 1999 | +3.00 | −3.90 |

Source: Banco Central.

growing deficits after 1996, mainly because of the new constitutional guarantees. The system also faces the basic long-term problem familiar to North Americans and Europeans: aging populations with longer life spans increasing the ratio of retired pensioners to active contributors. The more acute problem for the near future, however, concerns public employees, where

Figure 7-10. *Fiscal Performance and Interest Rates, 1989–99*

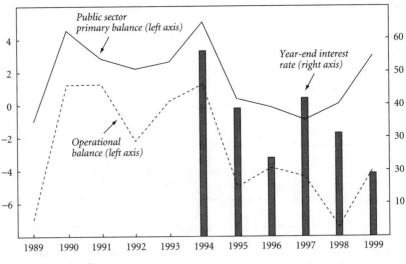

Source: Banco Central.

social security deficits have been much larger and abusive privileges more prominent.[27] In 1998, when the total social security deficit rose to 4.7 percent of GDP, the public sector accounted for more than 80 percent of that deficit, although serving a much smaller number of pensioners. Hence the salient role of social security reform in the macroeconomic crises of 1997–99 and in the struggle to preserve stabilization under the real.

It is, of course, the operational deficit, not the primary deficit, that determines the need for additional governmental borrowing and the consequent upward pressure on domestic interest rates. The total stock of Brazil's public debt, amounting at the end of 1999 to less than half the annual GDP, is not unmanageable by general international standards, but its enlargement discourages overall economic growth through its upward pressure on interest rates and absorbs budgetary resources badly needed for education, health care, and public infrastructure.

Alongside the balance of payments and fiscal deficits, the third great testing area for the Real Plan was the real economy: levels of production and employment, living standards, and the distribution of income. There again, the record since 1995 has been mixed. Figure 7-11 shows two critical indicators: overall output per capita and open unemployment.[28] Compared with the previous six years, 1993 and 1994 looked encouraging, but the trends became disappointing as the Real Plan progressed, even before the crises of 1997–99. Per capita output growth of 3 to 4 percent, while far below the rates of the miracle era, would double incomes in twenty years, but at 1 to 2 percent the doubling time rises to more than forty years. Business investment was being depressed by the high interest rates needed to finance the fiscal deficits. The stabilization policies came under increasing criticism, both domestic and foreign, as being too rigid in defending an overvalued exchange rate, whose relaxation might improve both external and internal macroeconomic performance without serious risk of a new inflationary

27. In its emergency fiscal reform message of October 1998, the Ministry of Finance noted that "the public system spends approximately R$40 billion per year to pay benefits to about 3 million retired employees, while INSS will spend about R$54 billion in 1998 on benefits for about 18 million workers." See *Programa de Estabilidade Fiscal* (Program for Fiscal Stability), October 28, 1998, p. 8.

28. The unemployment measures are the annual averages of monthly measurements by the National Statistical Institute (IBGE) in six major metropolitan regions of persons effectively seeking work during the previous thirty days and not employed in the previous seven days. They are generally considered more conservative than conventional unemployment statistics in advanced countries and are always much lower than the estimates of a respected trade union institute (DIEESE) in Greater São Paulo. Brazil's very high share of jobs in the informal labor market creates serious technical obstacles to accurate measurement of unemployment. Nevertheless, the IBGE figures are a good indicator of trends over time, which is the key point in the discussion here.

Figure 7-11. *Slowing Growth and Rising Unemployment, 1985–99*

Percent

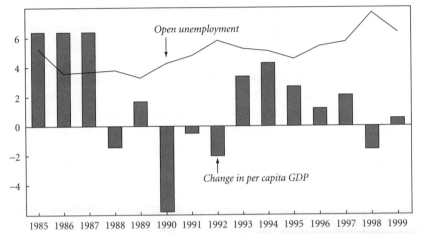

Sources: GDP change calculated from data published quarterly by IBGE. Unemployment data collected and published monthly by Fundação Getúlio Vargas, Instituto Brasileira de Economia.

cycle. Perhaps because of reluctance to "rock the boat" during the electoral season of 1998, in which the sitting president could now stand for reelection, remedial action was put off until forced by dramatic changes in the international capital markets.

## The Crises of 1997–99

At its very beginning, the Real Plan had been threatened by a "tequila effect" spillover from Mexico's foreign exchange crisis of 1994, but that danger passed almost without trace. The late 1990s were a different story, with capital flight triggered by crises in southeast Asia (1997) and Russia (1998) even though Brazil had little interaction with those economies. As shown in figures 7-12 and 7-13, tracing developments month by month, the macroeconomic impacts and policy responses in Brazil were strikingly different in the two cases.

The Asian crisis of 1997, starting with Thailand and then spreading to Korea, Indonesia, and beyond, surprised and shocked the international investment community but had no obvious relevance to Latin America. Until that September, Brazil seemed on a stable course, with international reserves in the range of $55 billion to $60 billion and interest rates gradually declining. Then in October, a wave of speculation against the real brought

Figure 7-12.  *The Crises of 1997–99*

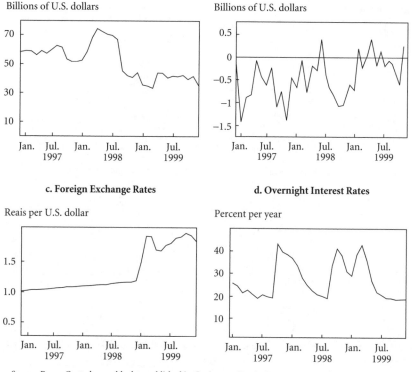

a. International Reserves

Billions of U.S. dollars

b. Trade Balance

Billions of U.S. dollars

c. Foreign Exchange Rates

Reais per U.S. dollar

d. Overnight Interest Rates

Percent per year

Source: Banco Central, monthly data published in *Conjuntura Econômica.*

reserves down by $8 billion in a single month. The central bank reacted by raising interest rates from 19 to 43 percent, while the Finance Ministry announced a package of fiscal measures increasing taxes and cutting expenditures. The tax side was effective, but in that election year for president, governors, and Congress, most of the expenditure cuts were resisted in Congress or abandoned by the government. Exchange rate policy remained unaltered.

For the short term, these policy measures were remarkably successful. As seen in figure 7-12, reserves rose steadily from November 1997 to April 1998, reaching an all-time high of $75 billion, while interest rates fell each month until by August they were lower than before the crisis. Then came a new external shock, this time from Russia's default on external debt and the major devaluation of the ruble. Since Brazil's economic links with Russia

Figure 7-13. *Growth, Inflation, and Fiscal Outcomes, 1997–99*

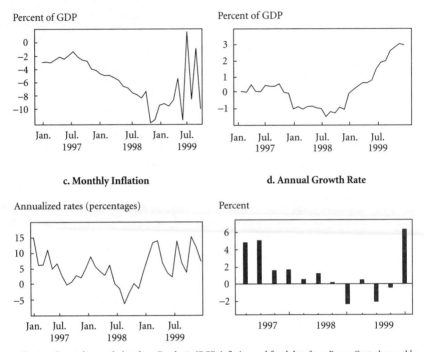

a. Operational Deficit, 1997–1999

Percent of GDP

b. Primary Balance

Percent of GDP

c. Monthly Inflation

Annualized rates (percentages)

d. Annual Growth Rate

Percent

Sources: Quarterly growth data from Fundação IBGE; inflation and fiscal data from Banco Central, monthly reports.

were even sparser than those with southeast Asia, the government apparently supposed that the experience of 1997 could be repeated. Their escape had been too easy and their optimism proved unfounded. Interest rates jumped to 42 percent and a renewed drive on fiscal deficits was promised. But this time the pressure on the exchange rate proved too strong. Reserves fell in September by $22 billion, a pace that would exhaust them in another two months. A detailed program for fiscal stability was announced in late October. Under the joint leadership of the U.S. Treasury and the IMF, an international financial support package of $41.5 billion was organized, contingent on Brazil's generation of a substantial primary fiscal surplus for the next three years (1999–2001). Then two almost adventitious events broke the exchange rate dam.

In December, just as the details of the international support package were published, the Chamber of Deputies rejected by a thirteen-vote margin a social security reform provision increasing taxes on higher-paid civil service pensioners. The world press construed the action as a rejection of the entire reform program. That view was mistaken and the same pension reform was passed a few weeks later, but the damage had been done. Reserves fell that month by another $8.5 billion. In January 1999, central bank president Gustavo Franco, who had been adamantly opposed to any devaluation, was replaced. His successor, Francisco Lopes, first tried to limit the depreciation to about R$1.40 per dollar (from R$1.20), following an obscure mathematical formula, but that did not satisfy market pressures and the rate fell close to R$2.00.

The second event was an announcement by former president Itamar Franco, newly elected to the governorship of the important state of Minas Gerais, that there would be a moratorium of ninety days on state debt payments, which included a Eurobond installment. Once again the world press misconstrued the event, treating it as a generalized governors' revolt against a central government lacking means of control. In fact, the central government had guaranteed the loan and it paid the installment on time. Moreover, no other governor followed Itamar's example, but the damage had been done. International credit rating agencies lowered their evaluation of Brazil and on "Black Friday," January 29, panic in the markets brought the real down to R$2.05 per dollar. Lopes was hurriedly replaced by Armínio Fraga, a former central bank official and Princeton-trained economist, who had moved to New York in charge of the George Soros investment funds for developing countries.

The immediate economic impact was a surge in inflation and a further drop in international reserves. The political impact was equally critical. Many observers, Brazilian and foreign, wrote obituaries on the entire Real Plan, foreseeing a return to indexation of prices and wages and an economic depression akin to recent experience in Mexico, Thailand, Korea, and Indonesia. Public opinion approval of President Cardoso dropped precipitously, in one regular monthly poll from 27 percent in January to 16 percent in March. There was a visible decline in Congress's willingness to support the administration, with many members treating the president as a "lame duck" despite his recent reelection on the first ballot. Looking back at year's end, Cardoso acknowledged that he had gone through a phase of demoralization, fearing that his capacity for leadership had been seriously impaired.

Well before year's end, however, experience showed that the pessimism had been grossly excessive. At the central bank, Fraga was remarkably adept at restoring foreign investor confidence in Brazil, with the result that capital once again flowed in. Reserve levels rapidly recovered to the range of

Table 7-4. *Brazil's Macroeconomic Performance, 1999*

| Indicator | Forecast, early 1999 | Actual outcome |
|---|---|---|
| GDP growth (percent) | −3 to −6 | +0.87 |
| Inflation, IPC-A[a] (percent) | 8 to 35 | 8.94 |
| Primary fiscal surplus | | |
| (percent of GDP) | −1.7 to +2.2 | +3.13 |
| Year-end exchange rate (R$/$U.S.) | 1.60 to 2.05 | 1.79 |
| *Balance of payments (billions of $U.S.)* | | |
| Current account | −14 to −16 | −24.4 |
| Trade balance | +7 | −1.2 |
| Net foreign direct investment | 24 | 30 |

Source: Forecasts were summarized by Orbis Publications (publisher of the widely respected newsletter *Brazil Watch*) in their *Brazil 1999 Country Report* (February 1999), pp. 18–21. Actual outcomes are from the Banco Central, except GDP, from the IBGE.

a. IPC-A (Indice de Preços as Consumidor-Amplo), a broad consumer price index prepared by the IBGE.

$40 billion to $45 billion while interest rates were brought down to the pre-crisis level of 19 percent. Then Fraga and Finance Minister Pedro Malan announced that the exchange rate would no longer be used as an "anchor" for price stabilization. Henceforth, the cardinal guidance for macroeconomic policy would be the actual rate of inflation, following the examples of the United Kingdom, Australia, and New Zealand. The central bank, however, did not abstain from intervening in the exchange market to counter movements it considered excessive, and at year's end it remained unclear how the inflation rate "anchor" would be managed. In practice, as seen in figure 7-12, the rate weakened somewhat during the second and third quarters, probably in response to the disappointing export performance, and then strengthened slightly to reach R$1.79 as the year ended.

On other major magnitudes, the results for 1999 were enormously better than the early forecasts, except for exports and the balance of payments. Table 7-4 provides the principal examples. The good economic news was matched in early 2000 by substantial improvements in the president's public opinion ratings and modest signs of congressional responsiveness to executive pleas for greater fiscal responsibility.

## The Outlook

As the new century opens, the Real Plan survives, with good prospects that annual inflation can again be kept in the single-digit range, barring some new imported crisis, while GDP growth in 2000 is forecast at +3 to +5 percent. High oil prices will worsen the balance of trade, but Brazil's greatly increased domestic production of oil will rule out the kind of adverse impact experienced in the 1970s and 1980s. The central bank appears to have become more skillful at containing external shocks. Foreign direct and port-folio investment are back in substantial volume. There is some renewed progress, even if halting, on tax reforms, expenditure controls, and the reduction of social security system abuses. It is no longer impossible to trim public payrolls when fiscal pressures so demand. The new Fiscal Responsi-bility Law applies a novel degree of discipline at the state and municipal levels.

On the other hand, it would be a gross overstatement to claim that macroeconomic policy has been consolidated, subject only to the vagaries that afflict most of the first world along with developing countries. With the fiscal balance still precarious, interest rates remain too high, dampening the prospects for sustained high-level growth. Brazil should surely continue to import capital, often accompanied by new technology and marketing skills, but long-term economic health calls for a higher proportion of domestically financed investment. State and local governments will continue to be ham-pered in providing badly needed social services, especially in education and health, as long as overemployment and showy projects for electoral gain absorb so large a share of available resources. For macroeconomic stability over the long-term future, political reform, on the lines discussed in chap-ter 6, appears an essential condition.

# 8

## Brazil and the World

Brazil's international position is almost unique among developing countries. Having separated peacefully from Portugal in 1822, it has no tradition of resentment against a former colonial master. The creation of Uruguay as a buffer state between Brazil and Argentina, the defeat of Paraguay in the war of the Triple Alliance (1865–70), and the negotiated settlement of all its northern and western borders early in the twentieth century eliminated potential threats to its physical security. Brazil declared war on Germany in World War I but remained a nonbelligerent. In World War II, it became Latin America's sole active participant in Europe, sending an expeditionary force of some 25,000 men to fight under American command in the difficult Italian campaign of 1944–45.

In nonmilitary relations, Brazil's large geographical extent, resources, and population, coupled with a high-quality professional diplomatic service, have given it a substantial voice in regional and world politics despite the lags in economic and social development. For over a century, Brazilian diplomats have participated in a variety of international arbitration proceedings and in the development of both global and inter-American institutions. In the decades following World War II, however, and especially since the ending of the cold war, the central focus of Brazil's foreign policies has been their contribution to economic development and modernization.[1]

1. An especially rich source for this topic is the symposium organized by the University of São Paulo's Research Unit on International Relations, of which two volumes have been published so far. Most of the authors are professional diplomats writing from firsthand experience; others are scholars in the field. See José Augusto Guilhon Albuquerque (organizer), *Sessenta Anos de Política Externa*

## Foreign Policy Tradition

In the period of Empire (1822–89) that followed Brazil's national independence, the country's great size and European-like superstructure of constitutional monarchy and titled aristocracy seemed to promise a future role on the world stage. With domestic political stability and secure borders, once the boundaries with Argentina and Paraguay had been definitely settled, the national elites could think of themselves as a potential international power, the equivalent at least of a second-rank nation of Europe. The aspiration to "greatness" (*grandeza*), however loosely defined, has remained a significant feature of Brazil's foreign policymaking through all the subsequent changes of regime.

At the start, foreign policy focused on stabilization of the Plata Basin on favorable terms. This aim was achieved with support from Great Britain, then the world's leading Great Power. Britain also provided the model for Brazil's constitutional monarchy and was the major factor in the marketing of its sugar and coffee exports and the supply of manufactured imports. For cultural inspiration, the Brazilian elites looked toward France, often sending their sons to French universities. They felt little kinship with Spanish America, with its frequent coups d'état and unstable successions of *caudillos*. Argentina was regarded as a troublesome rival. The United States was friendly but distant, certainly in no way a threat to Brazilian territory or interests and more likely a partner in warding off potential threats from Europe or from Brazil's Spanish-speaking neighbors.[2]

The seemingly stable constitutional monarchy, unique in Latin America, gave rise to a professional class in law, medicine, engineering, and the sciences. Under the Old Republic (1889–1930) this class provided the basis for an elite corps of diplomats, known to this day as Itamaraty for the mansion in Rio de Janeiro where it was originally housed. Their role model was the Baron of Rio Branco, the scholarly negotiator of Brazil's northern and west-

---

Brasileira (1930–1990) (Sixty Years of Brazilian Foreign Policy [1930–1990]) (São Paulo: Cultura Editores Associados, 1996). Subsequent references in this chapter are simply to *Sessenta Anos*. For a well-documented historical survey in English, including chapters on the views of Brazilian intellectuals and of military officers and diplomats, see Roger W. Fontaine, *Brazil and the United States: Toward a Maturing Relationship* (Hoover Institution, 1974).

2. Later in the nineteenth century and periodically up to the present time, rumors have circulated in Brazil of U.S. territorial designs on Amazônia, followed by denunciations of "Yankee cupidity." In recent years, they focus on proposals by some environmental NGOs that portions of the Amazon forest should be "internationalized" because of their vast capacity to absorb atmospheric carbon dioxide, proposals that have never been endorsed or supported by the U.S. government.

ern frontiers, who served as minister of foreign affairs from 1902 to 1912 and shaped the main guidelines of foreign policy for the following half century.

In this period, the constitution had been remodeled on American lines and the United States had become the leading purchaser of Brazilian exports (mainly coffee), although Britain remained the larger supplier of imports until World War I.[3] Spain had been driven out of the Western Hemisphere and the Panama Canal was under construction. For a statesman of Rio Branco's caliber, it was evident that the United States was emerging as a leading power, not only in the Western Hemisphere but globally. He took the initiative in making it Brazil's principal diplomatic partner, a cornerstone of Brazilian foreign policy until the late 1950s, although somewhat qualified during the run-up to World War II.[4] It should be emphasized, however, that Rio Branco saw in this partnership the best means for promoting Brazilian national interests; he did not advise unconditional adherence to American policies. In words often quoted by a leading midcentury diplomat, Brazil should be "with the United States, but not in tow."[5]

This background has led to some ambivalence in Brazilian-American relations, manifested in varying intensity up to the present. Objectively, the partnership has always been unequal, involving great disparities in military and economic power, in technological sophistication, and in influence with most third countries. Brazil figures only modestly in the spectrum of American foreign policy interests, while the United States is uniquely important to Brazil as a trading partner and source of technology, capital, and cultural influence. One simple measure of those disparities—the relative significance

3. Imports and exports with each of Brazil's principal trading partners are tabulated at decade intervals from 1842 to 1872 and annually from 1901 on in *Estatísticas Históricas do Brasil*, pp. 526–34.

4. There were three other major components in Rio Branco's policy initiatives, all also involving closer relations with the United States: (1) to enhance Brazilian national prestige in Europe and North America; (2) to assume leadership in South America in contrast to the earlier separatism from the Spanish-speaking countries, while also serving as a bridge to the United States; and (3) to engage in international activism, as demonstrated in the formation of the Pan-American Union. The Legations in Washington and Rio de Janeiro were raised to embassy status in 1905, and in 1906 Rio was the host for Secretary of State Elihu Root's first official visit overseas, to attend a Pan-American conference. See E. Bradford Burns, *A History of Brazil*, 2d ed. (Columbia University Press, 1980), pp. 323–30.

5. The phrase was originally coined by Lauro Müller. See Vasco Leitão da Cunha, *Diplomacia em Alto-Mar* (Diplomacy on the High Seas) (Rio de Janeiro: Editora da Fundação Getúlio Vargas, 1994), pp. xxiii–xxv, 176–80, 226–27, 290. This condensation of oral memoir transcripts taken in 1985 is a very rich source for understanding the evolution of Brazil's foreign policies in the entire period 1930 through 1968. See also Keith Larry Storrs, "Brazil's Independent Foreign Policy, 1961–1964," Ph.D. dissertation, Cornell University, 1973, p. 115.

as trading partners—is illustrated vividly in table 8-1 and figure 8-1, which also shows the modest reduction in Brazil's dependence on American supplies and markets since the 1960s.

Nevertheless, subjectively, Brazil's large size and resource potential have often made its well-educated diplomats and many other opinion leaders resentful of American power, especially when tactlessly displayed. As a result, differentiation from American initiatives can almost become an end in itself, as a desirable expression of Brazilian nationalism, even when the two countries are agreed on substantive policies. The well-known prickliness of American relations with France, especially with diplomats of the Quai d'Orsay, is sometimes attributed to the nostalgia of a former Great Power. At times it appears matched by Brazilian prickliness, especially among diplomats of Itamaraty, in anticipation of becoming a future Great Power.

Major decisions on Brazil's foreign policy, of course, are no longer made by professional diplomats; they rest with the political leadership and are greatly influenced by domestic politics, in which nationalist appeals always secure some response. Moreover, as in the United States and many other countries, professional diplomats do not control all governmental relations with other countries; they are often dwarfed by the economic ministries. And in recent decades, a dense web of nongovernmental relations has developed, including business and finance, educational exchanges, and a growing number of private not-for-profit institutions, the so-called NGOs.

During the 1930s, when economic depression and political revolution under Getúlio Vargas were reshaping society, there was a gradual weakening of Brazil's pro-American tradition, involving both political and economic factors. Vargas succeeded in repressing Brazil's communist and fascist totalitarian movements, both of which made armed bids for power in the 1930s, but his own appeal was also based in part on populist nationalism.[6] His Estado Novo dictatorship (1937–45) instituted a form of corporative organization for industrial labor relations based on the Italian fascist model. As Europe moved toward World War II, and especially after the fall of France, his close advisers were sharply divided between sympathizers with Britain, notably Foreign Minister Osvaldo Aranha, and Germanophiles, the

6. This aspect of Vargas's personal philosophy appeared again in his famous suicide testament-letter of 1954. Typical phrases included the following: "decades of domination and plunder on the part of international economic and financial groups"; "national freedom in the utilization of our resources by means of Petrobrás"; "I fought against the spoliation of Brazil; I fought against the spoliation of the people." For the full text in English translation, see John W. F. Dulles, *Vargas of Brazil* (University of Texas Press, 1967), pp. 334–35.

Table 8-1. *Trade Dependence between Brazil and the United States, 1940–98*
Percent

| Year | Trade with U.S. as share of Brazilian world trade | | Trade with Brazil as share of U.S. world trade | |
|------|---------|---------|---------|---------|
|      | Exports | Imports | Exports | Imports |
| 1940 | 39.9 | 45.3 | 2.8 | 4.0 |
| 1945 | 47.5 | 48.8 | 2.2 | 7.5 |
| 1950 | 52.8 | 33.6 | 3.6 | 8.1 |
| 1955 | 44.5 | 20.9 | 1.8 | 5.6 |
| 1960 | 45.4 | 31.7 | 2.3 | 3.9 |
| 1965 | 32.1 | 31.1 | 1.2 | 2.4 |
| 1970 | 24.5 | 29.5 | 2.0 | 1.7 |
| 1975 | 15.4 | 24.9 | 3.2 | 1.4 |
| 1980 | 17.4 | 18.5 | 2.1 | 1.4 |
| 1985 | 27.1 | 19.5 | 1.3 | 1.9 |
| 1990 | 24.6 | 19.8 | 1.1 | 1.5 |
| 1995 | 18.9 | 21.1 | 2.0 | 1.2 |
| 1998 | 19.4 | 23.6 | 2.2 | 1.1 |

Source: Instituto Brasiliero de Geografia e Estatística (IBGE), *Estatísticas Históricas do Brasil, Séries Estatísticas Retrospectivas*, vol. 3, *Séries Econômicas, Demográficas e Sociais, 1550 a 1985* (Rio de Janeiro, 1987), pp. 524–25; U.S. Department of Commerce, *Historical Statistics of the United States* (1975), pp. 903, 905; International Monetary Fund, *Direction of Trade Statistics* (various issues).

latter including War Minister Eurico Dutra (later president) and Army Chief of Staff Góes Monteiro. Vargas himself, however, consistently stated that Brazil was joined with the other American republics in collective defense against extracontinental threats. There was also concern about possible disaffection among the large numbers of Italian, German, and Japanese immigrants, concentrated in the southern states.[7]

In World War I, Brazil had followed the American example, sympathizing with the Allies but remaining neutral during the early years and then declaring war against Germany in October 1917 after German sinkings of Brazilian merchant vessels. It did not become an active belligerent, although a medical team was sent to France. The World War II experience was more complex. After Germany gained control of the European continent in 1940, Brazil came under increasing American pressure, first to make available air and sea bases in the Northeast to ward off possible German attacks and later

7. On this matter, see Ricardo Seitenfus, "Quatro Teses sobre a Política Externa Brasileira nos Anos 1930" (Four Theses on Brazilian Foreign Policy in the Thirties), in *Sessenta Anos*, pp. 115–60.

Figure 8-1.  *Brazil and United States, Reciprocal Trade Dependence,*
*1940–98*

### a. Brazil's American Trade as a Share of Brazil's World Trade

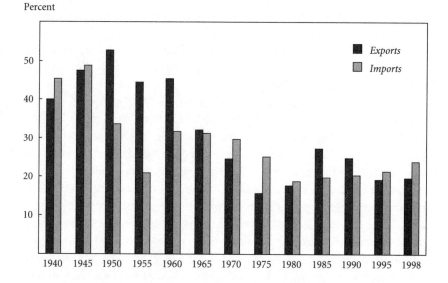

### b. United States' Brazilian Trade as a Share of U.S. World Trade

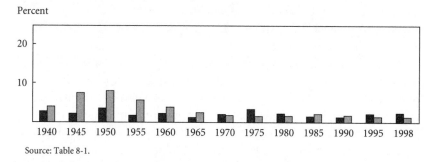

Source: Table 8-1.

to sustain the South Atlantic air link for the invasion of North Africa. Vargas sought for a time to remain neutral. He accepted the demand for bases
but bargained hard for American military equipment and financial and
technical assistance in the building of Brazil's first steel mill, the famous
Volta Redonda.[8] After Pearl Harbor, he affirmed Brazil's "solidarity" with

8. The evolution of Vargas's attitudes toward the war can now be traced in his personal diary, covering the years 1930–42, which was released by his granddaughter for publication in 1995. See
Getúlio Vargas, *Diário*, 2 vols. (Rio de Janeiro: Siciliano/FGV, 1995).

the United States and then broke diplomatic relations with Germany, Italy, and Japan at the Inter-American Conference in Rio in January 1942. Brazil did not declare war at that stage and was not yet considering active participation in hostilities. It bargained successfully for Lend-Lease assistance and cooperated with the United States in antisubmarine patrols, which led to multiple ship sinkings by German submarines and a declaration of war in August. Brazil also cooperated actively in the provision of strategic war materials, such as manganese, iron ore, and rubber, and in the denial of strategic materials to the Axis powers.

In 1942, the modernization and reequipment of Brazil's armed forces was organized through joint military commissions in both Washington and Rio de Janeiro—an arrangement reaffirmed by a formal agreement in 1952 that lasted until 1977.[9] The decision to send troops to fight in Europe, however, was an entirely Brazilian initiative. The scale was too small to make an important difference to the military outcome, but the purpose was long-range and eminently political. In the words of a leading diplomatic historian: "The Brazilian Expeditionary Force was thus the core of a political project intended to strengthen the Brazilian armed forces and to give Brazil a position of preeminence in Latin America and substantial importance in the world as a special ally of the United States."[10] The troops arrived in Italy in July 1944 and made a creditable record, including significant casualties, in the difficult campaign up the West Coast of Italy in 1944–45. The air force and navy also took active parts in the fighting.

As participants on the winning side of the greatest war in modern history, Brazil's officer corps and its civilian leaders emerged from this experience with very high expectations of a new role in the postwar world. The democratic constitution of 1946 removed the quasi-fascist dictatorship as an obstacle to such a relationship. The term "special ally" of the United States was widely used, in some minds almost equivalent to the Anglo-American relationship. In reality, however, the Brazilian expectations or aspirations were unrealistically ambitious and the euphoria generated by the Italian campaign was bound to be frustrated. Disappointment at the U.S. failure to offer economic assistance for the region's development, on a par with Marshall Plan assistance to European reconstruction, was shared by Latin America as a whole, but Brazilians felt especially aggrieved because of their active engagement in the war.

9. See Sonny B. Davis, *A Brotherhood of Arms: Brazil-United States Military Relations, 1945–1977* (University Press of Colorado, 1996).

10. Gerson Moura, "O Brasil na Segunda Guerra Mundial: 1942–1945" (Brazil in the Second World War: 1942–1945), in *Sessenta Anos*, pp. 99–100 (informal translation).

Brazilian diplomats had also taken a significant part in drafting the Havana Charter for an International Trade Organization, including provisions for commodity price stabilization. Having backed the American-sponsored multilateral approach instead of a Latin American regionalist alternative, they were frustrated by the charter's failure of ratification by the U.S. Senate. Another setback was the American postwar preference for collective arrangements with all Latin America, including parity for Argentina, instead of special bilateral arrangements with Brazil. Although President Eurico Dutra clearly sided with the West as the cold war against the Soviet Union took shape, relations were sufficiently soured by the absence of development aid to make Brazil refuse insistent American requests for troops in Korea, a refusal confirmed after Getúlio Vargas regained the presidency in early 1951 through free elections.[11]

On the economic side, the Truman administration had made a significant positive move by agreeing to a Joint Brazil–United States Economic Commission, which undertook the first comprehensive survey of Brazil's needs for developmental infrastructure and listed projects intended for financing by the World Bank or the U.S. Export-Import Bank. In the American perspective, however, this effort was a low priority matter compared with European reconstruction or the war in Korea. Washington also felt discouraged by the more strident nationalism of the Vargas presidency, with its strong bias against foreign participation in petroleum and minerals development. In early 1953, just as the Joint Commission completed its work, the Eisenhower administration took office in Washington. It was opposed in principle to large-scale governmental financing of overseas development, once again disappointing Brazilian expectations.

These events gave growing strength to sectors of Brazilian opinion skeptical of the traditional deference to the United States. An overt change in foreign policy, however, was postponed for a few years by the suicide of President Vargas. The immediate successor, Vice President João Café Filho, and the next elected president, Juscelino Kubitschek, were more sympathetic than Vargas to foreign private investment, and American industry was welcomed as a participant in Kubitschek's thrust for accelerated development, aiming at "Fifty Years in Five" (see chapter 2). After 1958, however, as growth rates slowed and inflation gained momentum, nationalist pressures again emerged strongly, some tinged with Marxist ideology and

11. See Stanley E. Hilton, "The United States, Brazil, and the Cold War, 1945–1960: End of the Special Relationship," *Journal of American History*, vol. 68, no. 3 (December 1981), pp. 599–624.

others asserting irreconcilable antagonism between first world and third.[12] Many Brazilian intellectuals and diplomats subscribed to the policy analyses developed at the UN Economic Commission for Latin America (ECLA, or CEPAL in Spanish), which coined the terminology of "center" and "periphery" and urged collective action by poorer nations to secure economic concessions from the richer. This view gained strength from Washington's cool response to Kubitschek's ambitious proposal for an American-financed hemisphere-wide development effort, termed Operation Pan-American.

In 1959, Kubitschek moved toward a more nationalist posture, epitomized by an outright break with the International Monetary Fund. Just at that time, the Eisenhower administration was becoming more responsive to Latin American demands for development assistance, having been shocked by the personal assaults on Vice President Richard Nixon in Colombia and Venezuela and then by Fidel Castro's assumption of power in Cuba. The changes in Washington included agreement to create the Inter-American Development Bank, a long-standing Latin American aspiration, and to establish a Social Progress Trust Fund under its auspices. They came too late, however, to forestall an overt shift in Brazilian foreign policy during the brief presidential tenure (1961) of Kubitschek's successor, Jânio Quadros.

## Brazil's "Independent Foreign Policy"

The "independent" policy proclaimed by Quadros was not as novel as advertised, but it did introduce some new themes that persisted for many years. It included a gross overstatement of Brazil's previous international "obscurity" and its alignment with "worthy though alien interests," meaning the United States. Its most dramatic departure from tradition was to withdraw support for Portuguese colonialism in Africa, which had been a long-standing exception to Brazil's general anticolonialism. In addition, while declaring Brazil "a predominantly Western nation" and acknowledging the Rio Treaty commitment to inter-American cooperation against extracontinental aggression, it emphasized new forms of common interest with underdeveloped countries generally, with Africa in particular, with the "nonaligned" movement, and potentially with eastern Europe, the Soviet Union, and the Chinese People's Republic.[13] There were even rumors that Quadros had been persuaded that

12. See Paulo Fagundes Vizentini, "A Política Externa do Governo JK (1956–61)" (The Foreign Policy of the Kubitschek Government [1956–61]), in *Sessenta Anos*, pp. 231–51.

13. See Braz José de Araújo, "A Política Externa no Governo de Jânio Quadros" (Foreign Policy in the Jânio Quadros Government), in *Sessenta Anos*, pp. 253–81. For an authoritative summary

the Soviet feat of launching Sputnik, the first man-made earth satellite, signified defeat of the United States in the cold war.[14] Shortly before his resignation, he made a symbolic challenge to the United States by conferring Brazil's highest diplomatic decoration on Che Guevara, Fidel Castro's most prominent political associate, who had just stormed out of the Alliance for Progress's founding conference in Uruguay.[15]

The basic theme of independence in foreign policy was maintained during the three troubled years of João Goulart's presidency.[16] In early 1962, Brazil conspicuously stood aloof from the American effort to suspend Cuban membership in the Organization of American States (OAS), although it did join in October in condemning the Soviet installation of nuclear missile bases in Cuba and endorsing the American naval quarantine against delivery of the missiles. Brazil reopened diplomatic relations with the Soviet Union and Eastern Europe and a trade delegation was invited from Communist China. There was only grudging and intermittent cooperation with President Kennedy's Alliance for Progress, offset by legislation severely limiting profit remittances by foreign investors; by late 1963, Goulart's attitude had become overtly hostile.[17] Brazil played an active part in creation of the United Nations Conference on Trade and Development (UNCTAD), assuming a substantial leadership role among "developing" nations.

## Foreign Policy under the Military Regime

The scarcely disguised anti-Americanism of Brazil's "independent" foreign policy was discarded immediately by the military regime that took office in April 1964. There was a prompt conclusion of negotiations for the purchase of American and Canadian electric utility companies, promised by Goulart

---

statement in English signed by Quadros himself, submitted on the eve of his unexpected resignation, see Jânio Quadros, "Brazil's New Foreign Policy," in *Foreign Affairs,* vol. 40 (October 1961), pp. 19–27. The phrases quoted in this paragraph are drawn from that article.

14. My personal recollection.

15. He also dispatched Vice President João Goulart on a trade mission to the People's Republic of China, even though Brazil was still following Washington's lead in recognizing the "Government of China" on Taiwan. Whether the motivation was another demonstration of "independence" in foreign policy or part of Quadros's resignation strategy will have to be left to future historians.

16. For my detailed account of the fluctuating character of Brazilian-American relations during this period, when I was serving as U.S. ambassador to Brazil, see U.S. Senate, Committee on Foreign Relations, Hearing on Nomination of Lincoln Gordon to be Assistant Secretary of State for Inter-American Affairs, February 7, 1966.

17. See Roberto Campos, *A Lanterna na Popa: Memorias* (The Lantern on the Stern: Memoirs) (Rio de Janeiro: Topbooks Editora, 1994), p. 539.

in 1962 but not carried through. The burden of foreign debt servicing was reduced through orderly negotiations in the "Paris Club" of creditor governments, without threats of unilateral repudiation. On the politically sensitive issue of foreign investment in mineral resources, the new regime promoted a tripartite solution sharing ownership among the Brazilian government, Brazilian private investors, and foreign private investors. Restrictions on profit remittances were sufficiently softened to induce a large flow of North American, European, and Japanese private investments, and Brazil became the world's largest borrower from the World Bank and from the United States through the Alliance for Progress.

In the international political arena, Brazil broke diplomatic relations with Cuba and the new foreign minister presided at the 1964 OAS conference that condemned Cuba for attempted aggression against Venezuela. In 1965 Brazil agreed to President Lyndon Johnson's proposal for "inter-Americanizing" the military intervention in the Dominican Republic, also accepting the nominal command of the Inter-American Peace Force, but only on condition that the intervention be legalized by a two-thirds vote in the OAS. When asked by President Johnson to join in the war in Vietnam, however, President Castello Branco made clear that any such action would require a previous formal vote in the UN Security Council or General Assembly, a condition with no prospect of fulfillment. Brazil continued to strengthen its ties with Europe and Japan and to develop common positions on international economic issues with other less developed countries. Special attention was given to trade relations and common infrastructure with South American neighbors, notably the huge hydroelectric project with Paraguay at Sete Quedas (Seven Falls).

Some Brazilian diplomatic historians condemn this period as a simple and retrograde subordination to the United States.[18] That was clearly not the view of the professionals in charge, led by Vasco Leitão da Cunha. In macroeconomic terms, the new policies resolved an immediate balance of payments crisis and helped lay the foundation for the economic miracle of 1968–74 (see chapter 3).

---

18. See, for example, Rodrigo Amado, "A Política Externa de João Goulart" (The Foreign Policy of João Goulart), in *Sessenta Anos,* p. 295. For the contrary view from inside, see Vasco Leitão da Cunha, *Diplomacia em Alto-Mar,* pp. 278–93. The negative interpretation may have been given some credence by an unfortunate public statement of Juracy Magalhães, the new regime's first ambassador to Washington and subsequent foreign minister, but not a professional diplomat: "What is good for the United States is good for Brazil." The intended and limited meaning is explained in Magalhães's memoirs, but it was widely misconstrued as an endorsement of indiscriminate subordination. See Juracy Magalhães and J. A. Gueiros, *O Ultimo Tenente* (The Last of the Lieutenants) (Rio de Janeiro: Record, 1996), pp. 325, 334.

In the late 1960s and into the 1970s, relations between Brazil and the United States chilled from both sides. In Washington, there was distress at the hardening of the military regime signaled in 1968 by Institutional Act No. 5 (AI-5) and by reports of human rights abuses in the battle against terrorism.[19] There was shock at the kidnappings of the American, West German, and Swiss ambassadors by leftist armed groups. Bilateral economic assistance became less important to Brazil and was less central to the Nixon administration's overall policies in Latin America. Trade disputes developed concerning Brazilian exports of soluble coffee, shoes, and textiles. On the Brazilian side, the "hard-line" faction within the military gained ground, especially under President Garrastazu Médici, reviving nationalistic objections to foreign participation in mining while promoting almost romantic concepts of Brazil's potential in information technology, atomic energy for both civilian and military purposes, and development of Amazônia. They formed a somewhat curious alliance with diplomats cultivating relationships with other less developed countries, envisaging Brazil as leader of the third world.

At the start of Ernesto Geisel's term as president (1974–79), the activist foreign minister, Antônio Azeredo da Silveira, set forth a new framework for Brazilian foreign policy under the rubric "responsible pragmatism." It revived many elements of Quadros's thrust toward "independence," including separation from American tutelage and special cooperation with third world countries although not with the communist bloc. Brazil became a leader in the effort to extract more resources from the richer countries through confrontation on "North-South" issues and the search for a New International Economic Order (NIEO).[20] At the same time, however, the minister cultivated a personal relationship with Secretary of State Henry Kissinger and negotiated a bilateral agreement for joint foreign policy consultations on a regular schedule. Those arrangements appear to have had more form than substance, and in any case did not survive into the Carter administration in Washington.[21]

---

19. See, for example, the Senate's "Church Committee," *States, Policies and Programs in Brazil,* Hearings before the Subcommittee on Western Hemisphere Affairs of the Senate Committee on Foreign Relations, 92 Cong. 1 sess. (GPO, May 4, 5, and 11, 1971).

20. For a generally sympathetic discussion, see Luis Augusto P. Soto Maior, "O 'Pragmatismo Responsavel,'" in *Sessenta Anos,* pp. 337–60.

21. The joint memorandum was publicized with a widely circulated photograph of a warm embrace between Kissinger and Silveira. Roberto Campos's memoirs describe a meeting in London in 1975 with British Foreign Secretary James Callaghan, in which Silveira repeatedly referred to "my friend Henry," prompting Callaghan to ask "Henry who?" (See *A Lanterna na Popa,* p. 951.) In Kissinger's own public memoir of his years as secretary of state, however, there is no reference to Silveira, and Brazil is mentioned only in connection with the fall of Salvador Allende in Chile.

## The Nuclear Saga

Brazil's policies toward the atom have been a microcosm of changing attitudes toward international relations more broadly. From the Hiroshima explosion on, governmental, scientific, and military circles showed a keen interest in the subject, taking into account the country's large mineral reserves of thorium, the possible contribution to energy supplies, and the once widely heralded potential for peaceful nuclear explosions.[22] Under the terms of Eisenhower's Atoms-for-Peace program, research reactors were installed at several Brazilian universities. While disclaiming any intention of developing weapons, Brazilian governments refused to sign the Nuclear Non-Proliferation Treaty (NPT) of 1968. They considered it a violation of basic international principle to accept permanent discrimination between acknowledged nuclear weapons states (which were also the permanent members of the UN Security Council with veto rights) and the rest of the world.[23] They accepted inspection of their civilian facilities by the International Atomic Energy Authority (IAEA), but chafed at the denial of capacity for fuel reprocessing and uranium enrichment that would make them completely self-sufficient in nuclear power production. In addition, there were clandestine "parallel" programs under military control, with the ultimate aim of a weapons capacity, which only became known to the Brazilian public and the world many years later.

Even before the oil shock of 1973 (action by OPEC to quadruple the price of crude oil), the Brazilian government contracted with the American firm Westinghouse to build a commercial-scale nuclear power plant, which was to be fueled with low-enriched uranium supplied by the U.S. Atomic Energy Commission (AEC, later the Department of Energy). In 1974, however, just after the oil shock, the AEC brusquely informed Brazil that it could no longer ensure fuel deliveries because of insufficient American enrichment capacity, a forecast that later turned out to be unfounded. For Brazil's policymakers, the oil shock had seemed to threaten a desperate crisis in the balance of payments. Energy consumption had risen rapidly during the economic miracle, but Petrobrás was having only modest success in finding oil deposits at home and there was little unexploited hydroelectric potential

22. As a member of the U.S. delegation to the UN Atomic Energy Commission in 1946, I recall the strong interest and active participation of the Brazilian delegation, led by Admiral Álvaro Alberto da Motta e Silva, later head of Brazil's National Research Council.

23. This theme was embellished in 1971 in a widely read article by former foreign minister João Augusto de Araújo Castro, then serving as ambassador to Washington, under the title "O Congelamento do Poder Mundial" (The Freezing of World Power), in *Revista Brasileira de Estudos Políticos*, vol. 17 (January 1972), pp. 7–30.

close to major markets. Atomic energy seemed to be an ideal solution, with the added attractions of participating in a major new field of technology and—in the minds of some military sectors—of paralleling or surpassing Argentina's clandestine weapons development.

In response to what seemed an American affront in both substance and mode of delivery, the Brazilians turned in 1975 to West Germany, which offered not only power plants and enriched fuel but also technical assistance in reprocessing and in providing Brazil a novel enrichment technology that might make the entire fuel cycle independent of outside supplies. That claim also later turned out to be greatly exaggerated, but at the time seemed to Washington to threaten the whole global effort to limit proliferation of "dual-use" nuclear technology (usable for weapons as well as peaceful applications). Strenuous American representations persuaded both Bonn and Brasília to accept a special safeguards arrangement with the IAEA to protect against diversion to military uses.

In 1977, however, the newly installed Carter administration in Washington initiated a more intensive effort at limiting proliferation. Its very first foreign policy venture was a mission by Vice President Walter Mondale to Western Europe and Japan. Without forewarning the Brazilians, the White House announced that the agenda in Bonn would include an effort to persuade Germany to cancel the program. Brazil's officialdom and press reacted vigorously against this example of "typical American hegemonism" and a follow-up visit by Deputy Secretary of State Warren Christopher was very coolly received. The Germans refused to back off, and the ground was laid for a deliberate breach in Brazil's relations with the United States.[24]

The pretext was an annual State Department report on human rights in Brazil required by the U.S. Congress with respect to any country receiving military assistance. When an advance copy was delivered to Itamaraty to avoid their first learning its contents through the press, Minister Silveira convened a special press conference, denounced the report as an unconscionable intrusion into domestic affairs, and said that he was "returning it" to the embassy as if it had been some kind of intergovernmental ultimatum. The action was acclaimed by the press and was widely popular. In March 1977, almost on its twenty-fifth anniversary, Brazil terminated the military

24. This episode, precipitated by faulty judgment and mismanagement in Washington, was in direct contravention of the Carter administration's hopes to develop special relations with Brazil as a "regional stabilizer" in Latin America. See Zbigniew Brzezinski, *Power and Principle* (Farrar-Straus-Giroux, 1985 ed.), p. 128.

accord of 1952, again with plaudits even from traditionally pro-American quarters.[25]

During the 1980s, however, the electric power side of the nuclear program encountered severe technical and managerial difficulties, including unstable foundations for the first German plant. Costs escalated, deadlines were missed, and output was minimal. Nationalist pride became focused instead on the eminently successful 10,000-megawatt power dam at Itaipú, near Sete Quedas, the largest in the world, which required complex negotiations with Paraguay and later with Argentina. On the military side, Brazilian Army and Navy units continued to work separately and secretly toward a capacity to produce nuclear weapons, although with occasional challenges from scientists, environmentalists, and enterprising journalists.[26] After the restoration of civilian rule in 1985, these latter groups proved sufficiently powerful to secure a clause in the new constitution providing that "nuclear activity within the national territory will be permitted exclusively for peaceful purposes and through approval by the national Congress."[27] But the major reversal of policy came in 1990, when newly elected President Collor ordered the shutting down of the weapons programs, dramatizing the decision before the cameras by pouring cement down a previously secret explosives testing shaft. Building on the new relationship with Argentina signaled by the formation of Mercosur, he then negotiated with President Carlos Menem a joint commitment to refrain from weapons development, to establish a bilateral technical institution to work with the International Atomic Energy Authority in enforcing full-scope safeguards against diversion of fissile materials, and to complete the ratification of the Treaty of Tlatelolco, making all Latin America a nuclear-weapon-free zone.[28] This signaled a wholly new era of special collaboration with Argentina in place of the traditional military rivalry. It also reflected the reality that there was no conceivable external threat to either nation's security that would justify the huge costs of building a capacity for nuclear deterrence.

Finally, in 1997, President Cardoso completed the policy shift by announcing Brazil's intention to subscribe both to the Nuclear Non-Proliferation Treaty and to the Comprehensive Nuclear Test Ban Treaty (CTBT) of 1996. In delivering the instrument of ratification of the latter to

25. See Davis, *A Brotherhood of Arms*, p. 203.

26. See Tania Malheiros, *Brasil: A Bomba Oculta* (Brazil: The Secret Bomb) (Rio de Janeiro: Gryphus, 1993).

27. Constitution of 1988, Article 21, para. XXIII.

28. For details, see "Denuclearization in Argentina and Brazil," in *Arms Control Today*, vol. 24 (March 1994), pp. 10ff.

the UN Secretary-General in 1998, he said (in free translation): "We do not want the atomic bomb. It would only create tension and mistrust in our region. It would destroy the process of integration which we are steadily deepening to the benefit of our peoples. For those reasons, we are rejecting this fatal option."[29] With this action, Brazil joined the 185 nations signatory to the NPT. It also joined the Missile Technology Control Regime, designed to discourage additional countries from developing long-range delivery systems for weapons of mass destruction. The principle of nondiscrimination was retained only in a reaffirmation of the ultimate goal of worldwide elimination of nuclear weapons (in my mind a chimerical goal). As to energy supplies, attention is now focused on accelerating domestic and off-shore petroleum discoveries and importing gas from Bolivia and oil from Argentina and Venezuela, both more economical in the short run than nuclear power plants. The secular tradition of hostile rivalry with Argentina has been reversed and replaced by trade affiliation through Mercosur and cooperation in nuclear research. Nuclear electric power remains a possible option for the longer run, but only under full-scope safeguards with IAEA inspection.

The dramatic transformation in nuclear policy is one aspect of a basic change in the 1990s in Brazil's attitudes toward the world at large. Similar transformations have taken place in environmental policies, especially in Amazônia, and in efforts to suppress narcotics trafficking. The goal of "greatness" among nations has not been abandoned, but fanciful or romantic ideas on how to achieve greatness have been replaced by a kind of sober realism—a recognition that greatness can be achieved only on the foundation of a modernized economy. With the collapse of the Soviet Union in 1989, any temptation to bargain between first and second worlds has evaporated. Brazil's lost decade of the 1980s, the surge in economic performance in East Asia (at least until 1997), the failure of negotiations for a New International Economic Order, and the growing evidence of mutual advantage from global interdependence have put an end to the idea of third world leadership as a centerpiece of Brazilian policy.[30] At the turn of a new century and millennium, therefore, foreign policy has focused on economic modernization and growth.

---

29. News report of Agência Brasil, July 13, 1998, no. 99.

30. A noteworthy commentary on these changes was made by Fernando Henrique Cardoso in 1994, shortly before he became a successful candidate for the presidency. See "Relações Norte-Sul no Contexto Actual: Uma Nova Dependência?" (North-South Relations in the Present Context: A New Dependency?), in Renato Baumann, organizer, *O Brasil e a Economia Global* (Brazil and the Global Economy) (Rio de Janeiro: Campus, 1996), pp. 5–15.

## Brazil in the World Economy

In the half century after industrialization began in the 1930s, the Brazilian economy was relatively closed to international trade and only selectively open to foreign investment. As shown in the two left-hand columns of figure 8-2, the surge in GDP during the miracle years was matched by a surge in imports, but with only a tiny increase in exports. In contrast with the East Asian miracles of the 1980s and the postwar recoveries of Germany and Japan, Brazil's economic growth focused on the domestic market. During the 1980s, the debt crisis demanded a push for exports in order to stave off national bankruptcy, but it was only in the 1990s, starting with President Collor, that economic opening to imports became a central policy objective, along with privatization. Taken together, they helped generate a competitive thrust toward modernization, beginning to make up for the previous lost decade. Their full promise, however, was thwarted by the failures on the inflation front and the miasma of corruption that brought Collor to impeachment. On the import side, a substantial degree of openness was achieved only in the mid-1990s, following the initial successes of the Real Plan.

Figure 8-3 compares Brazil's degree of openness in 1997 with an array of other countries of substantial size and varying degrees of economic development. Korea's export-driven economy and Canada's symbiotic relationship with the United States make them almost irrelevant for comparison, while Italy and Spain, like other small and crowded European countries, are heavily engaged in intra-European trade analogous to internal (interstate) trade in Brazil or the United States. Lying in the same bracket as the United States, China, Argentina, and Japan, Brazil's economy can no longer be regarded as extremely closed.

There are still areas of special protection, notably in the automotive and informatics industries, and export incentives have been introduced to compensate for ongoing exceptional costs of transportation and port services (the "custo Brasil"). On the more open side, however, after decades of contention about royalties on technological innovations, especially in pharmaceuticals, Brazil has enacted fairly liberal legislation for intellectual property protection, although the United States still considers it short of World Trade Organization standards. Brazil has taken a leading role in the General Agreement on Tariffs and Trade (GATT) and its successor World Trade Organization (WTO) from the foundation of those international institutions.[31] Its

---

31. I recall a conversation in Geneva in the 1970s with the deputy secretary-general of the GATT during the Tokyo Round of multilateral trade negotiations, in which he rated the national dele-

Figure 8-2.  *Brazil's Gradual Opening, Trade as Fraction of GDP, 1970–98*

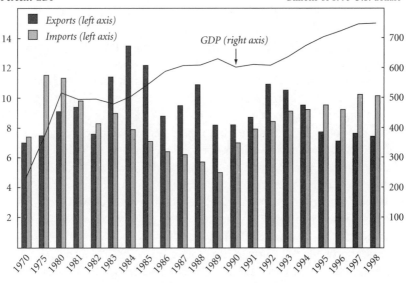

Source: World Bank, *World Development Indicators 2000* (on CD-ROM).

Figure 8-3.  *Trade as Share of GDP, 1997*

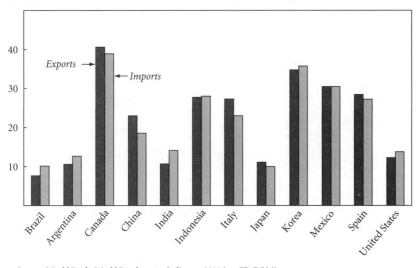

Source: World Bank, *World Development Indicators 2000* (on CD-ROM).

shift of position in the early 1990s toward inclusion of services in trade negotiations and strengthened enforcement procedures in the newly emerging WTO was a significant element in the success of the Uruguay Round.

A second cardinal aspect of Brazil's external economic relations is their geographical diversity. Figure 8-4 shows the changing patterns of export destinations and import sources since 1970. They now cluster in fairly equal quarter-shares among North America, Europe, Latin America, and the rest of the world, with Asia moving up rapidly. Europe is slightly in the lead and Latin America rising dramatically. The Middle East spike in 1980 reflected the oil shocks, still a serious risk but less acute since oil now comes mainly from domestic or nearby Latin American sources. The remarkable growth in trade within Latin America results in large part from the success of Mercosur as a regional market and the expansion of trade with other South American countries. Africa's modest shares confirm the unreality of the foreign policy pronouncements of the 1960s and 1970s that looked to Africa as an important partner in Brazilian economic growth.

As seen in table 8-2, foreign direct investment has risen to major proportions in the larger Latin American countries during the 1990s, especially Mexico and Brazil.[32] Mexico was an earlier convert to the new wave of macroeconomic reform and was therefore by far the larger recipient until the peso crisis of 1994, but has been overtaken by Brazil since the success of the Real Plan. In this competition, Mexico has the advantage of proximity to the United States and special trade access under the North American Free Trade Agreement (NAFTA), while Brazil has the advantage of a much larger domestic market and special trade access to Argentina and other nations of South America. In the 1990s, over 70 percent of FDI in Brazil represented new investment, mostly in new plants in the automotive, electronics, and chemical industries. The remainder involves privatization of existing facilities, especially telecommunications, financial services, and public utilities. The overall total will probably be reduced after 2000 as privatization of large-scale public enterprises passes its peak.

The sources of foreign direct investment in Brazil are diversified. Like the pattern of trade, they include Europe, Canada, and Japan, although the

---

gations by their quality as negotiators. He put Canada first, Brazil second, and the United States third. Specialists from Itamaraty have always been very highly regarded among professional trade negotiators.

32. See UN Economic Commission for Latin America and the Caribbean (ECLAC), "Brazil: Foreign Direct Investment and Corporate Strategies," in *Foreign Investment in Latin America and the Caribbean, 1998 Report* (Santiago, Chile, 1999), pp. 145–93.

Figure 8-4.  *Changing Patterns of Brazilian Trade, 1970–98*

**a. Export Destinations**

Percent of merchandise exports

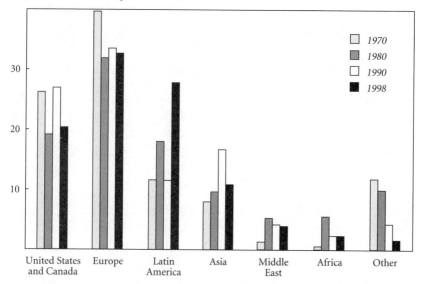

**b. Import Sources**

Percent of merchandise imports

Source: Calculated from data in International Monetary Fund, *Direction of Trade Statistics*, various dates. Note that in 1970 and 1980, the Soviet Union and some of the communist-governed eastern European countries were in the category "other."

Table 8-2. *Foreign Direct Investment in the Larger Latin American Countries, 1987–98*
Millions of U.S. dollars

| Country | 1987–92 average | 1993 | 1994 | 1995 | 1996 | 1997 | 1998 |
|---------|-----------------|------|------|------|------|------|------|
| Argentina | 1,803 | 2,763 | 3,432 | 5,279 | 6,513 | 8,094 | 5,697 |
| Brazil | 1,513 | 1,294 | 2,589 | 5,475 | 10,496 | 18,745 | 28,718 |
| Chile | 927 | 1,034 | 2,583 | 2,977 | 4,724 | 5,417 | 4,792 |
| Colombia | 464 | 960 | 1,444 | 968 | 3,123 | 5,701 | 2,983 |
| Mexico | 4,310 | 6,715 | 12,362 | 9,526 | 9,186 | 12,831 | 10,238 |
| Peru | 50 | 687 | 3,108 | 2,056 | 3,225 | 1,786 | 1,930 |
| Venezuela | 553 | 372 | 813 | 985 | 2,183 | 5,087 | 3,737 |

Source: United Nations, *World Investment Report, 1999* (New York, 1999), annex table B.1, pp. 478–79.

United States greatly outranks Germany as the largest single country. Table 8-3 presents the data for 1995–97.[33] During the 1970s, a much smaller wave of foreign investment generated widespread concerns about excessive "foreign penetration" and the "de-nationalization" of the Brazilian economy. There were echoes of these views in the 1998 campaigns of left-wing opponents to the Cardoso government. Although greatly diluted in the current "era of globalization," some degree of nationalist reaction along these lines can be found in all large countries, not excluding the United States. It remains to be seen whether the gains to Brazil from technological transfer and market expansion, as well as financial capital, will rule out a revival of constraints on foreign investors. At this writing, the foreign investment community seems prepared to take that risk.

## Mercosur

The most striking innovation in Brazil's foreign economic policy during the 1990s has been the negotiation and deepening of Mercosur,[34] the embryonic common market with Argentina, Uruguay, and Paraguay, which also has special linkages with Chile and Bolivia. In previous decades, Brazil had participated in the wider Latin American groupings known as ALALC (Latin

33. The ECLAC tabulation also shows substantial amounts from Caribbean tax-haven countries, which are evidently not the true sources of the funds.
34. In Brazil, the organization is generally referred to by its name in Portuguese, Mercosul. Since American readers are generally more familiar with the Spanish name, Mercosur, that form is used here.

Table 8-3. *Main Sources of Foreign Direct Investment in Brazil, 1995–97*
Millions of U.S. dollars

| Country | Stock | | Flow | |
|---|---|---|---|---|
| | 1995 | 1997 | 1996 | 1997 |
| United States | 10,852 | 17,210 | 1,975 | 4,382 |
| Germany | 5,828 | 6,236 | 212 | 196 |
| France | 2,032 | 4,237 | 970 | 1,235 |
| Netherlands | 1,535 | 3,549 | 527 | 1,488 |
| Japan | 2,658 | 3,193 | 192 | 342 |
| United Kingdom | 1,793 | 2,067 | 92 | 182 |
| Canada | 1,819 | 2,004 | 118 | 66 |
| Belgium/ | | | | |
| Luxembourg | 966 | 1,562 | 402 | 193 |
| Spain | 251 | 1,383 | 587 | 546 |
| Italy | 1,259 | 1,328 | 12 | 57 |
| Portugal | 107 | 990 | 203 | 681 |
| Sweden | 567 | 962 | 126 | 269 |

Source: UN Economic Commission for Latin America and the Caribbean, *Foreign Investment in Latin America and the Caribbean: 1998 Report* (Santiago, Chile, 1999), p. 154.

American Free Trade Association, formed in 1960) and ALADI (Latin American Integration Association, replacing ALALC in 1980), but without notable enthusiasm and with very modest results. The governmental focus on Mercosur, in contrast, has been sustained, intensive, and strongly supported by the business community and public opinion media. A common external tariff was agreed at the end of 1994, with general exceptions until 2001 for Uruguay and Paraguay and exceptions for all on some sensitive items, including special arrangements for the automotive and sugar industries, until 2006. The overall results until 1999 far exceeded the expectations of 1991, when the Treaty of Asunción was signed by the four presidents.[35] In 1996, Chile became associated with Mercosur through a free trade arrangement; Bolivia did likewise in 1997.

The effect on regional trade has been far-reaching, as shown in Table 8-4. Argentina has moved up from tenth position to replace Germany as Brazil's second trading partner. Joint ventures and intra-industry trade exchanges

35. An excellent analysis can be found in Antônio Salazar P. Brandão and Lia Valls Pereira, organizers, *Mercosul: Perspectivas de Integração* (Mercosul: Prospects for Integration) (Rio de Janeiro: Fundação Getúlio Vargas, 1996). See also Paulo Roberto de Almeida, *Mercosul: Fundamentos e Perspectivas* (São Paulo: Editora Ltr., 1998). A monthly bulletin including official documentation is published in São Paulo.

Table 8-4. *Brazil's Trade with Mercosur, 1991, 1997, and 1998*
Millions of current U.S. dollars

| | 1991 | | 1997 | | 1998 | |
|---|---|---|---|---|---|---|
| *Type of trade* | *Amount* | *Share (percent)* | *Amount* | *Share (percent)* | *Amount* | *Share (percent)* |
| *Exports to* | | | | | | |
| World | 31,620 | 100.0 | 52,993 | 100.0 | 51,152 | 100.0 |
| Argentina | 1,476 | 4.7 | 6,767 | 12.8 | 6,747 | 13.2 |
| Paraguay | 496 | 1.6 | 1,406 | 2.7 | 1,249 | 2.4 |
| Uruguay | 337 | 1.1 | 870 | 1.6 | 881 | 1.7 |
| Mercosur total | 2,309 | 7.3 | 9,043 | 17.1 | 8,877 | 17.4 |
| Chile | 677 | 2.1 | 1,196 | 2.2 | 1,023 | 2.0 |
| Bolivia | 256 | 0.8 | 719 | 1.4 | 676 | 1.3 |
| Mercosur plus | 3,242 | 10.2 | 10,958 | 20.7 | 10,576 | 20.7 |
| *Imports from* | | | | | | |
| World | 23,210 | 100.0 | 67,583 | 100.0 | 57,558 | 100.0 |
| Argentina | 1,747 | 7.5 | 8,932 | 13.2 | 8,028 | 13.9 |
| Paraguay | 223 | 1.0 | 584 | 0.9 | 349 | 0.6 |
| Uruguay | 446 | 1.9 | 1,078 | 1.6 | 1,048 | 1.8 |
| Mercosur total | 2,416 | 10.4 | 10,594 | 15.7 | 9,425 | 16.4 |
| Chile | 528 | 2.3 | 1,094 | 1.6 | 809 | 1.4 |
| Bolivia | 22 | 0.1 | 30 | <0.05 | 22 | <0.04 |
| Mercosur plus | 2,966 | 12.8 | 11,718 | 17.3 | 10,256 | 17.8 |

Source: International Monetary Fund, *Direction of Trade Statistics* (various issues).

have become common practice between Brazilian and Argentine firms. All four governments are developing ambitious plans for linking their transportation and energy systems. In a sense, the natural geographical unity of the Plata Basin may at last be permitted to overcome the political obstacles that have kept these economies apart over the centuries.[36]

36. An econometric analysis concludes that up to 1994 Mercosur accounted for more trade diversion than trade creation and was detrimental to both member countries and outsiders. The author recognizes, however, that these short-term static trade effects may be more than offset by dynamic effects on both production and trade. See Alexander J. Yeats, "Does Mercosur's Trade Performance Raise Concerns about the Effects of Regional Trade Arrangements?" *World Bank Economic Review*, vol. 12 (January 1998), pp. 1–28.

Nevertheless, it would be unwise to underestimate the obstacles to Mercosur's full development. Devaluation of the real in early 1999 was a traumatic shock, ending Argentina's bilateral trade surplus and raising challenging issues of financial coordination between dollarized and flexible exchange rates. Even the completion of the common external tariff is proving difficult in the absence of fully coordinated macroeconomic policies. Capital markets indicate doubts that a genuine common market is possible when one major partner maintains a flexible exchange rate while the other ties its currency to the dollar. Nevertheless, the political commitment of both major partners appears too strong to permit abandonment of the basic Mercosur objectives.

In the dimension of depth, Mercosur's stated goal is not merely a customs union but a full common market, based on the model of the European Union and including the possibility of a common currency. The structure of negotiating committees corresponds to that ambitious objective, although many policy areas such as the free movement of capital and labor have not yet been broached. As to breadth, Brazilian diplomats aim at the inclusion of all South America, at least in a free trade area, and Mercosur is already (1999) in serious discussions with the Andean Group. At this stage in Mercosur, progress is easier than for Europe in the EU's early decades because Argentine-Brazilian relations are so dominant, but that will become less true as other nations are added. Nor is it yet clear that the two key partners themselves are prepared for the kind of social and economic policy harmonization which required four decades of intensive effort in Europe.

Beyond South America, Mercosur has negotiated a "framework agreement" with the European Union, although Europe's Common Agricultural Policy poses major difficulties for that relationship. In the words of a leading Brazilian diplomat in this field: "For Brazil, the success of Mercosur, both in political terms (affirmation of democracy) and in economic and commercial terms (Mercosur is already an attraction for trade and investment), provides an enlarged projection of South America in the international context and an enhancement of the country's specific gravity in the concert of nations."[37] In the same article, however, the author recognizes the

---

37. Informal translation from "O Mercosul no Contexto Regional" (Mercosul in the Regional Context), by Rubens Antônio Barbosa, then Brazilian ambassador in London (now in Washington) and former national coordinator of Mercosur's Brazilian section. The article was published in 1998 through the Internet link of the Ministry of External Relations.

problem of competing priorities between Mercosur and the proposed Free Trade Area of the Americas (FTAA).

## Western Hemisphere Free Trade?

Under the slogan "From Alaska to Tierra del Fuego," the FTAA was originally suggested by U.S. President George H. W. Bush in 1990. In 1994, at a Western Hemisphere summit meeting of presidents in Miami, it was unanimously adopted as a goal to be negotiated no later than the year 2005, with "concrete progress" toward its attainment by the end of the twentieth century. It was the central topic at the follow-up summit meeting in Santiago de Chile in 1998.

During the years between the two summits, the nature of that interim progress and the part to be played by Mercosur became issues of acute tension between Brazilian and American trade negotiators. Washington's team, after its success in securing congressional ratification of the North American Free Trade Agreement, looked toward building the FTAA through successive admission of additional Latin American countries, starting promptly with Chile. Brasília, in contrast, sought first to expand Mercosur, ultimately enlarging it to include all of South America in a kind of South American Free Trade Area. That would be beneficial to Brazil if FTAA prospects should falter and could also provide the groundwork for a mainly bilateral final negotiation between NAFTA, led by the United States, and a South American grouping, led by Brazil, with the smaller Central American and Caribbean countries perhaps first joining with NAFTA. In the American scenario of 1997, Mercosur was an intrusive nuisance, which should disappear, but in the Brazilian scenario, it would play a decisive part. Despite the huge improvement in Brazilian-American bilateral relations on other issues, this question of long-run trade policy threatened a serious new downturn.

Behind the attitudes of trade diplomats lay real differences of opinion within both underlying political communities. The Mexican peso crisis of 1994 and consequent shift to a trade surplus with the United States cooled American enthusiasm for NAFTA, leading in 1997–98 to the failure of President Bill Clinton's request to Congress for renewal of "fast-track" trade-negotiating authority. In Brazil, the political left has been opposed to economic integration with the United States on any terms, while the business community is divided, some elements fearing unprotected exposure to American competition while others welcome the prospect of unimpeded access to the huge American market, nine times that of all South America.

In preparations for the Santiago summit, American negotiators pressed for substantive interim steps while Brazilians preferred to move ahead with Mercosur and hold back on FTAA.[38]

The troubled atmosphere was transformed in the course of President Clinton's visit to Brazil and Argentina in October 1997. In a joint press interview with President Cardoso, Clinton stated unequivocally that the U.S. government sees no conflict between Mercosur and FTAA, looks favorably on Mercosur's progress, and will cooperate with Brazil in moving toward the FTAA. The way was thus cleared for harmonious meetings of trade ministers in Costa Rica in March 1998, of the presidents in April at the Santiago Summit, and again of trade ministers in Toronto in 1999. The areas for implementation by the year 2000 were less ambitious than American trade negotiators might have liked, but Washington's bargaining power was limited by the absence of "fast-track" authority. On the other hand, Brasília has retreated from the foreign minister's earlier statement that all progress toward FTAA had to await congressional approval of fast track. Instead, the first follow-up meeting after Santiago agreed on a workmanlike structure for ongoing negotiation in which Brazil and the United States appear as equal cochairmen. That arrangement has been welcomed by both governments and approved by the specialized trade press, apparently marking an end, or at least a pause, in mutual suspicion and recrimination. Nevertheless, the question whether FTAA is really a viable project for agreement by the year 2005 evidently depends on election outcomes for presidents and Congresses in the United States in 2000 and Brazil in 2002.

## Brazilian-American Relations in the Late 1990s

The diminished tension on long-term trade strategy has brought Brazilian-American relations to their most amicable condition in several decades, if not ever. There are, of course, continuing specific trade disputes, as there are between the United States and Canada. Some are inherently insoluble because of the power of special interests on one side or the other. Two favorite Brazilian examples are the heavy U.S. tax on imported orange juice and the system of sugar import quotas, both gross exceptions to the much

---

38. A sophisticated analysis of Brazil's problems in preparing for FTAA, with a clear preference for giving priority to the consolidation of Mercosur and perhaps never adopting free trade with the United States, can be found in Sérgio de Abreu e Lima Florêncio, "O Modelo Brasileiro de Industrialização Diante das Novas Realidades da Integração no Hemisfério: Mercosul e NAFTA" (Brazil's Industrialization Model in the Context of the New Realities of Integration in the Hemisphere: Mercosul and NAFTA), in *Sessenta Anos*, vol. 2, pp. 79–102.

proclaimed openness of the American economy.[39] In 1999 the United States imposed antidumping penalties on imports of Brazilian steel, only to have them reversed by an administrative court. The American pharmaceutical industry is still dissatisfied with Brazilian arrangements for patent protection. Some American automobile exporters object to the special tariff on imports by companies without production in Brazil, but those with Brazilian plants are supporters of the arrangement, which certainly raises questions of conformity with WTO rules. Issues of this type are commonplace among industrialized democracies and have little effect on the overall tone of relationships.

That tone today seems mature and free of ideological strain. It differs from the Rio Branco tradition of Brazilian deference to American leadership but also differs from the Jânio Quadros notion that Brazilian dignity requires demonstrative anti-Americanism. In strategic matters such as nuclear nonproliferation and limiting missile technology dissemination; in efforts to control drug trafficking; in environmental protection in Amazônia or on the high seas; in strengthening of international institutions, especially for the promotion of democracy and human rights—the hallmark is an effort to identify mutual interests and cooperate in their pursuit, but without pretending that the national objectives are always shared.

Is this relationship too good to last? It depends heavily on continued success in Brazil's political and macroeconomic reforms, including progress in the social and political areas analyzed in chapters 5 and 6. It also depends on the maintenance of economic prosperity and a broadly internationalist outlook in the United States. If the ambitious goal of Western Hemisphere Free Trade comes to pass, it might even be intensified, approaching the "special relationship" sought by Brazil during World War II. On the other hand, the tensions of the 1970s and 1980s are by no means beyond resurrection. Chapter 9 provides an overall assessment of Brazil's prospects in the new century.

39. Early in the year 2000, the Brazilian embassy in Washington published a comparison of Brazilian and American tariff levels on the fifteen principal products involved in each country's bilateral imports, showing average rates of 14.3 percent for Brazil against 45.6 percent for the United States. The analysis was disputed by U.S. government trade officials.

# 9

## The Prospects

At the opening of a new century and millennium, Brazil has not yet achieved the goal of first world status described in the opening chapter. It has moved a long way in that direction since the failure of the "first chance" in the 1960s, but by fits and starts, more backward than forward during the bitter lost decade of 1981 to 1994. In the early 1990s, a major forward step was signaled by economic opening to international competition and privatization of the steel industry. Since 1995, price stability under the Real Plan has wrought a genuine sea change, a fundamental shift toward first world standards in attitudes and expectations. In this recent period, confidence in democratic institutions has also been strengthened. Yet public opinion remains divided on whether the nation is on the right track. Slow rates of economic growth, increased unemployment, and urban violence have undermined the popularity of the Real Plan and the Cardoso administration, even though no one openly advocates a return to high inflation. There is no effective consolidation of political coalitions even to define the right track. Much therefore depends on the quality of leadership that will emerge from Brazil's national and statewide elections in 2002.

The main policy challenges to be faced, before as well as after those elections, can be grouped under four headings: (1) maintenance of macroeconomic stability and renewal of sustained high rates of economic growth; (2) major reductions in poverty and in income disparities; (3) consolidation of economic relationships with South America, North America, Europe, and Asia; and (4) reform of political party structures and electoral mechanics.

Success in all four would permit achievement of first world status within the coming two decades.

## Macroeconomic Stability

In mid-2000, most of the short-term indicators were very encouraging. Inflation through May was at the record low annual rate of 3.4 percent, with 6.0 percent expected for the full year.[1] The central bank had lowered the basic interest rate from 19 percent at New Year's to 16½ percent in early July. Fiscal performance at all levels of government continued strong, with a primary surplus exceeding the targets agreed with the IMF. The partial social security reforms had tempered the deficits from that quarter. Industrial growth through April was 6.6 percent ahead of 1999; employment was rising and unemployment falling, even though still too large. Overall growth for the year 2000 was projected at about 4 percent. Exports through June were running 17 percent ahead of 1999 and imports only 10 percent ahead, making for a modest six-month trade surplus of US$856 million. The overall current balance of payments for the half year was in deficit by only $11.4 billion, mostly covered by capital imports. Net foreign direct investment was at the high level of $12.7 billion and reserves were almost $28 billion, worth about seven months of imports.

Except for the disappointing trade balance, those were good results, putting a definite end to the crises of 1997–99 and portending a resumption of significant overall growth without inflation. The direction was positive, but the pace still insufficient. Chapter 4 compared Brazil's per capita GNP in 1998 at $6,460 with Korea's at $13,286. For Brazil to achieve that Korean level by 2010, overall economic growth would have to average 6.2 percent, plus 1.1 percent for expected population growth, a total of 7.3 percent a year. Even to achieve Korea's present level by 2015 would require sustained annual growth at 6 percent. Those rates are low compared with the economic miracle, but high by more recent standards. Since the Korean economy would presumably not be stagnating, achieving those rates would not close the gap. Together with a major improvement in income distribution, however, they could provide first world living standards for the vast majority of Brazilians.

A central prerequisite is the maintenance of reasonable price stability. The discussion in chapter 7 shows how truly revolutionary it is for Brazil to

---

1. The macroeconomic data on the early months of 2000 are drawn from the Presidency's report, *Seis Anos do Real* (Six Years of the Real), and the Ministry of Finance's *Boletim de Acompanhamento Econômico* for July 2000, transmitted by Internet.

enjoy near-zero inflation. Any friendly observer must hope that it is there to stay. A return to fiscal laxity or to indexation of wages and contracts would rule out sustained high growth rates. A far-reaching Fiscal Responsibility Law passed in May 2000 is very promising. It applies to all three levels of government and sets new standards for systematic budgeting, auditing, and expenditure control, with substantial penalties for noncompliance. It promises to put teeth in the limitation of personnel expenses to 60 percent of revenues, to prevent interinstitutional borrowing and other self-dealing as escapes from budgetary limits, and to rule out profligate inauguration of new projects, especially in election years. If fully applied, it will mark a real transformation in long-standing Brazilian habits of fiscal maladministration for political or personal gain.

On the side of badly needed tax reform, however, the outlook is much less favorable, since some of the emergency tax measures are expiring while basic reforms of the system, including some form of value added tax, have been bogged down in the Congress. The social security accounts have improved, but the structure has not yet been adapted to the prospect of an aging population. Privatization in industry and services has been hampered by judicial orders and controversy over conditions of sale, with repeated delays in the test case of the former state-owned Bank of São Paulo (Banespa).

Higher overall growth rates and increased exports are overlapping goals, which call for further reductions in transport and port handling costs ("custo Brasil") and further improvements in productivity in both agriculture and industry. Brazil will not want to compete in exports with low-wage, low-technology, low-value-added textile and toy industries typical of South and Southeast Asia. It needs a major enlargement and diversification of capacity to compete in high-technology manufacturing, now represented mainly by automotive products and small aircraft, and in the dynamic new wave of service industries. Productivity improvement requires not only physical investment in plant but above all the upgrading of human capital, including basic, vocational, and scientific education. Success on those fronts would create the most effective path to higher overall economic growth. It would also expand the modern sector at the expense of the traditional—the most durable approach to Brazil's second great challenge.

## Reductions in Poverty and Income Inequalities

Chapter 5 sketched the main dimensions of Brazil's continuing backwardness in social development. Poverty levels, inequalities in landholdings and income distribution, and standards of education and health care remain substantially worse than in other nations with comparable economic output. Even on these fronts, however, the late 1990s brought significant improvements. One dimension concerns public awareness, reflected in press coverage, popular and scholarly attention, and political responses at all governmental levels. The shift in focus toward poverty reduction and other social issues at both the World Bank and the Inter-American Development Bank have enhanced that awareness and provided substantial support for remedial measures.

Data released in mid-2000 indicate that revolutionary changes in social conditions are taking hold, notwithstanding the limitations on public programs imposed by fiscal austerity. An energetic minister of education, with strong backing from the international development banks, has pressed for decentralization of primary school control to the municipal level, supplemental resources in the poorer states, upgraded educational materials and teacher quality, educational applications of radio, television, and the Internet, and systematic testing of results. Major strides are also under way to broaden public secondary education, where attendance is rapidly growing.[2] Educational progress, however, still falls far short of what is needed to participate fully in the current revolutions in technology and economic globalization. That would require first world educational standards, including secondary education for all and university education for half or more of the relevant age cohorts, with emphasis on science and technology.

The annual household sample study for 1999 showed only 4.3 percent of seven- to fourteen-year-old children not in school, compared with 9.8 percent in 1995. Child labor was correspondingly reduced. The Gini coefficient of inequality in income from work had fallen from 0.630 in 1989 to 0.567 in 1999, still very unequal but significantly better.[3] A recent updating of José Pastore's pioneering study of social mobility (see chapter 3, note 26) shows a continuing high rate of upward mobility even though overall inequality remains very high.[4] Pastore notes that education has become a more important factor in upward mobility than the social status of the father. Most strikingly, he finds that in 1996 fewer than 20 percent of the upper class were children of parents from that class. That finding points to the development

2. See Claudio de Moura Castro, "Education: Way Behind but Trying to Catch Up," *Daedalus* (Spring 2000), pp. 291–314, an issue devoted entirely to Brazil on the 500th anniversary of Cabral's landing from Portugal.

3. IBGE, National Household Sample Survey (PNAD), 1999, by Internet.

4. See José Pastore and Nelson do Valle Silva, *Mobilidade Social no Brasil* (Social Mobility in Brazil) (São Paulo: Makron Books do Brasil Editora, 2000), pp. 12–13.

of a new elite, based not on inherited wealth or standing but on education, energy, and ability. That kind of elite is prone to accept new ideas in place of ancestral modes of thought and practice.

Income gains under the Real Plan in the poorest segments have also improved living conditions (see table 9-1). Since the middle and upper classes already enjoyed these amenities, the improvements apply wholly to the lower classes. In a period of stagnant overall per capita incomes, those are significant achievements.

The concentration of poverty in the Northeast continues as a major challenge to public policy. The 1999 household survey shows that 40 percent of workers in that region receive less than twice the minimum wage, compared with 24 percent in the Southeast. The disparities persist despite decades of subsidies and special incentives to regional development, with a new "big push" on those lines announced by the president in mid-2000. Previous programs have suffered from diversions of public funds for personal or political gain; it remains to be seen whether the new fiscal responsibility legislation provides an adequate antidote. A less promising trend involves competition among individual states to attract large-scale foreign investment projects by major tax concessions, a form of fiscal warfare that tends to become self-defeating and a danger to state solvency.

Worldwide experience shows no inherent incompatibility between accelerated economic growth and reduced inequality in incomes. Gini coefficients in the first world cluster in the 0.25–0.35 range, with the United States

Table 9-1. *Household Survey Gains between 1995 and 1999*
Percent

| Amenity | 1995 | 1999 |
| --- | --- | --- |
| Piped water | 76.3 | 79.8 |
| Sewerage connection | 60.0 | 64.6 |
| Garbage collection | 72.1 | 79.9 |
| Electric lighting | 91.8 | 94.8 |
| Telephone | 22.4 | 37.6[a] |
| Refrigerator | 74.9 | 82.8 |
| Washing machine | 26.7 | 32.8 |
| Radio | 88.9 | 89.9 |
| Television | 81.1 | 87.7 |

Source: Instituto Brasileiro de Geografia e Estatística (IBGE), National Household Sample Survey, 1999, as reported on the Internet.
a. Rising rapidly with privatization.

at 0.40; Brazil in 1995 stood at 0.60.[5] Those comparisons should reassure Brazilians who fear that achieving first world conditions would forever doom their society to gross inequalities. Brazil's present focus on upgrading education is clearly the indispensable priority. It needs to be matched by technological upgrading in all economic sectors, a task mainly for private enterprise but one that can be assisted by government. The key, as stated in chapter 5, is the incorporation into higher productivity employment of excluded groups, whether they are illiterate peasants, dark-skinned day laborers, or manual workers in industry and services at jobs better performed by machines. Along the way, poverty should be progressively reduced, with what remains treated by public and community "assistencial" (welfare) policies and programs.

## Brazil and Globalization

The closing decades of the twentieth century witnessed two forms of tectonic change in worldwide economic relationships. In three basic areas of technology—electronics, genetics, and globalized information (the Internet)— new knowledge and new applications of knowledge were being created at a truly revolutionary pace. Their application and dissemination were not confined to one or a few countries; they were global and increasingly managed by genuinely multinational corporate and intergovernmental institutions. The pace of Brazil's move into first world status will be greatly influenced by the extent and depth of its participation in these transformations.

The economic openings since 1990, along with privatization of steel, telecommunications, and other public enterprises, provide a promising basis for that kind of participation. In many cases, foreign participation in ownership has brought with it direct access to first world technology. This is a far more promising route to new technology than the misguided informatics experiment of the 1970s and 1980s.

The attractiveness of Brazil as a large national market and production base for South America as a whole has increased direct foreign investment to record levels, only briefly interrupted by the financial crises of 1997–99. This attractiveness is amplified by the success so far of Mercosur (see chapter 8), despite the setbacks of 1999, and the prospect of at least partial adherence of South American countries in addition to Chile and Bolivia. In late 2000, Brazil is leading a new initiative for systematic South America–wide

5. Data for most of the world, taken in years ranging from 1982 to 1994, are shown in World Bank, *World Development Indicators, 1999*, table 2.8.

cooperation on common political and economic challenges, including human rights, smuggling of arms and drugs, and environmental protection, but it is too early to speculate on the possible impact on trade and investment.

The truly great challenge concerns trade and investment relations with the United States, or North America as a whole, where markets and economic capacities are in a vastly larger order of magnitude. Brazil alone accounts for over half the South American economy, but the North American market outranks Brazil's by more than eleven times; the United States alone by ten times.[6] A genuine Free Trade Area of the Americas would greatly accelerate Brazil's achievement of first world status. As noted in chapter 8, hemisphere-wide agreement by the target date of 2005 depends heavily on election outcomes in both the United States (2002 and 2004) and Brazil (2002), including Congresses as well as presidents. On the U.S. side, public opinion today is less favorable to NAFTA than at its inception, but that may be altered by the change in Mexican leadership. A souring of U.S. relations with the European Union might enhance congressional interest in FTAA, even though South American markets are much smaller than European markets.

For Brazilian negotiators as well, there is interaction between North-South and East-West trade dealings. In their view, renewal of fast-track arrangements in Washington is an indispensable precondition for final negotiations. Even in the best of prospects, full implementation of Western Hemisphere free trade would surely be spread over a multiyear transition period. FTAA would open vast new perspectives for Brazil but would require at least a decade to become a major contributor to economic and technological progress. In that time frame, as much or more can probably be achieved through global negotiations in the WTO. The critical issue of policy is the maintenance of active engagement with the world's most advanced economies, firmly resisting a reversion to inward-looking nationalist protectionism.

## Political Reform

The analysis in chapter 6 pointed to weaknesses in Brazil's political party structures and electoral mechanics that work against the consolidation of democracy and obstruct the paths to sustained economic growth and

6. Calculated from data in World Bank, *World Development Indicators, 2000*, table 1.1.

enhanced social justice. The hope for structural political reform in the wake of President Cardoso's reelection in 1998 was dashed by the ensuing international financial crises. The country now faces major political questions in two time frames. In the short term, through the super-elections of 2002 (president and vice president, both houses of Congress, governors, and state assemblies), will an effective coalition be formed with sufficient electoral appeal to maintain the price stability and fiscal sanity achieved through the Real Plan? Will such a coalition become dedicated after those elections to basic reforms in constitutional and legislative provisions governing party formation and electoral mechanics? If both choices are in the negative, the hopes for rapid and consistent progress toward first world conditions are almost certain to be frustrated. If the first is positive and the second again deferred, political weaknesses will continue to cast doubt on both democratic consolidation and sustained social progress.

In mid-2000, the economic and social gains summarized here have not yet been matched by public endorsement of the Cardoso administration's record or completion of needed reforms in the economic structures. Nor has there yet emerged the widespread first world pattern of two dominant parties or coalitions, one right of center and the other left of center, but both sharing a large middle ground in economic and social policy. Much of the left is still mired in a backward-looking nationalistic populism, protecting entrenched privileges and obsolete modes of governance. The fractionated array of parties and the undue influence of state political machines have worked against the emergence of creditable new candidates for effective national leadership.

Brazilian public opinion is volatile, and continued near-term economic and social progress may resuscitate the popularity of Cardoso and his team. It should not be forgotten that in April 1998 the polls predicted a clear victory—perhaps even a first-round victory—for the opposition led by "Lula" da Silva, only to be confounded by Cardoso's first-round reelection in October. Much will depend on the still unidentified candidates for election in 2002. The fractionated party system lends itself to charismatic individual candidates of dubious qualifications for the presidency, as demonstrated by Fernando Collor, but better qualified names have emerged from six years of successful anti-inflation experience and serious reform efforts in education, health care, and market practices. There is obviously no certainty that the gains since 1994 will all be preserved, but the odds on their preservation after 2002 are at least 50:50.

Political structural reform is mainly for a longer time frame. There is considerable support in Congress for a minimalist program, focused on eliminating tiny parties, making it difficult for members of Congress to switch parties, and encouraging durable coalitions, if not party fusions. Some action on these lines is possible in 2001. It would constitute a significant improvement over the present political party chaos. Reform of electoral mechanics is a much more difficult proposition, not to be imagined before the political "honeymoon" of early 2003. The new president-elect would have to give it a high priority for political action, and it would require a sustained effort in the interim to educate the general public and the political elites on its crucial importance. Its adoption would speed the day of Brazil's full incorporation into the first world.

In the seven decades since the Great Depression and World War II, Brazil has experienced three fundamental alterations in economic structure, social conditions, and political attitudes. The Vargas era (1930–54) marked the decline of patrimonial society, almost to the vanishing point. The period from Kubitschek through the economic miracle made economic development the central priority for national policy. The innovations of the 1990s in economic opening and macroeconomic stability herald a new Brazilian relationship to the first world—not as dependent, not as antagonist, but as an increasingly important participant.

# Index

Page numbers followed by letters *f*, *n*, and *t* refer to figures, notes, and tables, respectively.